Religion and Folk Cosmology

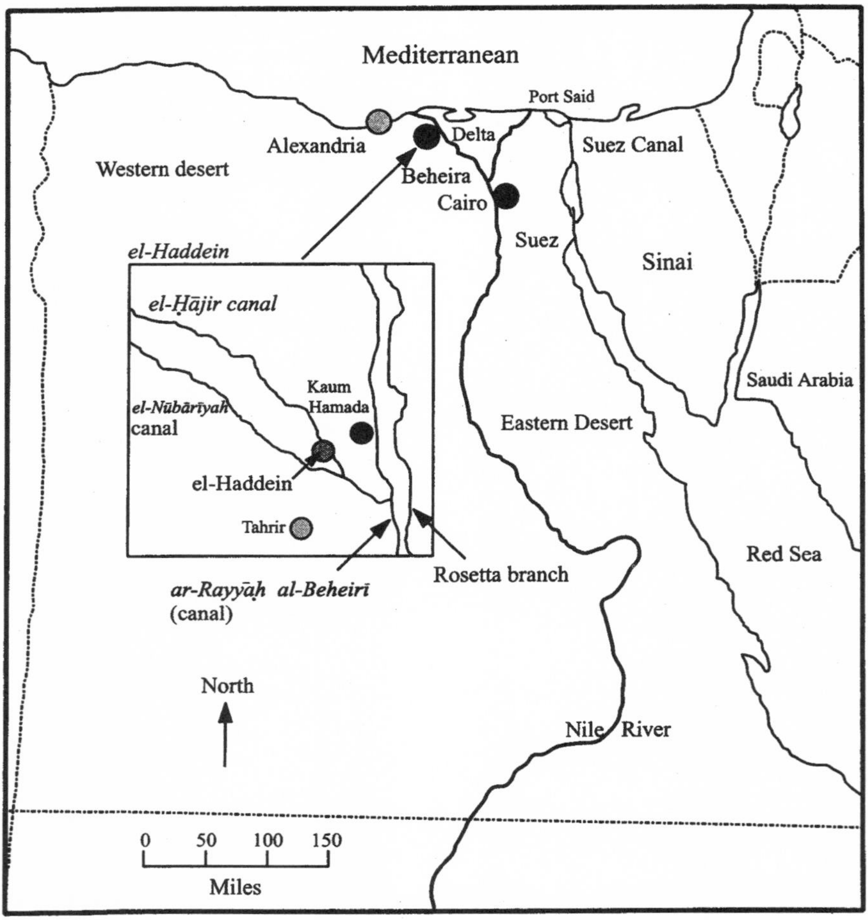
Mediterranean
Port Said
Alexandria
Delta
Suez Canal
Western desert
Beheira
Cairo
Suez
Sinai
el-Haddein
el-Ḥājir canal
Kaum
Hamada
el-Nūbārīyah
canal
el-Haddein
Tahrir
Saudi Arabia
Eastern Desert
Red Sea
ar-Rayyāḥ al-Beheirī
(canal)
Rosetta branch
North
Nile River
0
50
100
150
Miles

Egypt

Religion and Folk Cosmology

scenarios of the visible and invisible in rural Egypt

EL-SAYED EL-ASWAD

PRAEGER

Westport, Connecticut
London

Library of Congress Cataloging-in-Publication Data

el-Aswad, el-Sayed.

Religion and folk cosmology : scenarios of the visible and invisible in rural Egypt / el-Sayed el-Aswad.

p. cm.

Includes bibliographical references.

ISBN 0-89789-924-5 (alk. paper)

1. Folklore—Egypt. 2. Ethnophilosophy—Egypt. 3. Islamic cosmology—Egypt. 4. Egypt—Rural conditions. 5. Egypt—Social life and customs. I. Title.

GR355.A89 2002

398′.0932—dc21 2002021659

British Library Cataloguing in Publication Data is available.

Library of Congress Catalog Card Number: 2002021659
ISBN: 0-89789-924-5

First published in 2002

Praeger Publishers, 88 Post Road West, Westport, CT 06881
An imprint of Greenwood Publishing Group, Inc.
www.praeger.com

Printed in the United States of America

The paper used in this book complies with the Permanent Paper Standard issued by the National Information Standards Organization (Z39.48-1984).

10 9 8 7 6 5 4 3 2 1

This book is dedicated to

MY PARENTS, MY WIFE, and MY SONS

There is an order in the cosmos but it is not immediately apparent. It requires hard thought and prolonged study to discern it and to construct an image of it. There are many orders below this cosmic order and they are difficult to discern.

EDWARD SHILS, *Tradition* (1981, 326)

contents

five

Symbolic Exchange, Gender, and Cosmological Forces,
109

six

Multiple Worlds,
144

seven

Conclusion,

figures and tables

TABLES

acknowledgments

For the past ten years I have been involved in developing and synthesizing a broad theoretical perspective aimed at facilitating the multifaceted understanding of the interplay between religion, local tradition, and globalization, a problem that is today deeply debated by the contemporary anthropological community. The project has required full dedication, intensive work, and prolonged research to capture the significance of the unique blend of universal and local forces represented in religious and cosmic beliefs and practices that, through the dynamic scenarios of the visible and invisible, have played a major role in creating a particular sense of identity attached to both the local community and the global Muslim community (*ummah*).

Special gratitude goes to the late Roy Rappaport with whom I interacted intellectually and personally during my graduate study at the University of Michigan in 1980s and from whose reflection on the constructive power of religious rituals and worldviews in the making of human life I greatly benefited. Comments from Nicholas Hopkins on earlier versions of papers led to their development into chapters in this book. I would also like to thank Dale Eickelman and Peter Gran for their perceptive comments and insightful remarks on the manuscript as a whole. I am grateful to Ahmad Abou-Zeid, Maxwell Owusu, Raji Rammuny, and Hasan El-Shamy for their ongoing advice and support.

Teaching at Wayne State University enabled me to converse with students and colleagues about the current situation in the Middle East. Particularly, discussions with Barbara Aswad confirmed the importance of people's own perspectives without imposing alien notions on them under any circumstances.

It would have been impossible for this work to come to fruition without the eager interest and assistance of the people of el-Haddein village who, upon seeing me come and go for long and short intervals, asked me on my leaving, when I would come back again.

Special appreciation is extended to the Greenwood Publishing Group, editor Jane Garry, and Robert Kowkabany for their help in publishing this book.

Many thanks go to my wife, Mary, and sons, Kareem and Amir, who patiently tolerated my absence and enthusiastically encouraged my efforts during these years.

notes on transliteration

The text follows the transliteration system of the *International Journal of Middle Eastern Studies* for Arabic words. Except for proper nouns, all Arabic words are printed in italics. Colloquial words and phrases are transliterated as spoken and pronounced by individuals; however, in certain contexts where it is necessary, their meanings, in brackets, are written in standard Arabic form.

1

Introduction

The folk song below, prayerfully alive, captures the divine unity and oneness underlying the apparent multiplicity and diversity of cosmological, social, economic, and psychological phenomena and presents a meaningful introduction to rural Egyptians' holistic cosmological thought:[1]

Water irrigates the trees, but their fruits are not one.
al-maya bi-tisgī ashshajar, lākin aththamar mush wāḥid.
Palm trees are alike, yet their fruits are not one.
wa an-nakhl yashbah li-baʿ ḍu lākin aththamar mush wāḥid.
Sea and river are water, but their taste is not one.
wa l-baḥr wa an-nahr maya, lākin aṭṭaʿ m mush wāhid.
The sky is highly elevated, but there is not one pillar.
wa as-samā marfūʿah, lākin balā ʿamad wāḥid.
All people are created from dust, but their forms are not one.
wa an-nās makhlūka min at-turāb, lākin ash-shabah mush wāḥid.
The stomach (uterus) is the same, but the offspring are not one.
wa l-baṭin wāḥida, lākin al-khalaf mush wāḥid.
Brothers are from the same blood, but their tempers are not one.
wa l-ikhwān yabgu ashigga, lākin aṭ-ṭabʿ mush wāḥid.
This life is transitory, and all people will drink from one cup (death).
wa ad-dunyā fāniya, wa kull an-nās shāriba min kās wāḥid.

Everything in the universe is created by One God.
wa kull shai' fī-l kaun khālagu ilāh wāḥid.
This is your wisdom in the universe, O God, O One.
wa dī ḥikmitak fī-l kaun yā Allah yā wāḥid.
Recall Allah, O believer, and maintain His Oneness.
udhkur Allah yā mu'min wa waḥḥid al wāḥid.

This study aims to discern the cosmological belief order of rural Egyptians as well as to understand its relationship to their religious, social, and economic lives.[2] Rural Egyptian cosmology and traditional knowledge[3] are profoundly rich and extremely complex and, therefore, require special attention and consideration. Though latent, shared cosmological beliefs influenced by Muslim tradition have played a decisive role in Egypt's social and political history and have manifested themselves powerfully in critical historical moments.[4] Folk cosmology is the peasant's powerful genius or indigenous paradigm that has helped him endure the tenacious grip of colonialism, the oppression of feudalism, the tyranny of socialism, and the chaos of the open supermarket economy of capitalism. Folk cosmology, in this era of overwhelming globalization, is about authenticity and cultural identity and needs to be explained rather than justified.

"Cosmology" refers to assumptions concerning the structure of the universe, and is extended here to include ecology and society as well as human and nonhuman beings and forces, both perceptible and imperceptible, as constituting integrated parts of that universe.[5] As Eliade (1957, 22) points out, "If the world is to be lived in it must be founded." This study concentrates primarily on the meaning and structure of the cosmos, *al-kaun*, or the universe, *al-ʿālam*, in its visible and invisible dimensions as conceived, ordered, and enacted by rural Egyptians.[6] Cosmology is fundamental in the construction of their thought, identity, and community relationships. The focus, therefore, is not on the private beliefs of each individual as such, but rather on commonly shared concepts or collective representations in which religious and cosmological concepts are fused together. "There is no religion that is not a cosmology at the same time that it is a speculation upon divine things" (Durkheim 1965, 21).

The main concern here is not merely with the intellectual aspects of the cosmological order, but also with the social domains in which individuals locate and define themselves in their relations to others. Put differently, people's cosmologies are dealt with not only as an ideological system, but also as a system of meanings generated and enacted in different courses of public and private scenarios concerned with visible and invisible domains of local community. The term *scenario* is used broadly, incorporating "discourse" as used in contemporary anthropology with reference to dialogue, negotiation, and debate (Asad 1986, 1993; Bowen 1993; Eickelman 1989; Rosen 1988), as well as to the social meanings implicit in daily practices, rituals, and bodily orientations (Bourdieu 1977). Within this comprehensive sense of scenario, the focus will be on discursive and nondiscursive dynamics of everyday interaction. It is the *living scenario*—not just words fixed in scripture or print—from which Egyptian belief systems can best be discerned. Rural Egyptians are fond of narrating stories in fluent scenarios, rendering their culture as, using Geertz's phrase (1973, 448), "a story they tell themselves about themselves."

The classic works of Lane (1836) and Blackman (1924, 1927) on urban and rural Egyptian communities, respectively, confirm the impact of traditional beliefs and practices on Egyptian lives. More than 70 years ago, Blackman anticipated that peasants' beliefs and related practices would vanish as a result of education. She claimed that "with the spread of education the old customs and beliefs are already beginning to die out" (Blackman 1927, 9, 11). Nevertheless, recent ethnographic evidence shows that despite the growing spread of education, most of these beliefs and practices still persist in rural Egypt (el-Aswad 1985, 1988, 1994). Tradition or traditional beliefs and practices cannot be depicted as being residual categories attached to premodern societies because of the fact that they are historically embedded, in different ways, in all cultures, modern and premodern alike. "Traditions develop because the desire to create something truer and better or more convenient is alive in those who acquire and pass them" (Shils 1981, 15).

In this study, the terms "folk," "peasants," "villagers," "rural people," and "*fallāḥīn*" are used interchangeably.[7] The word *fallāḥ*, however, is not restricted to its occupational definition as an independent or hired laborer who works on his own or another's land, but rather is used as a unifying concept reflecting the social values and worldviews shared by those both born and who live in the rural community. Occupational and economic differentiation among people of the village does not prevent them from identifying themselves with the values of the *fallāḥīn*, or from calling themselves *fallāḥīn*. Those who are not directly involved in the agricultural economy have kin, friends, and neighbors who are. The associations of the concept implicit in *fallāḥ* are so omnipotent that the term itself is manipulated by nonagricultural workers in their attempt to convince the *fallāḥīn* that they share their values.

Yet, Egyptian peasants have been depicted in sociological and anthropological literature as being politically passive, backward, and superstitious, notwithstanding the fact that most Egyptians, including the majority of those who live in urban environments, have their roots in rural society.[8] Talal Asad points out that studies dealing with Muslims have "no place for peasants. Peasants, like women, are not depicted as *doing* anything . . . they have no dramatic role and no religious expression in contrast, that is, to nomadic tribes and city-dwellers" (Asad 1986, 10 [emphasis in original]).[9] Ayrout mistakenly argues that because the *fallāḥ* "lives in the present, he is neither in a hurry, nor ambitious, nor curious. He is mild and peaceful because he is patient, and patient because he is subject to men and events, and for these very reasons he has become like the Nile, indifferent rather than idle. His mind is passive and fatalistic; he accepts things as they are" (Ayrout 1963, 143).[10] This kind of misleading stereotype of the peasant was also reflected in contradictory Eurocentric statements by Blackman in the discourse of Orientalism that "had the epistemological and ontological power virtually of life and death, or presence and absence over everything and everybody designated as 'oriental'" (Said 1983, 223). It is inadequate for Blackman to state, in one place, that "the *mental outlook* of most of the villagers is *low*. As far as the women are concerned, there is nothing to raise it" (Blackman 1927, 43 [italics added]); and in another, that "Egyptian peasants . . . are as a whole a wonderfully cheerful and content people. They are *very quick of comprehension*, of ready wit, dearly loving a joke, even if directed against themselves, usually blessed with *retentive memory*, light-hearted, kindly and very hospitable" (Blackman 1927, 23 [italics added]).

The point here is that Blackman and those who follow the dominant Eurocentric paradigm are confined to the view that the West or Europe, the center, is definable solely as being opposed to the peripheral non-European societies, depicted as premodern, unsophisticated, underdeveloped, or exotic (Gran 1996, 5). Moreover, the claim that Egyptian peasants are politically passive and indifferent mirrors the bias of the dominant paradigm and lacks substantive evidence.[11] Historical accounts have explicitly shown that Egyptian peasants were involved in revolutions such as those of 1882 and 1919 that resisted colonialism and state oppression (Binder 1978; Brown 1990; Burke 1991; Goldberg 1992; Vatikiotis 1985). My argument here is that the life of Egyptian peasants, in general, and their cognition of the world, in particular, need further investigation, detached from misleading impressionistic and ethnocentric generalizations. The principal objective therefore is to explicate the cosmology from below as conceived, reconstructed, and enacted by the unjustly and unjustifiably overlooked Egyptian peasant.

In examining the belief system of Egyptian folk, several questions come to mind. Why do old customs and beliefs still persist? What do they mean to people? Are they considered as superstitions? Do they meet specific needs of the folk? Are they used as a social, intellectual, or cosmological paradigm for mobilizing certain actions and explaining certain events? Are they part of their cosmological order? Are they sanctified or refuted by religious statements? Do they form a kind of folk religion?

One of the serious predicaments facing the studies of the Arab societies is that anthropologists and Middle Eastern scholars[12] correlate the concepts of orthodox and nonorthodox Islams with elite/folk, formal/informal, scripturalist/nonscripturalist, literacy/illiteracy, and great/little traditions, respectively. These ideological antitheses, however, express the views of those scholars who fail to examine them from the *emic* perspective of the folk people themselves (el-Aswad 1988, 1994). It is not uncommon that "many ethnographers . . . are content to record that their subjects are Muslims and to note ways in which their customs differ from Islamic prescriptions" (Tapper 1984, 247). The terms "folk Islam" or "popular religion" are not accepted or even recognized by folk people or villagers. They imply a less-valued category of religion associated with the majority of mass population, as opposed to the religion of the high culture or elite. "What stands as a consequence of focusing on elites is a dehistorization of the mass population" (Gran 1996, 4). "Orthodoxy" is a problematic concept viewed and defined differently by scholars. While some scholars take it to mean a set of religious doctrines (Gellner 1981), others see it within a distinctive relationship of power that regulates or requires correct practices as well as condemns the incorrect ones (Asad 1986, 15).[13] Politically, "orthodoxy" has become identifiable more with the official, institutional, and administrative systems than with religious doctrine. For example, orthodox Islam was used by British colonialism (and is still used by the state) for political and administrative reasons, basically to suppress religious or Muslim groups opposed to them. The *ʿulamā*, Muslim scholars mostly of al-Azhar, have been manipulated by the state to justify or legitimize its regime. However, history reveals that *ʿulamā*'s submission to the state, during Nassser's secular regime for instance, was superficial, mostly because of the extreme political constraints imposed on them (Zeghal 1999, 374).[14]

Dividing religion into orthodox and nonorthodox or *folk Islams* is a contradiction in terms and hardly applicable to the local context of the community. For both elite or literate and popular or illiterate Muslims, there can be only one Islam.[15] The differences that might exist between them are considered here as surface variations of the deeper and hierarchically structured unity. Access to divine scriptures does not necessitate a specialist in religious knowledge. Any person able to read, no matter how simply, has access to the text both individually and collectively. Even those who are illiterate have access to the sacred text through listening to the ongoing recitation of the Qur'an that forms a distinct feature characterizing the atmosphere not only of the local community but also of the entire Muslim world. To be more specific, the sacred text and the interpretation of Muslim tradition are approachable and accessible through various public and private channels including, for instance, mass media (radio, television), audiocassette tapes, Friday sermons, and attending religious sessions in mosques or inside the house, in addition to daily prayers and funerary rituals (el-Aswad 2001b). Unlike Western societies in which loud noise coming from speakers is viewed as disturbing the peace, microphones hanging on the minarets of mosques are used loudly and assertively at least five times a day for prayer callings, allowing people, men and women, in their public and private spaces to hear them. To overlook such an audio phenomenon is to neglect an essential character of the Muslim community.

It is also irrelevant to accept the distinction between orthodox and non-orthodox Islams as represented, respectively, in the *ʿulamā*, Muslim scholars, and *Sufis*, leaders of religious (mystical) orders, because there is no such distinction in the social reality.[16] Here, one should emphasize the fact that "the membership of the body of the *ʿulemā* was and is in many cases drawn from all levels of society" (Gilsenan 1983, 34). It is arguable to claim that religious scholars, even those of al-Azhar, monopolize religious exegeses despite the fact that they have a great influence in religious public domains. "The *ʿulamā* no longer have, if they ever did, a monopoly on sacred authority. Rather, Sufi shaykhs, engineers, professors of education, medical doctors, army and militia leaders, and others compete to speak for Islam" (Eickelman and Piscatori 1996, 211).

Another problem implicit in that dichotomy is the generalization that Islam is an otherworldly religion and embraces irrational elements such as magic and mysticism (Weber 1958, 1964).[17] Such a statement relegates Muslim culture to an antiquated and inferior status. If Weber views Islamic culture as being otherworldly and in opposition to rational or Western culture, others mistakenly argued three decades ago that Islamic culture was moving away from its religious context. The claim that "Islamic culture like Western culture is being gradually weaned from its religious roots" (Trimingham 1968, 125) raises skepticism and is inapplicable to present Muslim societies.[18] The experience of rural Egyptians, presented in the ethnographic material, puts such a view to the test.

My point of departure is fundamentally cosmological insofar as cosmology encompasses a totality of the universe, society, and person. This study, however, is not concerned with what is so-called "orthodox Muslim cosmology," which is textual in nature,[19] but rather with the lived cosmology of rural Egyptians as influenced by three interrelated factors: First is the exegeses of the *ʿulamā* concerning the constituents and construction of the cosmos; second is the tradition of sainthood and related beliefs derived from various Sufi orders; and the third factor concerns local tradition and the specificity of the community as it is related to its history, social structure, location, and ecological features. These factors, inseparable in the context of social reality, are theoretically analyzed (el-Aswad 1994). The cosmology of rural Egyptians represents a uniquely ordered synthesis of many differing views.

It is important to assert that one cannot deny or underestimate the great influence the *ʿulamā* have had on the peasant construction of the cosmos through ongoing interpretations and reinterpretations of the *Qurʾan* and Muslim literature. These interpretations are made simple and intelligible so as to reach a great number of people. They are delivered through the national media and published in simply written and inexpensive books.[20] Much of their thought is concerned with the dominant religious theme of *al-ghaib*[21] (the invisible, the divine secret, the unknowable) and such related issues as the creation of the world, man's place in it, the potential means for improving social conditions, fate, death, resurrection, the afterlife, magic, envy, blessing, invisible beings (souls, spirits, jinn), and unseen forces without and within human kind. It is true that this orthodox discourse aspires to be authoritative. However, because "authority is a collaborative achievement between narrator and audience, the former cannot speak in total freedom: there are conceptual and institutional conditions that must be attended to if the discourses are to be persuasive. That is why attempts by social scientists at rendering such discourses as instances of local leaders manipulating religious symbols to legitimize their social power should be viewed skeptically" (Asad 1993, 210). The *shaikhs* or *ʿulamā* possess information that, by definition, their followers may neither possess nor fully understand. However, the major patterns which organize the concepts dealt with in this study can indeed be found in the discourse of ordinary peasants and religious experts alike. This is not a matter of simple political or economic domination—it is a matter of collective representations refracted in individual beliefs and worldviews that subordinate politics and economics within the larger whole.

In summary, through focusing on the folk cosmology of rural Egyptians, this study avoids the problematic consequences of applying the misleading terminology of folk Islam. That is, we can address the folk cosmology within a Muslim context without generating further contradictions implicit in the "folk versus orthodox Islam(s)" argument. The fundamental thesis here is that rural (Muslim) Egyptians are deeply influenced by the overarching Muslim sacred cosmology. But the cosmological view of both Muslim intellectuals and common persons, which endows them with a unique imaginative sense of engagement with a transcendent and superior reality, accentuates the theme of a divine, cosmic, invisible higher power surpassing any other. Such a belief represents an inexhaustible source of spiritual and emotional empowerment, which may be in certain critical circumstances politically mobilized. Within this context, the peasants' political resistance to British colonialism as well as to state domination can be viewed as a religious or holy struggle, a *jihād*.

The Ethnography of Invisible Domains

This study contributes to both general anthropology and Middle Eastern scholarship. What distinguishes this from contemporary ethnographic monographs is in its concern with the neglected topic of the social and symbolic implications of the cosmology, with its visible and invisible spheres, of traditional societies, particularly those of rural Egypt. More generally, except for textual cosmology, studies that deal with Middle Eastern cosmologies as lived by the people themselves are scant. Moreover, compared to the rich anthropological studies of the invisible dimensions of human experience (Graham 1995; Hanks 1996; Irvine 1982; Keane 1997; Metcalf 1989; Stoller 1989; and Wiener 1995, among others), little attention has been given to the ethnography of invisible domains in the Middle East although they overwhelmingly dominate people's everyday lives. Invisible things and unseen forces are flatly depicted as superstitions and never considered as critical aspects of identity, society, and the cosmos (el-Aswad 2001, 2002b).[22] People's perceptions of themselves and of the worlds in which they live have been given less attention than their political ideologies and economic activities. Moral aspects of Middle Eastern people, including honor, generosity, and hospitality, for instance, have been mostly studied either as part of the politics of domination and manipulation or as being isolated from the holistic (cosmological) context within which they acquire their meaning. Within this broader framework, this work is a departure from the limited inquiry of the moral features of people, to focus on the cosmic and holistic views of their lives.

At the theoretical level, there is not a generally accepted cross-cultural method or theory for investigating and comparing patterns of thought, cosmology, and worldviews. Structural anthropology is limited by its formal, synchronic, and abstract nature. Cognitive anthropology is confined to the formal, abstract, and taxonomic aspects of natives' thought. The connection between systems of meaning and action is not clearly defined in much of symbolic anthropology in which more attention has been given to moral or ethical dimensions than to the cognitive.[23] In its emphasis on the social structure or society as the sole model of universal categories, classification, and religion, Durkheim's sociology (1965) overlooks the semantic aspects of social phenomena. The claim that the body is the existential ground of culture and self (Csordas 1990) emphasizes one aspect, the visible or corporal, at the expense of the other, the invisible. The argument that "embodiment" is "an intermediate methodological field defined by perceptual experience and mode of presence and engagement in the world" (Csordas 1994, 12) deflects attention from the discursive, speculative, and reflective domains of human experience.

Folk cosmology, with its visible and invisible zones, can be explicated by examining villagers' daily scenarios or discursive and nondiscursive actions of varied arrays of similes, practices, rituals and ceremonies, attitudes toward time, space, and cardinal points, concepts of the person and the body, and the forms of their built environment. Rather than starting with preconceived concepts of people's cosmologies and worldviews, this study focuses on conceptual definitions and distinctions that people themselves make in constructing their own cosmology and identity.

As an inner-meaning system, however, the cosmology of rural Egyptians is addressed within a framework that deals with both content and structure. A symbolic-hermeneutic approach is employed that deals with culture as "an historically transmitted pattern of meanings embodied in symbols, a system of inherited conceptions expressed in symbolic forms by means of which men communicate, perpetuate, and develop their knowledge about and attitudes toward life" (Geertz 1973, 89). Within this framework, a hermeneutic or symbolic interpretation is used when the cosmos or universe and its constituents are described by people who attach values to, or express their attitudes toward, them. Description of the cosmos or universe "usually implies and entails evaluations and moral premises and emotional attitudes" (Tambiah 1985, 4). And values are a category of meaning, and a hierarchy of values is a hierarchy of meaning (Rappaport 1979, 156; 1999, 224–28).

In this study, however, attention is paid not only to the content of villagers' ordered cosmology, but also to the formal principles upon which that cosmology is symbolically constructed. In order to highlight the structural aspect of cosmology, emphasis will be on the relationships between its underlying principles that are asymmetrically and hierarchically ordered in opposite but complementary concepts. "To bring order is to bring distinction, to divide the universe into opposing entities" (Bourdieu 1977, 124). The structural analysis is based on Dumont's idea of hierarchical opposition (1980, 1986), distinguished from the binary symmetric opposition of Lévi-Strauss (1963) in which two terms or opposites have equal status, in that it is asymmetric and refers to the opposition between a whole and a part of that whole. This opposition contains a double relation of identity and contrariety and can be used to analyze contradictory aspects belonging to different levels.[24] On the one hand, there is a distinction within an identity; on the other hand, there is an encompassing of the contrary. Hierarchical opposition necessitates the attachment of a value to one of two opposites. That is, a highly developed idea, to which a value is attached, contradicts and includes a lower idea. For example, what makes the right hand superior to the left hand in their relation to the whole (or the body), and what makes it stand for the whole, is the value people attribute to it (Dumont 1986, 227, 228, 252). Through the application of the notion of hierarchy, the one part or principle that stands for the whole, or the universe, can be made evident. The application of Dumont's structural-hierarchical approach can lead to significant conclusions regarding a Middle Eastern society that have been hitherto unrealized.

This ethnographic study has led the author to assign importance to the notion of "invisibility" in its relation to what is visible.[25] It is theoretically significant to note that

> with the decline of structuralism, it has become common for anthropologists to criticize the use of dichotomous categories. But it is worth stressing that there is nothing *essentially* wrong with them. The absurdity lies only in assuming that all dualities have the same logical status, or in insisting that all thought can be reduced to dualities. It cannot *always* be wrong to counterpose "mind" to "body," or "reason" to "emotion," or "life" to "death regardless of context." (Asad 1997, 45n7 [italics in original])

Egyptian villagers' cosmology and patterns of thought and action can be understood by focusing on the distinction they themselves make between *aẓ-ẓāhir*, the visible (apparent), and *al-āṭin*, hidden, or *al-ghaib*, the invisible and unknowable.[26] Concentrating on this opposition facilitates the study of the complicated cosmological order by starting with this simple grounded principle and moving toward the cluster of principles of thought and action built upon it. Although the details of different modes of thought are not comparable, the principles by which collective representations are organized may be generalized (Evans-Pritchard 1933, 1934, 1974; Horton 1967; Lienhardt 1954, 1961; Tambiah 1973, 1985, 1990).

This study examines to what extent the distinction between the visible and invisible corresponds to the distinctions between the public and private, social and psychological, outward and inward, objective and subjective, physical and spiritual, and natural and supernatural. The themes of private, invisible or inward, *bāṭin* and its opposite public, visible or outward, *ẓāhir*, have important meanings in the context of people's interactions with one another. What is inward is associated with intent, *niyyah*, that constitutes a core element according to which people's actions can be designated as social, economic, religious, or political. Peasants' actions, for instance, can be identified as political if their intent is concerned with issues of justice, legitimacy, and allocation. Theft for economic reasons is different from theft for political motive, whereby the victim's wealth is viewed as unfair profit from an illegitimate and exploitative system (Brown 1990, 1991). In specific social contexts, the word "*bāṭin*" means that which is hidden and secret. Secrets are private matters that are intentionally kept from the public view. A person whose secrets are unveiled, especially those that have negative moral or social implication, is called *mafḍūh*—shamefully exposed. In this connection, the concept of *satr*, cover, is socially significant. To maintain his social dignity and honor, a person not only endeavors to act honorably in order to demonstrate his worthy attributes, but also to painstakingly hide his moral defects and imperfections from the public. The one who succeeds in achieving his goals by behaving honorably and concealing his mistakes is called *mastūr*—covered. Keeping the private affairs or secrets of a person, family, or group concealed is their own responsibility. This study, then, attempts to delineate the boundaries between public and private scenarios. A significant contribution of this monograph is in recognizing that the antitheses of the visible and invisible upon which Egyptian folk cosmology are built are conducive to understanding the dynamics of public and private scenarios that occupy a major space in current scholarly discussion.

The ethnographic material found here was obtained through four fieldwork tours of varying lengths conducted between 1980 and 1999. I discovered that these short and long intervals of ethnographic study had many advantages: First, it kept me thinking about the village and about the data I had collected. Second, I completed (or tried to complete) what I had unintentionally overlooked in previous fieldwork. This point is related to the nature of the complicated topic of people's cosmology that required, at least in this study, a lengthy period of time to understand and assimilate in terms of both its underlying principles and content. Third, these intervals helped me to discern whether there were any changes in the village social, economic, political, religious, and cultural domains, especially in the last decade, which has witnessed the rise and spread of globalization. Peasants, viewed by many as being locally oriented, have become interested in faraway countries and events (Muslim and non-Muslim), enticed by the reach provided by mass media, advanced means of communication, and expedient transportation. They also have to cope with the growing expansion of globalization, secularization, and consumerism on the one hand, and with the demands of maintaining their Muslim identity on the other.

Along with library research, archives, government documents, oral history, and textual tradition, I used in-depth interviews, participant observations, and longer-term observations to collect data. The number of persons I interviewed totaled 145 and included members of eleven families (six extended families, or *Dārs*, and five small families, or *dārs*) with whom I interacted extensively. These families were chosen from different descent groups representing dissimilar or diverse economic levels as well as rival political affiliations. Folk tales, songs, and sayings of both adults and children, males and females, were recorded and analyzed in the social contexts from which they sprang. This explains my extensive quoting of folk utterances: sayings, poems, and songs of the people themselves. In this study, as I did in previous works (1987, 1988, 1990a, b, 1994), I treat folk sayings or traditions as part of social life, not as a form of oral literature or verbal art separate from its

FIGURE 1.1 A gathering for religious teaching, *dārs*, in the village mosque.

social reality. To deal with folklore as a mere category of archived material is to strip it from its social and cultural contexts as well as to relegate it to an epiphenomenal category.

In the mosques of the villages I discussed religious principles, concepts, and values with religious leaders, *shaikhs*, or preachers and their followers (see figure 1.1). Preachers are chosen on the basis of their competence in religious knowledge, whether it is achieved through formal *Azharī* education or self-education. It is worth noting that with the exception of two preachers, there were no full-time official religious leaders, *imāms*, appointed by the Ministry of Religious Endowments to teach people Islamic principles or lead them in prayer. In addition to Friday sermons, which are structured and delivered in classical Arabic, there are two kinds of religious teaching that are delivered in an informal way: The one held in the mosque, the other in the homes of religious leaders or their followers. First, except on Fridays, a religious lesson, *ad-dars*, attracting several dozen attendees, is delivered everyday at the mosque after sunset prayer, *al-maghrib*, and lasts until evening prayer, *al-ʿishā*. Different religious and social issues are addressed, thus allowing those present to participate through discussion, argument, and questions.[27] Second, religious teachings, however, are not confined to mosques,

FIGURE 1.2 A gathering for religious teaching, *dārs*, in the *shaikh*'s house, in which the author (center) was participating.

but are sometimes taught in the homes of religious leaders or their followers where the texts, the holy *Qur'an* and interpretations of scripture, are read and commented on. I participated in both kinds of these religious lessons or sessions (see figure 1.2). The number of those who attend religious sessions in homes is less than those at mosques. However, home sessions are more intimate and longer than those at the mosque. Inside the house, attendees, sit on mats around a wooden table, *ṭabliyyah*, where the religious leader reads and interprets books related to Muslim tradition, *turāth*. Except for their religious knowledge, there is no particular dress or symbol that distinguishes *shaikhs* from the other people in attendance.

Although they are not affiliated with particular political parties, local preachers, through sermons and religious sessions, have been involved in public debates criticizing and opposing the intrusion of the central government in people's lives. The informal and spontaneous way through which preachers interact with members of the community has resulted in the formation of small moderate groups interested in discussing religious issues with political implications.

It is an important fact that religious teaching is not restricted to gender. *Shaikha* Badawiyya, a revered and knowledgeable woman, served as a religious teacher, using the hall and one room of her house as a *kuttāb*, a local

FIGURE 1.3 *Shaikha* Badawiyya (center), with her daughter (carrying her child) and a neighbor.

institute for teaching and memorizing the *Qur'an*. She represents a substantial challenge to those who unjustifiably claim that Muslim women do not participate in religious spheres.[28] Her house was a center of attraction and children from around the village would attend her *kuttāb*. Adults and parents would also visit her to either seek advice or gain information about their children's religious education (see figure 1.3). *Shaikha* Badawiyya was not only a great reservoir of information and folk narration, but was also an excellent social mediator through whom I had the opportunity to interview both women and children directly in her *kuttāb*.[29]

Organization of This Book

This book is divided into seven chapters, including the introduction and the conclusion. Throughout, people's paramount assumptions concerning the cosmos, including those of visibility, invisibility, sanctity, inhabitability, hierarchy, reciprocity or symbolic exchange, time, space, and cardinal points through which the universe is ordered are extensively discussed. In order to construct a universe there must be inhabitable space (visible or invisible), entities and forces existing within that space, cosmic time, events, and cosmic signs revealing hidden dimensions of that universe. The relationships existing among various phenomena, objects, and events are explored.

Starting with the relationship among the physical, visible, and social components of the surrounding environment, chapter 2 delineates the cosmological implications embedded in village location, architecture, ecology, economy, and oral history that evidences religious significance. The villagers' notion of the cosmic capital implicit in the concept of *as-satr*, divine cosmic shield or cover, as a source of security in both public and private meanings is also addressed.

The dynamic and hierarchical relationship among visible and invisible spheres of the cosmos and related notions of superordination and subordination is dealt with in chapter 3. It is not only the cosmos but also the social world that is hierarchically divided and ordered through the dominant dichotomy of visible and invisible. This dichotomy coincides with other socially significant opposites related to the relationships among men and women, outside and inside, open and closed, and public and private.

The antithesis of visible/invisible is reflected not only in the macrocosm and in society but also in the person or microcosm as will be shown in chapter 4. As hierarchy orders the cosmic totality, it also constructs the totality of the person. Personal, social, and cosmological dimensions are fused in the person, as symbolically and hierarchically constructed by Egyptian culture. However, the Egyptian holistic view of self-hood with its hierarchical implications does not necessarily result in the lack of an autonomous or independent sense of personhood. Rural Egyptians endeavor to connect the known with the unknown at multiple levels of the universe, society, and person.

As hierarchy orders the cosmic totality and the totality of the person, it also generates gender distinction within the social whole. In chapter 5, special attention is given to gender hierarchy as represented in men–men, men–women, and women–women relationships maintained through socialization, gift exchange, and religious and secular rituals and ceremonies such as the *zikr* and *zār*. Symbolic exchange encompasses personal, social, and cosmic-mystical zones and goes beyond the mere exchange of gifts to include the constant reciprocity of material and immaterial symbols (words, incantations, or prayers) among people and invisible beings. These invisible beings and forces exist to evoke imaginative knowledge, while possibly obscuring the limits of ordinary religious experience.

Rural Egyptians do not consider the visible and tangible world as the only accessible world of experience; rather, as is discussed in chapter 6, there are multiple invisible and imaginary worlds from which possible worlds emerge. In effect, the notion of invisibility and related concepts of spirituality provide the possibility of a more complete cultural and religious experience. This chapter refutes the Western dominant paradigm of modernity by showing that rural Egyptians have their own paradigm of secular modernism that does not negate religious nor sacred orientations. Villagers' concepts and beliefs concerning this world, the world of the tomb or death, *ʿālam al-qabr*, and the world to come are interwoven and integrated, together forming a holistic cosmic view. Religious concepts and beliefs are not just parts of these worlds, but eventually make up these worlds. However, this holistic cosmic view is challenged by the penetration of secularism and globalization, whose negative impacts are viewed as signs of cosmic corruption leading to the annihilation of this world, that will be followed by another world in which nothing will be corrupted, hidden, concealed, or invisible.

In summary, this volume attempts to delineate the correlation among people's concepts of the person, society, and universe within the framework of their cosmological belief system. It is the dynamic and hierarchical antithesis of the seen/unseen, apparent/hidden, or visible/invisible through which public and private scenarios in rural Egypt are demarcated. Egyptian folk cosmology is consistent in many significant aspects with the overarching religious (Islamic) conceptual system. This holistic cosmic view has been maintained by both men of religious learning and common people against the ongoing corruption by secularism and globalization. The future of folk cosmology, one concludes, is not a matter of purely local concern, but is bound up with the future of tradition and religion in Egypt as a whole.

Notes

1. Folk cosmology or peasants' world views have had a great impact on poets, and novelists who have drawn genuine pictures of the life of the countryside. This influence is explicitly and implicitly shown, for example, in the work of Abdel Rahman al-Sharqawi, Yusuf Idris, and and Abdel-Hakim Kassem. In his foreword to al-Sharqawi's novel *al-ard* (*Egyptian Earth* [Cairo: Dar al-Katib al-Arabi, 1954]; translated into English by Desmond Stewart [London: Saqi Books, 1990]), Robin Ostle says that with "the genration of al-Sharqawi and Yusu Idris, the world is viewed from the perspective of peasants themselves" (pp. x–xi). Likewise, in his foreword to Abdel-Hakim Kassem's story *ayyam al-insan al-sabah* ("The Seven Days of Man," translated into English by Norment Bell [Evanston, IL: Northwestern University Press, 1996]), Ahmaed Abdel-Muti Higazi (p. x, emphasis added) points out that "Kassem is loyal to his experience and to his perceptions in the minutest detail. *The village in his perspective is the capital of the universe. Everything he sees is measured by its standards, and everything he writes springs from its life.* . . . In Kassem's language poetry is blended with prose in such a way that *the novel takes on the character of authentic folk literature.*" Also, he (pp. ix–x) appreciates the novelist's unique way of depicting

> the image of the village, the faces of its people, the characteristic traits, the distinctive expressions, the penchants and the homes they live in-their wives or their husbands, their children, their animals, and their belongings. The fields surrounding the village, the palm trees and the willows, the water wheels and the lanes, the feasts and the festivals, the love and affection that bind its people together, the strife and enmity that at time divide them. The house and animal pen, the mosque and graveyard, the slaughtering of animals and the baking of bread. The bond between husband and wife, the relations between fellow wives, the flowering of full-fleshed adolescence. Day in the village and evening in the village, the guest house and the coffeehouse, weddings and funerals, degrading poverty and indomitable spirit. How the sun rises, how the shadows retreat, the burning of the noonday heat, and the fall of evening. Cries and whispers, sounds and echoes, the harshness and the tenderness on the men, the misery of the women and their occasional little joys. The fatigue of the day, the ecstasy of the *zikr*, and the dreams of the journey to the feast of Saint Ahmed Bedawi in Tanta.

2. Studies that deal with Middle Eastern people's cosmologies are woefully limited and scant. When reviewing the rich and well-established ethnographies of cosmologies and worldviews of different societies in various parts of the world (Barth, 1987; Goodenough 1986; Howell 1989; Kearney 1984; Kiernan 1981; Kluckhohn 1949; Ohnuki-Tierney 1968, 1969, 1972; Redfield 1941, 1960, 1968; Reichel-Dolmatoff 1971; Tax 1941; Traube 1986, among others), no apparent substantial study of the cosmologies of Middle Eastern people, particularly those of rural Egyptians, has been conducted.

3. According to Shils (1981, 12 [emphasis in original]), tradition "means simply a *traditum*; it is anything which is transmitted or handed down from the past to the present." In another place Shils emphasizes that tradition "includes material objects, beliefs about all sorts of things, images of persons and events, practices and institutions. It includes buildings, monuments, landscapes, sculptures, paintings, books, tools, machines. It includes all that a society of a given time possesses and which already existed when its present possessors came upon it and which is not solely the product of physical processes in the external or exclusively the result of ecological and physiological necessity" (1981, 12). Shils regretfully criticizes the way tradition has been neglected, saying "[if] we read an analysis of a contemporary social scientist of what happened in a given situation, we see that the pecuniary 'interest' of the participants are mentioned, their irrational fears are mentioned, their desire for power is also mentioned; internal solidarity of groups is accounted for by irrational identifications or by interests; the stratagems of their leaders of the constituent groups are mentioned; tradition is seldom mentioned as having anything to do with important things. Realistic social scientists do not mention tradition" (1981, 7). He points out that social scientists "avoid the confrontation with tradition and with their omission of it from explanatory schemes by having recourse to 'historical factors.' In this way, they treat tradition as a residual category, as an intellectual disturbance which is to be brushed away" (1981, 8).

4. As happened, for example, in the dramatic case of the formation, from below, of Islamic movements in Egypt in the mid-1970s.

5. Cosmological assumptions or axioms refer to "the paradigmatic relationships in accordance with which the cosmos is constructed" (Rappaport 1999, 264). Although

these assumptions are not identified with "values," "values may be implicit in them, entailed by them, or even derived as theorems for them" (Rappaport 1999, 264). Cosmology and worldview are differentiated from each other by Redfield. He argues that worldviews are formed by the folk or the majority of people, while cosmologies are constructed and articulated by the erudite elite (Redfield 1960, 91; 1968, 88). To emphasize this distinction, Redfield (1968, 89) points out that "the gap between the ordinary man's worldview and the scientific cosmology is very great indeed." This distinction, however, is connected to the basic dichotomy Redfield makes between *Little Tradition*, characterizing common people or the folk, and *Great Tradition*, belonging to the reflective intellectuals (Redfield 1960, 41–42). Redfield's distinction, however, proves to be insufficient. With reference to Egyptian society, for instance, the intellectuals share with the folk or the majority of people the common cosmological concepts and values, though they might reject or elaborate on some of them.

6. Rural Egyptians or peasants constitute the majority of the population of Egypt; however, anthropological studies concerning them are fewer than those concerning other groups. In his review of "Anthropology in Egypt," Hopkins states that, "Over the years there has been considerable interest in *two marginal groups*, the Nubians around Aswan and the Bedouins of the northwest coast and of the Sinai peninsula" (Hopkins 1998a, 50 [emphasis added]).

7. For further discussion of the term *fallāḥ*, peasant, see chapter 2.

8. Also, historical and social misrepresentations of and prejudices against the peasant were made by urban intellectuals in seventeenth-century Egypt (Baer 1982, 13–20).

9. "Among the figure in the scholarly imagining of the post-colonial world, 'the peasant' is a strange kind of presence" (Mitchell 1990, 129). Mitchell offers a meticulous criticism of misleading and racist statements about Egyptian peasants made by Critchfield, Ayrout, and Le Bone. Historical and social misrepresentations of peasants have been reflected in the Egyptian media and writings of intellectual elite. Abu-Lughod (1998a) points out that images of rural Egyptians as ignorant and backward created by Egyptian state officials and urban elite, including television and textbook writers, are not true (el-Aswad 2000a). See also, Fred H. Lawson (1981, 131–53), who differentiates between peasants' and artisans' revolts in rural Egyptian society in the period between 1820 and 1824.

10. In the same vein, Mayfield, quoting an Egyptian expert, says, "The fellaheen as a rule cannot be hurried into adopting new ways of doing things" (Mayfield 1971, 180). Ayrout's conclusion (1963, 141), which reminds us of Levy-Bruhl's theory of primitive mentality, can be summed up as follows: "The truth is that the fellah does not think outside the immediate present, he is referred to the moment. No time and place except the present have much effect on his mind, because they have none on his senses. He is like a primitive or child; his intellect is controlled by the things he is feeling and doing. He looks for causes and effects not in the rational, but in the visible order." These inadequate and false statements lack material evidence.

11. Burke (1991, 24) argues that "the historical literature has emphasized the nonrevolutionary character of the Middle Eastern peasantry, stressing the fatalism of peasants and the oppression of corrupt governments and landowners. The elite bias of many sources and stereotypes about the nature of Islamic societies account to con-

siderable extent for this view." However, the statement that Egyptian peasants are politically passive has been refuted by scholars (Baer 1962, 1969; Brown 1990; Goldberg 1992; Schulze 1991), who give numerous examples of the *fellāḥīn*'s revolts and rebellions against the government during the eighteenth and twentieth centuries. For example, for almost two months—March and April 1919—Egypt witnessed "one of the great peasant revolts of her history and of the twentieth century. Contemporaries viewed it as having international importance because it was the result of thirty years of European domination, and its resolution would be likely to affect all Western colonial empires. For us, it marks the emergence of Egyptian liberalism and the construction of the modern state" (Goldberg 1992, 261).

12. See, for example, Trimingham (1965, 1968); von Grunebaum (1955); Antoun (1968); Geertz (1968); Gellner (1969); and el-Zein (1977).

13. If "orthodox" Islam refers to tenets or doctrines and practices of the *Qur'an* and tradition (of the prophet) as interpreted by the *'ulamā*, religious scholars, these basic doctrines and practices (including the five pillars: *ash-shahāda*, the testimony of the oneness of Allah and Mohammad is His prophet; *aṣ-ṣalāt*, five-times daily prayers; *az-zakat*, alms-giving; Ramadan fasting; and *al-hajj*, pilgrimage to Mecca) are observed by ordinary Muslims regardless of their occupations or education.

14. Zeghal (1999, 372) argues that "[b]y creating a state-controlled religious monopoly, the Nasserist regime brought the ulema to heel and forces them into complete political submission in 1960s, but gave them, at the same time, the instrument for their political emergence in the 1970s."

15. Addressing the same issue, Abu-Zahra (1997, xii) argues that the "assumption that the common person cannot relate his practices to the Islamic tradition, and that the Islamic text is not available to the common man deflect from investigating and comparing the different ways in which people relate their practices to the Islamic tradition in diverse Muslim societies."

16. For further information concerning this point, see el-Aswad (1988, 1994).

17. For further criticism of Weber's theory of Islam, see B. Turner (1974). See also Gran's insightful study (1979) in which he asserts the Islamic roots of capitalism.

18. Concerning the problem of Western misrepresentation of the other (the oriental or the Muslim), see Edward Said (1979, 1981), and Bernard Lewis (1966).

19. For a review of Muslim orthodox cosmology, see Burkhalter (1985); Heinen (1982); Izutsu (1964); Nasr (1964); Netton (1989); Rahman (1960); and Wan Mohd Nor Wad Daud (1989).

20. For example, the late Muhammad Mitwally al-Sharawy, a former minister of religious endowment in Egypt and a widely known and respected scholar, is an excellent example of the *'ālim* who published a series of small books through Akhbar al-Yaum (Today News) Press. Some of these books are *al-Ghaib* (The invisible or the divine secret) (1990); *as-Siḥr wa al Ḥasad* (Magic and envy) (1990); *al-qaḍā' wa al-qadar* (Fate and divine decree) (1989); and *Nhāyat al-'ālam* (The end of the world) (1990).

21. The concept of *al-ghaib*, the unseen and unknowable, is a fundamental principle in Islamic theology; however, it has a profound impact on Muslim's daily lives.

22. Western scholars tend to question the credibility of unseen and magical dimensions of experience while appearing to approve and even reaffirm it. Lane informed

us that he attended in Egypt a special sort of "magic mirror of ink" in which a young boy was asked by the magician to describe what he saw in the ink. After observing many experiments, Lane, referring to the magician, said:

> He now addressed himself to me; and asked if I wished the boy to see any person who was absent or dead. I named Lord Nelson, of whom the boy had evidently never heard. . . . The magician desired the boy to say to the Sultan—"My master salutes thee, and desires thee to bring Lord Nelson: bring him before my eyes, that I may see him, speedily." The boy then said so; and almost immediately added, "A messenger is gone, and has returned, and brought a man, dressed in a black suit of European clothes: the man has lost his left arm." He then paused for a moment or two; and, looking more intently, and more closely, into the ink, said, "No, he has not lost his left arm; but it is placed to his breast." This correction made his description more striking than it had been without it: since Lord Nelson generally had his empty sleeve attached to the breast of his coat: but it was the *right* arm that he had lost. Without saying that I suspected the boy had made a mistake, I asked the magician whether the objects appeared in the ink as if actually before the eyes, or as if in a glass, which makes the right appear left. He answered, that they appeared as in a mirror. *This rendered the boy's description faultless.* (1966, 252–53 [emphasis added])

Despite such a document, Middle Eastern or "oriental" people's beliefs in the supernatural have been viewed as backward and exotic. However, one must mention "the quite striking proliferation of U.S. television programs in which aliens, angels, and supernatural beings solve social and even individual problems in what is at the same time proclaimed to be a technology-driven scientific and rational society" (Bahl and Dirlik 2000, 4).

23. According to Ortner (1984, 129), "'Geertz' heart has been more with the 'ethos' side of culture than with the 'world view,' more with the affective and stylistic dimensions than with the cognitive."

24. It is significant here to note that "Gregory Bateson is one of the rare anthropologists who clearly saw the necessity of organizing a hierarchy of levels" (Dumont 1986, 23).

25. The notions of visibility and invisibility constitute inseparable domains of rural Egyptians' daily lives (el-Aswad 1987, 1988, 1993, 1994, 1997, 2001a, b, 2002a, b). Also, they are reflected in folk literature such as *Arabian Nights* that consist of "four categories of folk tales: fables, fairy tales, romance, and *cosmic as well as historical anecdotes*. . . . The essential quality of these tales lies in their success in interweaving the unusual, the extraordinary, the marvelous, and the supernatural into fabric of everyday life. Animals discourse and give lessons in moral philosophy; normal men and women consort or struggle with demons and, like them, change themselves or anyone else into any form they please; and humble people lead a life full of accidents and surprises" (Haddawy 1992, xiv [emphasis added]). In *Arabian Nights* one reads such tales that deal with visible and invisible spheres as the tale of "The Merchant and the Demon"; "The Fisherman and the Demon"; "The Envious and the Envied"; and "The Enchanted King" (Haddawy 1992). It is worth noting that anthropologists have found similar notions to be part of empirical reality in different societies. In an insightful account, Jackson pointed out that

> [e]xperiences we tend to gloss as belonging to the unconsciousness—an abyssal region of the mind-are conventionally construed in many preliterate societies as belonging to the unknown-a penumbral, inscrutable space. Thus, in Polynesia, the world of light . . . is contrasted with the darkness. . . . For the Kuranko of northeast Sierra Leone, the contrast between daytime and darkness is suggestive of a more far-reaching distinction between secular authority and "wild" power. . . . In Central Australia, the contrast between waking and dreaming worlds also conjures up with a distinction between the patent, visible world of quotidian existence and the latent world of Dreaming from which all life comes and into which all life ultimately returns. . . . However, none of these distinctions implies that domains of darkness, wilderness, or Dreaming are other-worldly, super-natural. On the contrary, they are worlds that enter experience of the lifeworld not ordinarily brought into consciousness, *but they are integrally part of empirical reality.* (Jackson 1996, 14–15 [emphasis in original])

26. Although not the focus of this study, political issues related to conspiracy and secret organizations in the Middle Eastern context might be better understood with reference to the predominant concept of concealment or invisibility.

27. See Gaffney's study (1994) in which he discusses the significance of religious lessons delivered by preachers in Upper Egypt. Also, Antoun (1993) provides a case study of religious lessons in the Jordanian context.

28. The role of females in religious teachings has been overlooked by scholars. Likewise, in the domain of folklore, El-Shamy points out (1999, 13) that "until recently, collectors, with few exceptions, have not paid sufficient attention to females as a source of Arab tales." See also, El-Shamy (1980).

29. Also, *Shaikha* Badawiyya possessed a remarkable memory that helped her not only in offering advice in daily matters, but also in participating in a local informal contest of the "memorization of the *Qur'an*," which she occasionally won. As part of that contest, two persons, usually men (still, the *Shaikha* was allowed to participate), recited a verse of the *Qur'an*. The second one recited another verse on the condition that he (or she) proceeded immediately from the last word of the first competitor. The same condition applied to the first person who, in reciting a different verse, was required to use the last word of the verse relayed by the second competitor.

2

The Village in a Sociocosmic Context

What follows is a descriptive account of how rural Egyptians have pictured to themselves the world, as well as the immediate environment in which they live, in unique representations in which religious and cosmological dimensions are interwoven. These representations invest with meaning the community's history, social units, physical structure, and economic life, as well as the community's names for adjacent communities. What is visible, physical, or material can be understood through explicating its relationship with what is invisible or imaginative, representing something beyond the natural physical or objective reality.

The Setting

El-Haddein is a village located in the Beheira governorate of Egypt's Western Delta (see frontispiece). The distance between el-Haddein and the town of Kaum Hamada (the capital of the district of Kaum Hamada) is about 9 kilometers. El-Haddein lies about 140 kilometers northwest of Cairo. At the local administrative level, it is one of eight villages that constitutes a unit, *waḥdah maḥallīyah*, whose local center is Dist el-Ashraf. El-Haddein is bordered by four villages: To the east there is Khirbita; to the southeast, Dist el-Ashraf; to the northeast, el-Qalawat; and to the north, Kafr Ziyada[1] (see figure 2.1). In 1976, the population of el-Haddein was 8,644. However, it more than doubled in ten years, reaching 18,238 in 1986.[2]

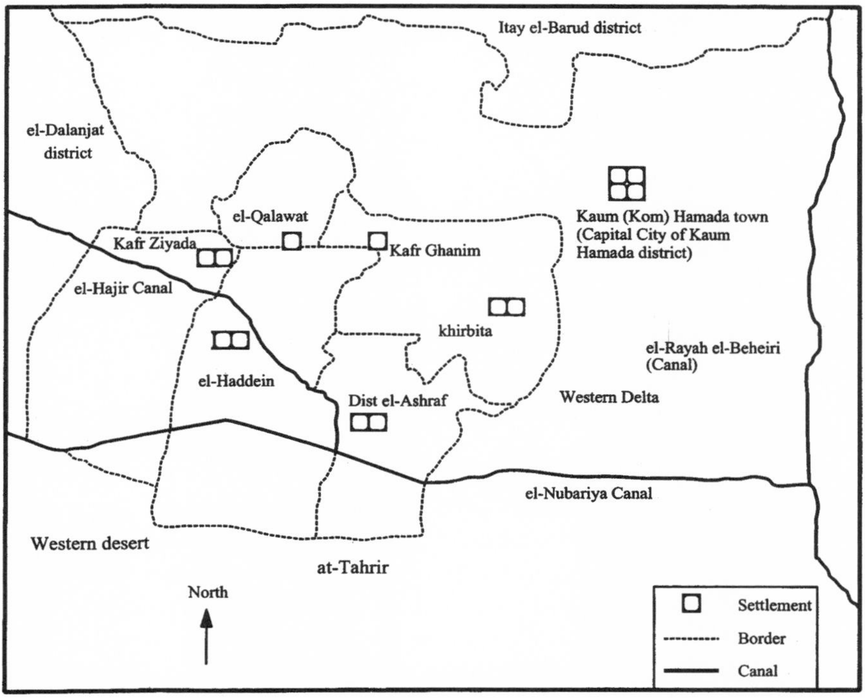

FIGURE **2.1** The borders of el-Haddein village.

Tanta, the capital city of the al-Gharbiyya governorate located 50 kilometers east of the village, is the largest and most active commercial center in the region. It is also a city endowed with religious significance, because it is home to both the shrine and mosque of the renowned Muslim saint and religious (folk) hero, al-Sayyid al-Badawī, a revered pillar, *quṭb*, at the level of the nation and the Muslim world. Folk songs praising al-Sayyid al-Badawi are frequently sung, as well as being available on audio recordings. Villagers travel to Tanta to pay homage to *Shaykh al-ʿArab* al-Sayyid al-Badawī and to buy goods, including roasted chick peas and sweets, *ḥummuṣ wa ḥalāwah*, for which the city is celebrated. Village shop owners purchase their wares and newlyweds shop for their furnishings and gold from the city. Educationally, Tanta University, established in the early 1960s, has been a distinguished provincial university, attracting a substantial number of students from the Delta and elsewhere in Egypt.

Although not the main concern of this study, brief mention can be given to the fact that rural communities of the Delta (referred to as Lower or North Egypt) and the Valley (referred to as Upper or South Egypt) share a national culture, notwithstanding significant differences between them. These differences, overlooked by social scientists, have historically and politically been founded on and categorized as *baḥarī* or *bihīrī*, which locally means both "sea" (with reference to the Mediterranean Sea located north of Egypt) and "north," and *ṣaʿīd* or *ṣaʿīdī*, which refers to Upper Egypt. Upper Egypt historically has been socially and economically underprivileged and neglected as compared to Lower Egypt, which with its geographical features (particularly of the Nile Delta) and location near important waterways has received greater exposure to Eastern (or Asian) and Western (or European influences) (el-Aswad 2002c). Although national projects such as sugar cane factories, universities, and the High Dam have recently been established in Upper Egypt, it continues to lag behind in terms of economic development, income per capita, education, entertainment, health, sanitation, electricity, and other community services.[3] As opposed to the rich and fertile soil of the Delta, the arid ecological conditions of Upper Egypt further inhibit its development. As such, it has become home to peripheral, marginalized and tribal social groups that are more conservative than those residing within the Delta. Being distant from the political center, it is also a location for active Muslim groups that are motivated toward resisting the central control of the state. Although peasants or *fallāḥīn* of both Lower and Upper Egypt have been the target of jokes made by urbanites and the elite, Upper Egyptians, *ṣʿāyda*, in particular have been targeted. They are, however, also recognized as being tolerant and showing a great sense of humor.

The division between Lower (North) Egypt and Upper (South) Egypt is prehistoric; however, Menes, in the fourth millennium, was the first ruler to establish a unified Egyptian kingdom. "There is no doubt that Lower Egypt dominated the Valley by the superiority of its civilization" (Moret 1972, 103).[4]

Archaic Egyptian cosmology (el-Aswad 1997), with its myths of Osiris and Isis, was manipulated to support such division.[5] The opposition between Lower and Upper Egypt, which nature had made both different and complementary, was reflected in the mythical rivalry between warrior brothers that was necessary for the life and equilibrium of the universe: "The Kings of the North, who maintained the tradition, call themselves the heirs and successors of Horus, Son of Isis . . . the Kings of Upper Egypt regarded themselves as the heirs of Seth. . . . Seth continued to be a dynastic god, though secondary all through the history of Egyptian civilization" (Moret 1972, 103). Horus was depicted as a falcon and served as a lord or divine symbol of the god of the Delta, while Seth, brother of Osiris, was depicted as a greyhound or anteater that survived as a symbol of the lord of Upper Egypt (Ions 1968; Moret 1972).

Oral History and Religious Significance

History is part of a larger totality that encompasses religious, cosmological, ecological, and social meanings and is used as a basis for ascribing meaning to the present, for defining identity, and for naming certain localities. As a source of indigenous experience, oral history provides knowledge of the broader context within which people become aware of changes that have occurred in time and place. A strong sense of locality is generated in the village whose identity stems from shared historical events as well as collective sentiments and face-to-face relationships. Villagers offer two interpretations for the name el-Haddein: one is an ecological explanation (to be discussed later), and the other is a historical interpretation that sheds light on people's imaginative construction of their history and the history of adjacent villages. Though oral-historical accounts vary from person to person, they all share in relating to significant past events. The fundamental concern here is more with people's own view and construction of their history than with the accuracy of the details.

History and geography are meaningfully interwoven through events viewed by people as significant because, for them, real history begins with the advent of religious (Islamic) faith, before which people lived in the era of ignorance, *jāhilīyya*. El-Haddein, according to local exegeses, means "two borders" that in the past separated people of the faith from their atheist enemies. The name "el-Haddein" becomes relevant when viewed within the historical context in which, as oral narratives suggest, the names of the adjacent villages, Kafr Ziyada, Dist el-Ashraf, Khirbitta, and Biban, were coined.

Within the context of the cosmic and political history of Islam, local folk narratives, supported by historical accounts offered by the educated of the community, tell us that an Arab commander (with reference to ʿAmr Ibn al-ʿĀṣ)[6] seized Egypt with a divine mission to spread Islam over the world.[7] Some time after he entered Egypt, this Arab commander marched northward toward Alexandria. On his way he destroyed the resistance of a strong defensive center that became known as *Khirbithā*, or Khirbitta. The vernacular Arabic word *khirbithā (kh-r-b)* means "ruins" or "destruction." In Khirbitta there is a mosque, *jāmiʿ Abūl-Haul*, named after a Muslim warrior killed in battle who became a legendary figure after his death. The name *Abūl-Haul*, meaning "father of horror," commemorates the fear and terror felt toward him by those he faced in battle. Creating a heartfelt image of the heroic martyr, the folk narration recounts that the Muslim hero never relinquished the battle, even using his detached, broken leg to continue fighting (el-Aswad 1990a).

Before the destruction of the village, the army leader chose a site to be a center of his command. This site was a place where food and provisions for the Arab army were prepared—today called "Dist el-Ashraf," which means "the place of noble people" (the Arabic word *dist* also means "cauldron" or "big pan made of metal used for cooking food"). The word "el-Ashraf" here designates the Arab or Muslim heroes, martyrs, and leaders who won battles in this region in the early days of Islam. Villagers contend that Dist el-Ashraf continues to be honored by being presently the mother village and seat of the local unit that administratively controls eight villages, including el-Haddein.

Not very far from Khirbitta exists a village known as "Biban." *Bibān* is a plural form of the Arabic word *bāb*, which means "door" or "gate." Biban acquired its name from the gates that were used for defending Khirbitta before its destruction. Muslim armies, the folk story tells us, destroyed both Biban and Khirbitta while fighting *al-kuffār*, the atheists or unbelievers, who fled to another center called Kafr Ziyada,[8] connoting a place where atheism abounded. One must mention here that villagers differentiate between the word *kafr*, meaning a small village, and *kufr*, which means atheism. Nevertheless, in some specific contexts as in the one discussed here, the two words are used interchangeably. (See figure 2.2, which accords with the story as told by the villagers.) Within this historically constructed scenario, the village of el-Haddein acquired its name from its strategic location between the Muslim armies and the village of unbelievers. In other words, the word "el-Haddein" refers to the borders that separated the Muslims, or the *Ashrāf*, whose camp was Dist el-Ashraf, located three kilometers southeast of the village, from their enemies, whose camp was Kafr Ziyada that was located two kilometers north of el-Haddein. The proximity of these villages attests to the aggressive march of the Muslim armies as they swept away their enemies. The events that are ordered in the oral history or narrative appear to be real insofar as they are incorporated into a meaningful order of moral existence (White 1987, 23). What makes these folk narratives significant is the fact that they reflect the locals' awareness of the prehistoric distinction between Muslims and non-Muslims as a defining marker of their identity.

In certain significant aspects, these folk narratives concur with the historical documentation of the Muslim–Arab advent in Egypt. According to written records, ʿAmr Ibn al-ʿĀṣ, after seizing Babylon in 641, marched northward to Alexandria along the western bank of the Nile where his army and cavalry had space to maneuver without being hindered by the canals and swamps of the Delta (Ibn ʿAbd al-Ḥakam 1961, 107; Butler 1978, 282). There were many historic battles fought in the western Delta between the Muslim and Roman armies (Egypt being a part of the Roman or Byzantine Empire).[9] One of these, the battle of Kaum Sharik, literally translated as "the mound of Sharik," was named after an Arab leader (Butler 1978, 286–87; al-Maqrizi 1970, 163). Kaum Sharik is presently the name of a village, admin-

Legend

⟶	Muslim armies
◆	Muslim armies and their alliance
☐	Center of Muslim armies in the area
○	Village
●	Kaum Hamada
●	Damanhur

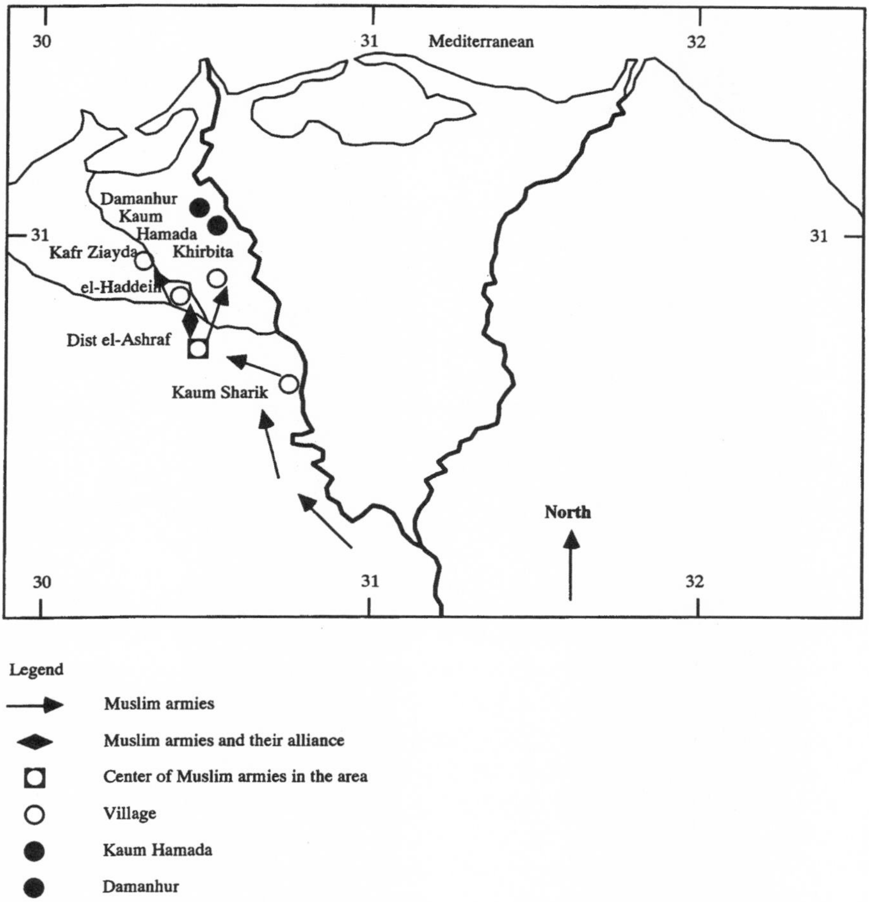

FIGURE 2.2 The course of Muslim armies as described by villagers.

istratively related to the Kaum Hamada district, located twenty-five kilometers southeast of el-Haddein.[10]

The region, Khirbitta, and adjacent villages witnessed some critical historical events when, after the assassination of ʿUthman Ibn ʿAffan (the third righteous Caliph), people revolted, demanding the punishment of the assassin (Zaytun 1962, 337). Moreover, the region became an attractive place for members of the holy family in the aftermath of this internal Muslim crisis, out of which the Shia sect emerged.[11] This crisis followed the murder of ʿAlī Ibn Abī Ṭalib, the cousin and son-in-law of the Prophet Muhammad and fourth Muslim Caliph. Although the inhabitants of the village define themselves as

FIGURE 2.3 The shrine of Sit Raḍiyyah.

ʿArab el-Haddein, the village as a whole is identified with a female saint, Sit Raḍiyyah,[12] a descendant of Fatima az-Zahra, daughter of the Prophet Muhammad and wife of ʿAlī Ibn Abī Ṭalib. A marble plaque mounted into the outside wall of the shrine identifies the saint as follows: "This is the sanctuary of the blessed ʿAisha daughter of ʿAli al-Raḍī, son of Musa al-Kazim, son of Jaʿfar al-Ṣadiq, son of Muhammad al-Baqir, son of ʿAbdullah al-Husain, son of Faṭima al-Zahraʾ, daughter of Muhammad, peace be upon Him"[13] (see figure 2.3). In Islam, "the reality of heredity finds expression in the existence of the shurafa or descendents of the prophet" (Stoddart 1984, 24). "El-Haddein" and "Sit Raḍiyyah" are names used synonymously by both residents of the village and pilgrims who come to visit the sanctuary of the saint.

Three festivals are held to honor and celebrate the venerability of this saint. The first one is on the second day and on the first Friday following *ʿĪd al-Fiṭr* (or *al-ʿĪd as-Ṣaghīr*), the feast of breaking of the fast of Ramadan. The second festival occurs on the second day and on the first Friday of *ʿĪd al-Aḍḥā* (or *al-ʿĪd al-Kabīr*), the feast of sacrifice. The third festival, which is celebrated at nighttime, is the saint's birthday celebration. A great number of people come to participate in these festivals, visiting the saint's shrine and donating money, among other things. These donations have been used for building two mosques in honor of Sit Raḍiyyah. The people of el-Haddein enjoy a reputation for being "a generous people," *ahl al-karam*, and for showing great hospitality to their guests, relatives, and friends who take advantage of these occasions to maintain their social relationships within the community.

Social Units: Cosmological and Sociological Implications

Hierarchy is reflected in various domains of everyday life. Generally, it is the hierarchy of values that both differentiates people from one another and maintains the similarity among them. The social organization and political life of the village can be understood within a holistic hierarchical framework encompassing kinship, residence, propinquity, economy, cosmology, and religion, and the values associated with them. This framework provides the arena within which individuals define their identities, interact with one another, and formulate their interests and act to achieve them.[14]

El-Haddein is organized in terms of social units called *dārs*. In its overarching cosmological and sociological sense, *dār* is used by villagers to mean a place (visible or invisible) in which people (alive or dead) and other entities or beings (visible or invisible) exist. The basic meaning of *dār* is simply a "house" in the sense of both an architectural structure and an inhabited place. The term *dār* can be extended to mean the family, village, and country as well as world. Egypt as a country is referred to as *dār al-miṣrīyīn*, home of the Egyptians.

Furthermore, *dār* can signify spatial and temporal dimensions denoting a place where people reside for a certain period of time. The "temporal forms and spatial structures structure not only the group's representation of the world but the group itself, which orders itself in accordance with this representation" (Bourdieu 1977, 163). In a word, the temporal and spatial meanings of *dār* are associated with birth and death in the sense that both the house and tomb are referred to as *dār*. In its cosmological significance, *dār* implies multiple interwoven meanings when used with other terms such as *dār ad-dunyā*, this worldly life, also referred to as *dār al-fanā'*, the inferior and evanescent abode, and *dār al-ākhira*, the otherworldly life, used synonymously with *dār al-baqā'*, the everlasting abode, which includes the world of the tomb (*barzakh*) where the deceased wait until the day of resurrection. Within this holistic context, members of the same *dār* will live together in this life, be buried together in the family tomb, and be together in the afterlife.[15]

Dār also connotes homogeneity in the sense of belonging to a village where most people are born, having regular interpersonal relationships with one another, and where along with their ancestors they are buried. For villagers, a city or urban environment in general is not viewed as a *dār*, because it is a heterogeneous place where foreigners from different regions live and interact formally rather than through face-to-face relationships with one another. In the village, by contrast, an outsider is immediately identified as a stranger, *gharīb*. If the stranger does not inform the village of his birthplace, he becomes suspect and referred to as "homeless" or an "alien." The *dār* is the social shelter in which individuals seek intimacy and protection. Leaving or deserting it for whatever reason could lead to humiliation and loss of dignity as expressed in the simile, "*man kharag min dāru yanggal migdāru*" (Who goes away from his home will loose his identity). This meaning is applicable to those who leave their house, village, or country.

As a social unit, *dār* is used locally with reference to three hierarchical but interconnected meanings: descent group, extended family, and small or nuclear family. In order to maintain the distinction among these three meanings of the social unit of *dār*, I will refer to the first meaning by using italicized capital letters, *DĀR*; to the second meaning by capitalizing the first letter of the word, *Dār*; and to the third meaning by using all lower-case letters for the word, *dār*. Recognizing that there are no capital letters in the Arabic alphabet, this convention is strictly an analytical and not a local distinction.[16] Patrilineality, or a patriarchal view of the world, is the core principle upon which the social relationships among members of the same *dār* in its triple meanings are regulated.[17]

The descent group, *DĀR*, includes members who share a common male ancestor. The *DĀR* is characterized by the following features: It is grounded on and organized by the patrilineal principle, although other factors such as seniority or elderliness, wealth, political position, and education, for example, influence hierarchical ranking among its members.[18] Members of a *DĀR* have obligations and responsibilities toward one another and are expected to cooperate and participate on various social occasions. For this reason, each *DĀR* has its own *mandārah* or guesthouse in which such social and public events such as dispute settlements, political-election campaigns, and funeral ceremonies take place. The *mandārah* is used exclusively by men and represents the public face of the *DĀR*. In social activities such as wedding ceremonies and death rituals women participate within the private zones of homes, but not in the *mandārah*. Despite the fact that members of one *DĀR*, motivated by a sense of duty and moral obligation, offer financial support to one another, the *DĀR* itself does not form an economic unit. Each one has its own tomb (or tombs) in the village cemetery. Married women are buried in the tomb of their husbands' *DĀR*.

The extended family, *Dār, aila*, is a patrilineally oriented social unit consisting of a husband and his wife, children (sons and unmarried daughters), and families of married sons. Although members of an extended family live in one residence, eat together from one dish, and participate in the household's activities, they constitute not a full economic unit, but a semi-unit. Families of married sons are not considered as independent or self-sufficient units, because they are residentially and socially dependent on the house of the father or the head of the *Dār*. Also, a deep sense of privacy is not completely obtained in the extended family. Occupational and income differences among married brothers living in an extended family cause economic inequality. The male heads of small families share the costs of common daily living, such as purchasing food or maintaining the household or property; however, they keep a part of their income for the personal and private needs of their own families, such as for clothes, medication, and education. In the extended family, wives of married sons are submissive to their *ḥamā*, or mother-in-law.[19] The one who shows independence from her mother-in-law is considered troublesome and her husband is asked to either control her or live independently, in a separate house.

The *dār* (*usra*), nuclear family, is the smallest social unit in the village and includes a husband, wife, and their children living within their own private space. This kind of nuclear *dār* differs from the extended *Dār* in significant respects. A *dār* or small family is considered to be an independent unit insofar as its economy and privacy of living are concerned. Both husband and wife of the same *dār* manage all the affairs of their household without interference from the husband's father or mother. The wife is depicted as *sitt ad-dār* or *sitt al-bait*, the mistress of the house.

Out of moral obligation, all members of a family should hierarchically follow or obey their father's or elder bother's advice and commands. However, the establishment of a *dār* is a powerful element in asserting independence from the hierarchical web. In one incident, a married son and his family had to leave the *Dār* because his father would not allow him to pursue a project to enlarge the cattle pen to raise calves for investment and commercial purposes. The son had asked his father's permission, but the father argued that the house was too small for the pen. Nevertheless, the son, motivated by the idea of improving and maximizing his interest, built a small house, next to which he attached a stable. The project succeeded and the son became the independent head of his own *dār* or small family.

Social and Political Differentiation: The *DĀR* and the *Aṣl*

Concepts of *dār* and *aṣl* form a significantly interwoven web within a system of social and cosmological meanings associated with both the politics and cultural values of the community. The word *dār* is derived from the root "*d-w-r*," which means to "circulate." Kinsmen, describing the unity of their blood, say *al-aṣl dāir*, meaning that the blood of the ancestor is circulating within the members of their *DĀR*. For villagers, *aṣl* is a multiple-meaning concept that can imply values and principles of rootedness, origin, descent, nobility, honor, self-sufficiency, or social status. By means of the different associations of the word *aṣl*, in addition to the meanings of the social groups *DĀR*, *Dār*, or *dār*, individual actors evaluate and differentiate themselves hierarchically from one another.

In their daily life, the *fallāḥīn* think and interact with one another in terms of *aṣl*. There are various interconnected forms of the term *aṣl* whose meanings vary according to the social contexts in which they are utilized. First, *aṣl* means "root" as related to descent, consanguinity, or blood, *dam*. All the members of one *DĀR* or descent group belong to one root, *aṣl wāḥid*, or male ancestor, whose blood still circulates within their veins, *ʿurūq*. In this sense, having *aṣl* is a source of pride, honor, and power. Strangers are called *nās bidūn aṣl*, "rootless people." When a stranger or man of unknown *aṣl* asks to marry a woman from the village, he is usually refused unless he proves he has relatives, *ahl*, or kin-root, *aṣl*. In a private scenario, a woman rejects such a proposal, saying that she cannot marry a man who "uncovers his head and whose kin do not exist," *qāliʿ rāsuh wa ʿādim nāsuh*. A person without *aṣl*, not belonging to the community, is treated as an alien or outsider *agnaby* (*gharīb*) and viewed with suspicion. Moreover, if the stranger is a troublemaker and violates the community's norms and values, he is quickly depicted as a bastard or illegitimate person, *ibn ḥarām*.

In a public scenario, for example, members of the same *DĀR* and its allies support their leader in the competition for political positions at both local and national levels—that is, for membership in the Local Popular Council, the Board of the Community Development Association, the National Democratic Party, or the National Assembly. Though conflict occasionally erupts between brothers or agnates, they are consistently reminded, in both private and public scenarios, that "blood never becomes water," *ʿumr ad-dam mā yabqā mayya*. Immediately following settlement of the dispute, one hears people cheerfully uttering the simile, "the blood (of brothers) flows toward each other," *ad-dam yaḥinn li-baʿḍuh*.

Second, *aṣl* refers to the noble and honorable actions achieved by the predecessors of a *DĀR* in establishing its reputation in the community. Implications of the meaning of *aṣl* here resemble those associated with the concept of honor, *sharaf*, a core virtue in most Middle Eastern societies.[20] In a public scenario, members of a *DĀR* stress their self-esteem and pride, in hierarchical terms, through recalling and enumerating the honorable deeds accomplished by their grandfathers and ancestors. Deeds such as holding prestigious positions in the village, building mosques, and donating resources for community projects including, for example, schools, health clinics, and telegraph buildings are politically significant. Members of *DĀR* Zaidan, for instance, proudly refer to the honorable action of their predecessors who offered the government a piece of land and a suitable building to establish the first primary school in the village. On the other hand, members of *DĀR* Shukr state that the reputable office of *ʿumdah*, head of the village, was held for the first time in the history of el-Haddein by their predecessor. Although the people of *DĀR* Nada do not disagree, they maintain that their grandfathers and fathers have held the office much longer than any other *DĀR* and that they have controlled the office consecutively for over fifty years.

Villagers differentiate between "nobility of blood," *aṣālat ad-dam*, and "nobility of action," *aṣālat al-fiʿl*. The classical Arabic phrase *ḥasab wa nasab* is used to refer to people who are known for their honorable deeds and noble kin.[21] A person who has root *aṣl*, or kin, *ahl*, is more honorable (*aʾṣal* or *ashraf*) than the one who does not, and a person whose predecessors are recognized as honorable (*maʿdan aṣīl*) is himself considered honorable. Descendants of notable people share the quality of *aṣl* insofar as they continue doing honorable actions. This statement is applicable not only to individuals, but also to any of the three levels of social units: *DĀR*, *Dār*, and *dār*. If the son of honorably rooted people, *awlād al-uṣūl*, misbehaves, villagers reprove his conduct by comparing it to that of his ancestors. Yet, if he corrects his behavior and acts respectably, people say that he has come back to where he belongs (to his noble root), *rajaʿ li-aṣluh*. Descendants of honorably rooted people are expected to be better socialized and disciplined than those with common forebears. Their misdeeds are criticized more severely than those of the offspring of ordinary ancestors or those who are considered rootless, *ʿadīm al-aṣl*. A person who does not have noble predecessors can establish his own honor and be called *aṣīl*.[22] Honorableness can be extended to a self-made individual who, through hard work and education, establishes himself in the community as a socially and politically influential person. Still, if he misbehaves, villagers, shaking their heads, say that he has returned to where he belongs, *rajaʿ li-aṣluh* (his inferior root).

The following event that occurred in May 1999 at the railway station of Kaum Hamada emphasizes the value of honor or *aṣl*, as related to an individual's action. In this event, the hero was not a member of an old generation or a dominant family, but was a nineteen-year-old university student and son of a very modest family. According to the story, a train coming from Damanhur stopped at the Kaum Hamada station, where the overcrowded passengers pushed one another to get out. Suddenly, an eight-year-old boy fell beneath a train car. Without thinking of the danger to himself, the student jumped down onto the tracks and rescued the boy. However, when the student tried to climb up from the tracks to the platform, the train began to move. In spite of the shouts and screams of the people to alert the conductor, it was too late to stop and the young man lost both of his legs. Women and men competed to donate blood to help the young man; however, all attempts were in vain. The student lost his legs in his effort to save a young boy from death. This event regenerated both public and private scenarios dealing with values of compassion, altruism, and honor and denouncing the emerging urbanized trends of disintegrating modes of egoism, selfishness, and apathy.[23]

Al-aṣl is not confined to men. Women and their behavior are evaluated in terms of *al-aṣl*. Before choosing a wife, a young man's relatives and friends privately advise him to "look for the honorably rooted woman" (*dawwar ʿalā al-aṣīla*), "take the deeply rooted (good) woman and you will be delighted or satisfied" (*khud al-aṣīla tirtāh*), and "take the honorably rooted woman even if you have to sleep on a mat (because of poverty)" (*khud al-aṣīlah wa-lau ʿalā al-ḥaṣirah*), because a poor but respectable woman is better than a rich but amoral one. A woman of noble manners, *bint al-uṣūl*, should not allow a strange male, or even a friend of her husband's, to enter the house when he is not there, unless there is an adult son present.

The image of the strong female character is reflected locally in the personality of ʿAziza or umm ʿAziz (the mother of ʿAziz), who established legendary distinction. ʿAziza's story began at her age of sixteen years when her mother died, leaving her in charge of two young sisters and a three-year-old brother. Two years later her father also died, leaving her with even more responsibility for her siblings. Because of the great fortune she inherited she was the center of village attention and gossip, especially when she refused many proposals from suitable young men, including close male relatives. Her refusals were because of her concern for her siblings and also her determination to obtain a high school diploma so as to enter business. Her troubles started when she found herself facing the problems of maintaining her land and livestock in addition to taking care of her siblings. She was known for working as hard as a bee, *naḥla*, exercising shrewd managerial skills, and determination. She was accused of being hardheaded, *mukhkh nāshif*, especially in dealing with the men working on her land and with her livestock. To protect herself she would carry a licensed gun, an action that seemed odd and viewed locally as masculine behavior. However, by hiring or finding jobs for the needy and through continuous donations supporting local public projects and services such as schools, mosques, and charitable societies, she gained the respect of the community. With complete self-denial she helped her two sisters not only to graduate and hold university degrees but also to get married, while the younger brother became a reputable lawyer. Behaving like a mother, though never married herself, she was, because of the community's respect, privately and publicly addressed as the "mother of ʿAziz" (ʿAziz being the name of her younger brother).

Third, *aṣl*, associated with birthplace, residence, territory, land, and place, connotes authenticity and rootedness in the village. Members of dominant *DĀR*s in the village assert that they and their ancestors are "the origin of the village," *aṣl al-balad*, and call themselves sons of the country or village,[24] *awlād al-balad*. The meaning of *aṣl* as a birthplace is associated with land, *arḍ*, also colloquially called *atar* (*athar*), meaning a mark or sign. The word *atar* is used to mean ownership of land or area as evidenced when a peasant says, "I am sitting in my place (land)," *anā gāʿid (qāʿid) fī atary*, or "this is my place that I inherited from my father and grandfather," *hādha atarī (makānī) abban ʿan jadd*. For the *fallāḥ*, the word *atar* implies tracing his land, territory, or house to its origin (i.e., to his grandfather or ancestor). It is worth noting that members of a group of blood relatives identify themselves not only with their *DĀR*, the honorable actions of their family members and their own private land, but also with their own residential section or neighborhood locality, *nāḥiyah* or *ḥittah*.

To summarize, the fundamental characteristics of the concepts of *aṣl* and *dār* are connected with the key notions of descent or consanguinity, action, and residence. To be a member of the community one must have roots (*uṣūl*), family (*dār*), kin (*ahl*), residence or house (*dār*), and act in accordance with people's expectations and principles. However, although the community is based on interconnected factors encompassing family, kinship, neighborhood, and residency, the shared cosmic-religious worldview and moral values are decisive factors in orienting rural Egyptians' social and political actions.

The Village, the House, and the Cosmos

The village consists of clusters of buildings and houses divided into a center and five sections, *nawāḥy* (sing. *nāḥīya*) or circles, *dawāʾir* (sing. *dāira*). To indicate a certain place, people say, *dāyr annāḥiya*, "around the residential section." The village boundaries are formed by the el-Hajir canal to the east; the drainage canal, *al-maṣraf*, to the west; *el-ʿizba el-baḥarīya* or the northern *ʿizba* (referring to *ʿizbat Ḥabbās*) to the north; and *el-ʿizba el-qiblīya* or the southern *ʿizba* to the south. ("*ʿIzba*" refers to an extended unit such as a farm that has been incorporated into the village.)

The center of the village, *wasṭ al-balad*, is comprised of over-crowded, single-story houses in which people from different kin groups or *DĀR*s live. There are also two mosques, one of which is named after the saint, Sit Raḍiyyah. The center of the village represents and encompasses the whole community. It recalls people's concepts of the center of the heaven. I was told that the center of the heaven is immovable and can be seen at all times from all directions. The center is considered to be the interior or heart, *qalb*, of the community, symbolizing values of intimacy, collectivity, and unity.[25]

To the east of the village center is the section of *DĀR* Nadā. This section encompasses the following structures: a mosque named after *DĀR* Nadā, a pharmacy, the Agricultural Cooperative Society building, and a telegraph. The head of *DĀR* Nadā, who is the chief man[26] of the Nada section of the village, held the position of president of the board of the Agricultural Cooperative Society for three decades. In the northeast region of the village center is the section of *DĀR* Shukr, which includes the houses and families of those related to that *DĀR* by kinship or political ties. This section also has two mosques named after *DĀR* Shukr, as well as an elementary school. To the north of the village center is the section of *DĀR* Habbās, and to the south, that of *DĀR* Zaidān. In the southern section of the village one finds a cemetery, four schools (of different levels: elementary, preparatory or middle, and religious *Azharī*), a health clinic, the location of the village leader, *dawwār al-ʿumda*, and the water supply. Meanwhile, along the western side of the village and close to the drainage canal, *maṣraf*, there are scattered houses belonging to different *dārs*, but mostly to *ʿizbat* or *DĀR* ʿIbīd. Hostility from competition between the northern and southern parts of the village occurs from time to time.[27]

Although the village is conceptually divided into sections, it is considered to be a unified community. The width of the village is described in spatial terms, "from the bridge to the bridge," referring to the distance between the two bridges built on the canals at the eastern and western edges of the village. Likewise, there are common or shared places and institutions that are available to all villagers. These include the marketplace, cemetery, health unit, agricultural cooperative society, telegraph building and schools.

The houses of el-Haddein village, like those of the rural Delta in general, are grouped densely together. The houses on one side of a street are so compact, they seem like one long building with many doors and windows. As such, villagers can walk or move easily on their roofs without being hindered by any space between them. This compactness strengthens the notions of kinship and propinquity or neighborhood. However, because of this density and because the roofs of these houses are used for the storage of straw, cotton, corn stalks, and *jillah* (cakes made of dung mixed with straw and used as fuel), fires could be fatal and threaten to destroy the entire village.

There are both traditional and modern houses in the village. Two fundamental differences between these types can be noted. First, the traditional house is built of bricks made of mud mixed with straw, while the modern house is built of burned or red bricks, *ṭūb aḥmar*, supported by cement or ferroconcrete and steel. Second, the traditional model has a courtyard while the modern house may not. When the modern house does have a courtyard, it is not attached to the house from the inside as in the traditional house, but rather is attached from the outside. Apart from these differences, the structure of the modern and traditional house is similar. They are, however, hierarchically differentiated according to size, building material, and location. Rich people only are able to build or own modern houses, though they keep their old houses for raising domestic animals such as water buffalo, camels, cattle, sheep, and poultry. Both traditional and modern houses are decorated with symbolic icons and phrases denoting cosmological and religious significance. Phrases written on the walls include: "In the name of the God" (*bism allah*), "Allah is the most great" (*Allahu Akbar*), "Thanks be to God" (*al-ḥamdu lil-lāh*), "The Protector (God) is existent" (*asstār maujūd*), and such similar ones. Also, handprints showing the five fingers of the hand are painted or stained on the walls of the houses for the purpose of warding off the evil eye.

All houses are alike in formal structure. This is because the traditional house is built according to an implicit plan or framework. However, this distinctive feature characterizing the plan as used in the Middle East and differentiating it from the structure, frame, or plan as understood in the West has not been unrecognized but rather underestimated by scholars. In the West, the plan is an abstract construct "set apart from 'things themselves' as a guide, a sign, a map, a text, or a set of instruction about how to proceed. But in the Middle East . . . nothing stood apart and addressed itself in this way to the outsider, to the observing subject" (Mitchell 1988, 32).[28] What is missing here is the fact that the plan of the traditional house is implicit or invisible, not explicit or visible. In other words, the traditional house of a specific society presents an order with an implicit plan, model, or framework (Rapoport 1969; Fathy 1989; el-Aswad 1996a). Without embodied plans it would be impossible for the dwellers to define the shape and form of their houses or to specify certain places or rooms to be used. Through these implicit plans, the distinction between the folk houses of Egypt and United Arab Emirates, for example, has been cross-culturally studied.[29] The embodied or implicit plan might not be as highly precise or professionally explicit as the Western or modern plan, yet it still guides people in selecting specific locations, in dividing the space, and in using certain materials. The meaning of the implicit plan or scheme[30] is presented in what Bourdieu (1977, 88) calls "apprenticeship through simple familiarization" with general patterns of daily practices. According to apprenticeship through familiarization, individuals are not taught specific rules, instructions, or plans, but rather they assimilate, embody, or internalize the general patterns of associations and oppositions by being involved in daily practices. Apprenticeship through familiarization can be demonstrated by the example of food preparation in the village. When a peasant woman prepares food for her family, she, assisted by her daughters or other females in the family, relies on what she has learned by observing her mother and female kin, and not on cookbooks or written recipes. The recipe, rather, is internalized, embodied, cognized, or existent in the woman's mind or body. Hence, one cannot say that the woman does not have a plan of what, when, where, and how to cook. Similarly, a peasant has in his mind a picture, plan, or model of the house he wants to occupy or build. Why does this mental plan not have equal status with a modern plan?

This form of embodied or internalized plan leaves room for individuals to react within the boundaries of what is socially and culturally acceptable. What keeps the traditional house alive amid ongoing changes is its flexibility and ability to uphold a constancy of pattern or model whose dynamics depend on the relationship among its constituting units.[31] "Departure from the pattern and a variation in identity can render the entire arrangement meaningless" (Shils 1981, 230).[32]

When people express a theory or view of their house, it often implies assumptions about the nature of both society and the cosmos. The cosmos as a whole is the core toward which villagers are oriented. However, villagers are highly concerned with building their houses in relation to the cardinal point of north.[33] North, *shamāl*, locally called *baḥarī*, is an adjective derived from the word *baḥr* or sea, which refers specifically to the Mediterranean Sea that is located north of Egypt. Though the general plan of the village is circular, northward expansion and housing development have resulted in its assuming a pear-shaped pattern. Most villagers who earned money in the last three decades through working abroad or in Arab Gulf countries bought land and built houses mostly in the northern part of the village. People prefer to build their houses with the fronts facing north, because of the northerly blowing breeze. Because houses are directed toward the north, major streets run from east to west.

The house as a whole is seen as a sanctuary,[34] *ḥaram*, and enjoys its respect, *ḥurma*. Individuals stress the sanctity and respect of the house, saying, for example, *ad-dār lahā ḥurmah* (The house has its own respect). Similarly, to show respect to the house and its dwellers, it is common to hear them utter certain phrases before entering, such as *dastūr yā ahl al-bait* or *dastūr yā ahl ad-dār* (Pardon, oh inhabitants of the house). If the house represents the interior, sacred, and private domains, the mosque, *bait Allah* (The house of God) represents the exterior, sacred, and public domains.

The main objective of both building a house and establishing a family, as is assertively expressed by villagers, is to inhabit the universe, *yʿammar al-*

kaun. To participate in the universe is to participate in cosmic inhabitation through biological and social reproduction that is to make the house or the cosmos full. In other words, "to marry is *ʿammar*, to be full" (Bourdieu 1977, 126). The "fullness of the house," a dominant notion in traditional societies of the Middle East,[35] is analogous to that of the pregnant woman, the granary, the fields, and the village. As described by an elderly man, the fullness of the house is shown in the oiled interior wooden lock, *ḍabbah*, of the door caused by the hands of women involved in milking and making butter and cheese, the purest, richest, and most blessed of food items. Inhabiting the universe is a divine objective that is to be fulfilled by God and His blessed creatures. Going beyond the social locality of their homes, villagers often refer to the "divinely inhabited house," *al-bait al-maʿmūr*, an invisible cosmic center located above the *Kaʿbah* toward which Muslims turn in prayer. In this sacred cosmic house, such invisible entities and forces as angels, spirits, and *baraka* (blessing) exist.

Cosmological invisible forces and beings, viewed in spatial and temporal terms, are drawn into people's everyday practices. The universe itself is constructed of visible and invisible components.[36] Concerning the invisible domain, the universe is existentially divided into three worlds: *ʿālam ar-rūḥ*, the world of the spirit; *ʿālam al-malāʾikah*, the world of angels; and *ʿālam al-jinn wa al-ʿafārīt*, the world of *jinn* and ghosts.[37] These three categories of invisible entities and forces are dispersed not only throughout the cosmos, but also throughout the person[38] and house. Concerning the structure of the house, however, specific divisions are connected to each category based on the distinction between purity, *ṭahārah*, and impurity,[39] *najāsah*.

Angels and benevolent spirits are believed to hover around places such as the entrance, the storage, and the granary, insofar as they are clean and closed. None of these places are seen opened except without good reason. The entrance, *al-madkhal*, is the signature, face, *wajh*, or the public aspect of the house that represents the family or household as a whole. The door of the entrance is the masculine shield that keeps the interior world of women and privacy covered up and protected. Metaphorically, it is always good to keep the door from which the wind blows closed, *elbāb illy yagy minu arrīḥ siddu wa-starīḥ*. However, at specific periods of time, before noon or before sunset, for example, it is acceptable that women undertake light work such as cleaning the wheat or rice as well as to entertain their children on the *masṭabah*, a mud brick bench against an external wall of the house.

People seek heavenly protection through the use of symbols such as arches, round objects, and written phrases that praise Allah. The space above the outside door takes the shape of an arch representing the cosmic arch of the heavens.[40] Here, villagers hang plates and horseshoes that are believed to be imbued with mythical and cosmic forces that protect them from the evil eye and vicious spirits. The *fallāḥīn* insist on keeping the entrance clean so as to maintain the respect and sanctity of the house as well as to attract good spirits, angels, and *baraka* (blessing).

If the entrance, particularly the gate, is the protective shield of the house, the threshold, *al-ʿatabah*, represents an ambivalent space uniting the contraries. The threshold is the place where rites of passage (Van Gennep 1960, 25) or transitions from one state to another—outside to inside and the reverse—are carried out. In other words, the threshold, a space used for crossing, is a symbolic intermediary through which the oppositions of outside/inside, open/closed, going out/coming in, secure/insecure, men/women, and public/private are linked together. Also, the threshold is a place endowed with magical potential, whether it be attached to a mundane or sacred building such as a mosque. For its ambivalent quality, the threshold is akin to a crossroads and used for magical purposes.

The storage room, *ḥujrat al-khazīn* or *al-khaznah*, where food items are stored, is a site for women's activities. Though food in general is a blessing (*niʿmah*), bread (*ʿaish*, which also means life), and milk (*laban* or *ḥalīb*, including milk products) are considered the most sanctified food items.[41] Like the storage room, the granary, *ṣawmaʿah*, containing wheat and maize for bread-making, is a place that must be kept full and clean. Located in the courtyard, the granary, reflecting the idea of the sacredness of stored crops, takes the shape of an erected arch penetrating the cosmic space. Angels and benevolent spirits are believed to visit the storage room and granary in which the most sanctified food items are stored. Peasants are careful to keep pieces of bread even in the living room and bedroom so as to maintain *baraka* (blessing) and to ward off the negative impact of dangerous spirits (see figure 2.4).

The courtyard, *al-ḥaush*, is referred to as the center of the house, *wasṭ addār*. It represents another ambivalent space encompassing such opposite qualities as purity/impurity, scared/profane, and angel/devil. For example, in the courtyard, the granary and storage, which are considered pure and hallowed places that attract angels, coexist with the lavatory and stable, which are impure and profane places that attract *jinn* and *ʿafārīt*. Also, the courtyard contains the oven, *furn*, which is a small square- or rectangular-shaped structure made of unburned or baked bricks. Among women there is a belief that *jinn* and *ʿafārīt*, as being created of fire, like to reside there. The woman, as she puts a loaf of dough in the oven, says "O pardon, O occupants of the place" (*dastūr yā sukkān al-makān*).

The profane parts of the house, which include impure and filthy places such as the lavatory, stable, or other areas where unclean material is disposed of, are treated with great caution. The impure objects represent a threat to the

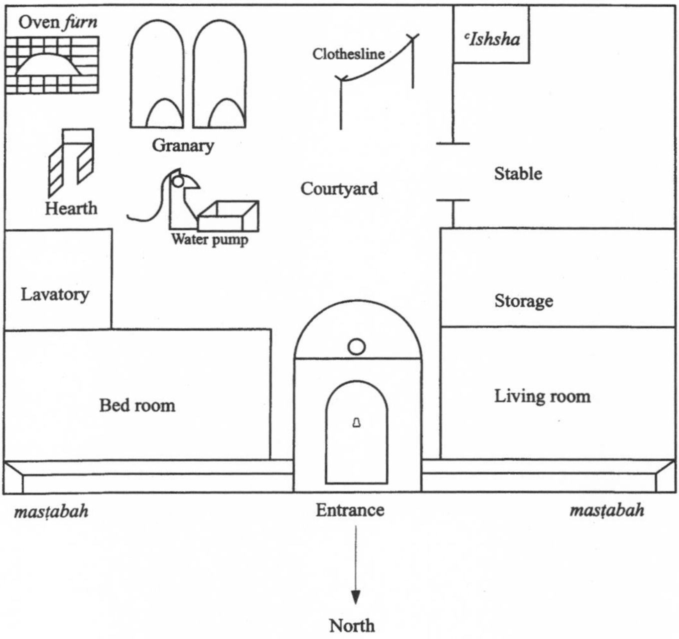

FIGURE 2.4 The structure of the traditional house.

social environment (Douglas 1966). Because of its uncleanliness, the lavatory is believed to be inhabited by malevolent spirits and jinn.[42] To protect themselves before entering the lavatory, villagers whisper, "*aʿūdhu beka min al khubth wa al khabāʾth*" (I seek God's protection against invisible wicked and malicious beings). It is prohibited to mention the names of God, prophets, and holy places or to carry sacred objects in impure and filthy places.

Ecology, Cosmology, and Economy: The Theme of *as-Satr* (Divine Protection)

Values attached to the landscape have a deep impact on people's cosmology as well as on ways through which they identify themselves with that region (Rappaport 1979, 116; 1999, 8, 458). The relationship between villagers and their ecology is ordered in both pragmatic and mystical terms. One of the most distinctive features of el-Haddein's environment can be understood by referring to the villagers' ecological interpretation of its name, different from the historical one discussed previously. As has been mentioned, the Arabic word *el-Haddein* means two sides or two edges. The village is located at the yellow edge of the western desert, on the one hand, and at the black edge of the fertile soil of the Delta on the other.[43] This is observed upon entering the village. Visible from the east is the black arable soil, *arḍ samrah*. As one moves westward through the village, a mixture of black and yellow soil, *arḍ ḥamrā* (red land), becomes apparent. This mixture of sand and soil fades as one continues on through the village and faces the yellow land, *arḍ ṣafrā*, of the desert from the west. The geographical location affects the economic activities of the village in that there is access to crops and plants that can be grown in different types of soil:

1. Black soil, *arḍ samrah*, is rich with mud and silt and useful for planting cotton, beans, sorghum, and vegetables.
2. Red soil, *arḍ ḥamrā*, is mixed with mud, silt, and sand. It is used for cultivating cereals such as wheat, barley, rice, sesame, and cotton.
3. Yellow soil, *arḍ ṣafrā*, also called "white land" (*arḍ baiḍah*), is comprised of only sand and is good for growing watermelon, melon, peanuts, potatoes, and orchard trees, including palm, mango, and citrus.

There is limited use of modern technology in farming; camels and donkeys are still important for agricultural activities.

In addition, there are three seasonal classifications of crops:

1. The winter crop, *al-maḥṣūl ash-shatawī*, planted during October and November and gathered in winter and spring, includes cereals such as wheat and barley, vegetables such as cabbage and cauliflower, and clover.
2. The summer crop, *al-maḥṣūl aṣ-ṣaifī*, planted during February and March and gathered in spring and/or summer, comprises watermelon, melon, rice, taro, potato, sorghum, *mulūkhīyah* (*Corchorus olitorius*), and cotton.
3. The Nile crop, *al-maḥṣūl an-nīlī*, planted during July and August and gathered in winter and spring, includes sorghum, potato, and garlic.

Some crops, such as tomatoes, are planted during all seasons. Also, there are two systems for watering the land. The first is by perennial irrigation according to which peasants use a three-crop rotation system called *daura zirā-*

ʿīya.[44] It is used effectively in growing crops such as cotton and wheat. The second is an underground water system, called *baʿlī*; this method is used for cultivating watermelon and tomatoes, for example.[45]

As a cash crop, watermelon is the main source of income for the village farmers. Unlike cotton, which is a source of income for nearby villages, watermelon is planted annually and is not restricted by the rotation system. The crop, however, is not regulated within the capitalist market economy, but rather within the traditional or precapital mode of production.[46] Peasants also raise pigeons not only for commercial and nutritional purposes, but also for agricultural reasons. Pigeon dung is used to fertilize the soil in which watermelon particularly is planted. El-Haddein is well-known regionally as *balad al-baṭṭīkh* (The country of watermelon).[47] As the main cash crop of the village, watermelon is sold in large quantities to merchants of Kaum Hamada, Tanta, Alexandria, and other cities. The wealth of some landowners and peasants is interpreted as being the result of the commerce of watermelon within local or regional markets. It must be asserted that the incompatibility of peasants' economic activities within the capitalist world market does not thus render them as part of the periphery, as the followers of the dominant paradigm claim (Gran 1996, 336).

Peasant families work together, although they observe a sort of division of labor based on gender and age. Men undertake heavy agricultural tasks such as land preparation, hoeing, plowing, threshing, fertilizing, planting, and irrigating, while women and children perform other tasks such as weeding, picking out harmful worms, and harvesting. However, this division is not rigidly observed, since women also participate in fertilizing and planting, while men partake in harvesting and weeding. However, working with heavy tools and machines is done exclusively by men. Although they are enrolled in school, children below sixteen years of age and even as young as ten constitute an additional source of the family's manpower. Agricultural work involves a practical sort of knowledge related to weather conditions, seasonal changes, positions of celestial bodies, types of soil, fertilizers, kinds of seeds, and so forth. The courses of such cosmological entities as the sun and moon are carefully observed because of their impact on agricultural activities.

Owning land is a source of social prestige and wealth. However, there is an inverse relationship between *owning* the land and *working* the land. Those who own a large amount of land—the notables (*aʿyān*)—are expected to work less than people who have small plots. In other words, people who inherit or own large amounts of land do not work or cultivate their land by themselves but rather hire and supervise agricultural laborers who work for them, while people who own small plots cultivate their land by themselves. In this respect, there are three hierarchically classified categories of people who are involved in agricultural activities: *farmers* or *big landowners* who are able to hire agricultural laborers; *peasants* or *fallāḥīn* who own land and cultivate it themselves; and *agricultural proletarians* (landless villagers, also called *fallāḥīn*) or *ajīr* who sell their work and who constitute the lowest stratum in the village.[48]

In addition to agricultural and other economic activities, almost all households of the village raise livestock. Villagers who own land also own draft animals such as water buffalo, cattle, camels, and donkeys. Camels play an important role, especially for those with farmland located in the western desert. Water buffalo, cows, and sheep are also basic resources for villagers' dairy subsistence. Peasants do not slaughter these animals, because of the milk on which they depend in their daily life. Nor are camels killed until they grow old, when they are sold to butchers. Poultry and small animals such as rabbits and goats are also important economic elements in villagers' lives. Moreover, people who are not landowners but who work as agricultural laborers are also engaged in raising poultry and small animals for subsistence.

The spatial layout of the village asserts the intimate relationship between ecology and cosmology. The ecology of the region is imbued with cosmological meaning. The different kinds of soil in the village are associated with different values and orientations. The combination of fertile soil and yellow sand has significant impact not only on the economic and agricultural activities of the villagers, but also on their concepts of the surrounding environment. The western edge of the village is referred to as "desert" and is associated with masculinity, dryness, and openness, while the eastern edge is referred to as "land," *arḍ*, and is associated with femininity, fertility, productivity, and closure. Villagers have developed a conceptual distinction that attributes a higher value to the desert in spite of the fact that it is economically less significant than the fertile soil. The desert is a place believed to be invested with invisible powerful beings and forces. It is also associated with sanctity. The Arabic word used to describe this view of the desert is *al-jabal*, or the mountain, which encompasses meanings of highness, strength, toughness, masculinity, and steadiness. A wise, calm, and brave person is described as being "as steady as a mountain." A camel—a strong, patient animal—is associated with both the desert and sainthood. From the local point of view, seeing or talking to a camel in a dream means that a saint has revealed himself to the dreamer. Desert attributes of dryness, cleanness, and openness fit the image peasants have about sacred places. This image of the desert is opposed to the image of the black soil or mud, which is devoid of spiritual and sacred values though it has significant economic value. To honor and welcome a dignitary, it is common to hear villagers say that they will pave the road with sand, *nafrish al-arḍ raml*, when he comes.

FIGURE 2.5 *Shaikh* Ghānim (middle) attracts visitors to his house for blessing.

As has already been mentioned, there are three shrines in the village. Located in the desert and slightly west of the village are two: one of the female saint Sit Raḍiyyah, and the other of a male saint about three meters away.[49] Located in the cemetery, south of the village, a third shrine belongs to *Sīdī* Ghānim, whose descendants are believed to have inherited his power of blessing (see figure 2.5). The reputations of the two male saints are limited to the el-Haddein region itself; they are less prominent in prestige and honor than the female saint, Sit Raḍiyyah, whose reputation has spread beyond the village to remote villages and towns. While visiting the sanctuary of this female saint, people collect and retain a handful of sand from inside. Sand is believed to have *baraka* (blessing) and the power of healing. Interestingly, peasants never collect dust (powdery earth), but for the purpose of having *baraka* from the saint they will touch it.

The relation of desert to black soil is akin to that of space to earth. The desert is a vast and mysterious place endowed with spirits, beings, and powerful forces. Globally, villagers emphasize their belief in the interconnected relationship between the desert and the transcendent by referring to the fact that the most sacred place, the *Kaʿbah*, the earthly home of God, is located in the desert. *Kaʿbah* is the center of the entire cosmos, toward which Muslims turn in prayer and at which they perform the rituals of the pilgrimage, *ḥajj*. Villagers affirm that it is a matter of the hidden and sacred wisdom of Allah that this arid region, having neither water nor vegetation, has become one of the wealthiest places on the earth, religiously and economically. Above the *Ka'bah* exists *al-bait al-ma'mūr*, the heavenly inhabited (cosmic) house where benevolent spirits and angels praise and worship *Allah* continuously. It penetrates all of the heavens and is the link between the heavens and earth.

The economic activities of villagers are inseparable from their symbolic capital (Bourdieu 1977) referring to their social, ethical, and religious principles. Before starting their daily work or commercial bargaining with one another, villagers say *ṣalāt an-nabī rasmālī wa maksabi* (Praising the Prophet is my capital and profit). Villagers view work, *al-'amal*, as a sort of worship, and idleness as a sort of impurity, saying in public *al-yad al-baṭṭālah nagisah* (The idle hand is impure). Hard work is considered to be a cardinal value that enhances people's symbolic and economic capital or social status and income. Nevertheless, the result of one's work depends completely on God's willing, *mashī'at Allah*. As *Shaikh* Shukry, a farmer and not a religious leader, contends, Allah bestows His blessing, *ni'mah*, on whom He chooses. Furthermore, each person is responsible for maintaining that blessing, which might be in the form of good health, well-behaved children, a faithful wife, a reasonable mind, good friends, an unsullied reputation, useful knowledge, a respectable position, wealth, or, most importantly, a graceful covering (secured, not shamefully exposed), *as-satr*.

It is not uncommon to hear people repeat the word *satr* with its various forms in different contexts. In their daily lives, villagers say *Allah yasturak duniyā wa ākhira* (May God cover you in both this life and the hereafter) to express gratitude toward a person who has helped or done them a favor. When Sabir, a peasant who obtained a loan from the bank to cultivate his land, expressed his anxiety about the productivity of his crop as well as about his ability to re-pay his debt, he said *illy satrhā fi al awwal yastrhā fi al'ākhir* (May who so protects at the beginning [implicitly God], protect at the end). The notion of covering is so dominant in people's discourse that when a man, moving from a public zone to private domain, approaches a house he calls loudly *yā sātir* (O, cover) to alert the inhabitants, especially the women, of his approach so that they may take their precautions in maintaining their privacy.[50]

The economic life of Egyptian peasants is guided neither by the image of the limited good (Foster 1965) nor by the image of the unlimited good (Dundes 1971), but rather by the concept of *as-satr*. Fundamentally, *as-satr* implies such multiple meanings as those indicating whatever can be invisible, veiled, covered, concealed, protected, guarded, and secured. These multiple meanings encompass economic, social, personal, spiritual, and cosmological dimensions, which can be phrased, "cosmic capital." Cosmic capital here is identified in terms of neither the moral economy defined by Scott (1976) nor the calculating and rational economy defined by Popkins (1979),[51] but rather is based on three core components: legitimate means of economic resources, industrious people, and the cosmic power of God. These conditions establish the balance between secular and religious domains characterizing peasants' own secular modernism.

In their secular, mundane, or economic activities, villagers work diligently to maximize their interests and incomes so as to enhance their social positions.[52] Their activities, however, are validated by the scheme of the cosmological notion of *ar-rizq*, livelihood[53] (daily bread), which belongs to *ʿālam al ghaib*, the invisible or unknowable world. The cosmic power dominated by God, the Provider, the Merciful and the Coverer, *Razzāq Halīm Sattār*, can be reflected in, for example, the heavens, the power of blessing, sacred objects, hallowed places, sanctified periods of time, and in human beings such as prophets, saints, and pious people. This cosmic potential asserts the assumption that cosmic capital is fundamental to cosmic structure. To support the notion that livelihood is governed by cosmic power, villagers say *igry gary alwūḥūsh ghair rizgaq lan taḥūsh* (If you run as fast as a beast, you will not achieve more than what is predestined for you). This statement, however, is not fatalistic, but rather signifies the existence of a divine omnipotent power that dominates the universe through mercy (*raḥmah*) and trancends human understanding.[54] Villagers assert that it is not the material accumulation, but the *baraka* (blessing) of what they have that matters. A little capital that is blessed might be better than a large but envied, *manẓūr*, or unblessed, *mā fīha baraka*, capital. People who help others, for example in finding a job, are considered to be mediators sent by God. I heard a mother say to her son who was going to work abroad, *rabunā ywaqqaf lak awlād al-ḥalāl* (May God help you through good people). The father supportively replied, *rabb huna, rabb hunāk* (The God here is the same God there).

When a source of living depletes or ceases, or an additional economic responsibility presents itself, people say it will be replaced or compensated for by something else (by God), *yagtaʿ hunā wa yūsil hunā*. Within this logic of divine mercy, villagers' attitudes toward having a large number of children despite their poverty and despite the government's ongoing campaigns for birth control are rendered intelligible. The debate between the government and the folk regarding the relationship between the size of the family and their economic resources reflects two different views. Each view attempts to explain the logic of economic activity. For villagers, a newborn infant is by divine mercy assured of his or her own livelihood regardless of the actual economic difficulties it faces.[55]

The cosmic capital of *as-satr* is founded upon a view in which a distinction between *ḥalāl*, what is legally and morally gained, and *ḥarām*, what is suspicious and illegally obtained, is sharply drawn. A rich person or a poor man who is content and refrains from asking people's financial support is considered to be socially and economically covered or secure (*mastūr*). A wealthy but greedy person, *jashiʿ*; however, is not considered covered, because his behavior displays his dependence and vulnerability. Metaphorically, the image of heaven as laying gracefully, powerfully, and evenly over the earth triggers the cosmic concept of shield or cover, *satr*, in a balanced order as represented in the simile, "Stretch your legs as far as your blanket covers you" (*ʿalā gadd liḥāfak midd riglayk*).

It is to be noted that *as-satr* is implicit in the villagers' subsistence ethics. There is not a minimum or maximum economic standard against which the state of *as-satr* is measured. If someone is asked about his financial condition, he is expected to answer, "It is secured (covered) and praise be to Allah" (*mastūra wa al-ḥamdu lil-lāh*). This may explain the peasant's unusual ability to smile cheerfully and spontaneously as well as to be receptive to jokes and humor while experiencing unbearable economic hardships. *Ḥajj* Hamid, a poor but witty and beloved guard (*khafīr*) in the village, recounted that if a household has only bread, its residents should feel secure and covered, *mastūrīn*. What he says becomes intelligible on knowing that the basic constituents of the *fallāḥīn*'s diet, whatever its quality and quantity, are bread, *ʿaish* (which also means life), and *ghamūs*, a dip or any other food item accompanying bread. *Ghamūs* might be milk, cheese, cooked vegetables, or just salt. However, *Ḥajj* Hamid asserted that he had to eat plain bread, *ʿaish ḥāf*, without any other kind of food for almost a week when he lost his previous job as worker in the village cooperative society. According to his story, bread symbolizes *as-satr*, which can be translated into contentment, self-sufficiency, protection, independence, and blessing. To emphasize the importance of bread, *Ḥajj* Hamid uses similes: "If bread is available, *misḥ* [brine of sour cheese] would be a delicacy," and "Who has bread and wets it, has all that is good" (*man kān ʿandu al-ʿaish wa ballahu ʿandu al-khair kullu*).

Eventually, cosmic capital is understood within a holistic cosmic vision based on religious outlooks and local traditions that relieves the individual and society from the increasing attitude and pressure of materialism and individualism. It maintains the balance between the rich and powerful and those who, in spite of their poverty, show a great deal of integrity and independence (el-Aswad 1990a, 126). If *as-satr* is a positive state of being that should be secured, the opposite state, *al-faḍīḥah*, shameful exposure, must be avoided. When it comes to the point where the subsistence or cosmic capital of *as-satr* is threatened, villagers revolt forcefully.[56] As far as people are socially and economically covered (*mastūrīn*), they will never be shamefully exposed. In a discussion with a poor villager concerning the expanding gap between rich and poor caused by the competition for possessing material goods, he said *illy yasturuh ar-rab mā yfḍaḥu al ʿabd* (The one whom God protects [or covers] will not be humiliated by man or slave).

Migration of the *Fallāḥīn*

Before the 1970s, it was rare to hear that a peasant had left his village to work overseas for an extended period of time. It was not long ago that people ironically commented on peasants who went outside the village borders as being lost in the world and not knowing what to do. Also, it was believed, as if it were formally written (*maktūb*), that peasants were destined to spend their lives within the confines of their village. However, there has been a tremendous change in the attitude toward the future. This change is manifested in the transition from static to dynamic views of space and time. Economically, peasants have become capable of planning for their own future by utilizing opportunities that go beyond their immediate environment or locality.

The migration of villagers to Arab countries started in the late 1960s when some teachers and craftsmen arranged to work in Libya. The experience of these people was so successful that other villagers, skilled and unskilled, were encouraged to migrate to other wealthy Arab countries such as Saudi Arabia, Iraq, Kuwait, and the United Arab Emirates. However, migration and work abroad were particularly facilitated after the government's call for *al-infitāḥ*, the economic open-door policy, in 1973.[57]

In the census of 1983, made by the Agency for Reconstruction and Development of the Egyptian Village, migrants from el-Haddein numbered two hundred persons. Sixty percent of these were working abroad. In 1987, based on fieldwork I conducted in the village, the number of migrants who worked abroad had increased to 311 persons. However, the number decreased in 1995 to 274. One might classify labor migrants into three categories. First are the government officials, including teachers, nurses, engineers, and so forth. These officials are formally allowed leaves for a certain period of time, ranging, more or less, from one to four years depending on the rules and regulations implemented by each government institution. Second are the migrants working abroad with private labor contracts (mostly skilled craftsmen, construction workers, mechanics, and agricultural laborers). Third are the migrants who enter the hosting country under tourist or visitor visas and then change these to working visas after finding a job. The majority of migrants who work as agricultural laborers are those who have small land ownership as well as those who used to work as migratory laborers in the village.[58] These people borrow money from wealthy relatives or friends in order to cover the cost of airfare, and when they find jobs, send money back to their families to pay their debts.

The proximity of Arab Gulf countries to the birthplace of Islam bestows meaning to this migration as being motivated not just by material interest, but also by the Islamic concept of *hijra*, or migration to sacred places. Migrants who work abroad maintain their relationship with their families and friends in the village through letters and tape recordings. Moreover, most visit their families at least once a year. Most remittances or earnings sent to families or brought home with workers are invested in domestic projects such as animal or poultry farms, repairing or building houses, or buying land, trucks, and agricultural tools like tractors and pumps. Although workers are concerned with budgeting and investing their money, they spend a considerable amount of it on purchasing consumer goods such as television sets, tape recorders, electric fans, and so forth. These goods have become new signs of status and prestige as well as indicators of the change in people's attitudes toward new lifestyles. In addition, video recorders, satellite dishes, computers, and mobile phones have become accessible to those who have succeeded in doing financially well. However, access to the Internet is a privilege only for the wealthy.

As a consequence of this open-door policy in which the gap between rich and poor has increased, peasants have been seeking other economic alternatives such as with involvement in more than one job. A peasant might cultivate his small piece of land as well as seek to work in a public career such as being a guard in an agricultural cooperative, school, or the like. For villagers, a fixed income (*dakhl thābit*), however low, is a reliable means of living. A government job is a good example of the kind of work associated with a fixed income, but because of the government's low salaries, an official (*muwaẓẓaf* or *afandī*) might also work as a *fallāḥ* and cultivate his own land.

Migration has had a profound impact on the villagers' views or attitudes toward other people as well as toward themselves.[59] As workers in a foreign or Arab Gulf country in which expatriates from all continents are found, villagers have to cope with people from different countries, with their different cultures and backgrounds. Migrant's attitudes toward aliens or foreigners have become increasingly open and flexible. However, as far as the family structure in the village is concerned, there is no evidence to conclusively show that the migration of male laborers has affected the social and structural relationship among members of the family.

The impact of migration on the village can be summarized as follows. First, economic change has lead to housing development, where new or modern houses have been built close to or have completely replaced older ones. Also, the quantity of technological advancements such as in the use of trucks, vehicles, and modern agricultural machines has increased. Second, return migrants have become interested in investing their money in "land market," not just in agriculture. As a result, the economic value of land has unexpectedly increased. In the 1960s, the price of one *faddān* of black soil was 800 Egyptian pounds, while in the 1970s and 1980s it exceeded 15,000. Moreover, in the late 1990s the price of the same *faddān* had tripled, reaching over 45,000 Egyptian pounds. This has a negative consequence on *fallāḥīn* who seek to purchase land for agricultural purposes. Third, the social and economic status of agricultural laborers has risen because of the agricultural labor shortages in the village.[60] And lastly, because of their temporary migration, villagers have been actively involved in experiences that have broadened and deepened their worldviews. Peasants have become aware of inside and outside forces that affect their economic and social conditions.

Conclusion

This chapter has attempted to explicate the overarching sociocosmological context within which el-Haddein village is located and defined. It has traced the cosmological implications embedded in the village's location, oral history, physical structure, ecology, economy (cosmic capital), and the local political system. It has demonstrated that the social history and ecological characteristics of the village, along with the symbolic cultural values attached to the social unit of the *dār* and the related multifaceted concept of *aṣl* (root), influence the way people conceive of themselves and others. Through ongoing usage of oral history and traditions, villagers define not only the name and location of the village but also their relationships to other adjacent villages as well as to the country as a whole. This chapter has also discussed the structure of houses within cosmological perspectives—that is, different spaces that constitute physical structures of both the village and the house have been depicted as being associated with cosmic orientations.

This study has shown that the cosmological, religious, and mundane spheres of people's thought and practices are interactive and coexistent. The relationship between villagers and their ecology and economy is ordered in both pragmatic and mystical terms. The economic system of the village is interconnected with and affected by regional, national, and international markets and economic policies. The village, however, is not a passive unit in its relationship with these outside forces. The local socioeconomic politics are selective agents or forces that not only adopt what is good for individuals and families, but also influence the application of specific formal regulations and laws made by the state to change or develop the countryside.

The economic or material changes that families have undergone has not affected the structure of the household nor has it altered people's deeply rooted social and religious values and principles. Villagers show a great deal of interest in improving their economic conditions through working in the village or working abroad. However, they prefer their symbolic or cosmic capital of *as-satr*—being economically and socially covered, even with the minimum income—to achieving the maximum income whose sources are questionable. The cosmic capital is understood within a cosmic worldview, based on religious outlook, that liberates the individual and society from the increasing attitude of materialism and individualism.

In their daily lives and interactions, villagers describe themselves as well as others in the following terms: *Aṣīl*, deep-rooted, noble, genuine, and knowledgeable about *al-uṣūl*, the principles and manners of the community. A person who demonstrates honorable manners is metaphorically described as being of an original or genuine metal, *maʿdan aṣīl*. Rootless, *ʿadīm al-aṣl, ghair aṣīl (mush aṣīl)*, meaning that the root, blood, and actions of a person or collectivity are neither recognized by the village nor exist at all. The stranger who imposes himself on the community for no reason, the individual who respects neither himself nor the other through gossip or unveiling people's secrets, and the one who abuses his power are examples of rootless people.

Hospitality (*ḍiyāfah*) and generosity (*karam*) are signs of a plentiful house inhabited with honorable people. In their daily interactions, people, in praising someone or persuading him to do a favor, say *Allah yʿammar baitak* (May God bless your house and make it full of good things). The opposite of this is destruction, *kharāb*. The mere notion of destruction is deeply feared by peasants. To curse or insult somebody, it is enough to say, "May God destroy or ruin your house" (*Allah yakhrib baitak*), indicating a wish to eliminate the root of the cursed one. An uninhabited space (*faḍā*) or ruined place (*kharāb*) is an ambiguous space that drives people to create different sorts of speculations and imaginations about it, making it, at least conceptually, inhabitable with unseen entities or forces.

Notes

1. According to official records of the local cooperative society, the total area of el-Haddein village is 3,117 *feddāns* (1 *feddān* = 1.038 acres). The size of the village settlement is approximately 180 *feddāns*.

2. According to the general population census of Egypt (1976) made by the Central Agency for Public Mobilization and Statistics, the population of el-Haddein

village was 8,644. There was another census made in 1983 by the Organization for Reconstruction and Development of the Egyptian Village, or *Jihāz Iʿādat bināʿ wa tanmiyat al-Qarīyah al-Maṣrīyah*, supervised by the General Administration on Statistics and Information. According to that census, the population reached 15,034. However, the general population census of Egypt (1986) revealed that the village population had more than doubled in ten years. The 1986 census stated that all residents of el-Haddein village were Muslims.

3. In a recent article, "*subul taʿẓīm at-atanwwuʿ fī Miṣr*" (Means of enhancing genuine diversity in Egypt), published in the *al-Ahram* newspaper (July 12, 2001, no. 41,856, p. 12), Samir Naʿim, an Egyptian sociologist, argues, without giving specific figures, that the conditions of life in Upper Egypt in terms of income per capita, education, health, sanitation, electricity, and other community services are very poor and unjustifiably neglected.

4. It was in the Delta that royal institutions, which first appear in a primitive form in the group of the Western Nomes at Sais and in the confederation of the Eastern Nomes at Busiris, developed until they became the "protectorship" of Anzti and the "kingship" of Osiris, followed by that of Horus, Son of Isis, which dominated the whole of Lower Egypt" (Moret 1972, 103).

5. In this context, it is important to indicate that "mythology represents the most archaic form of universe-maintenance, as it indeed represents the most archaic form of legitimation generally" (Berger and Luckmann 1966, 110).

6. It is worth stressing that except for a few educated persons, villagers are not familiar with the name of this renowned Arab leader, though they mention some other names in their folk narratives such as Abul-Haul, a legendary hero.

7. The Arab conquest of Egypt goes back to 640–641 A.D. (Butler 1978, 280).

8. The identity of those who opposed and fought against the advancement of the Muslim army (whether they belonged to the Roman Empire or not) was not given or specified in the narrative.

9. It is interesting to note that Arabic became the official language by the beginning of the eighth century and "the first Arabic document of the Nile Valley was dated from 709 A.D." (Meinardus 1965, 7).

10. According to villagers' folk narratives, the enemies of Muslim armies were retreating northward, a fact documented in the written history. Butler (1978, 287), describing the advancement of the Muslim army, points out that "[s]teadily pushing the enemy before him, Amr now probably marched northeast, still following the canal which borders the desert, till he reached Dalingât, and from that point struck due northwards in the direction of Damanhûr." The city of Dalingât is located 25 kilometers north of el-Haddein. Damanhur, the capital city of Beheira governorate, is located 45 kilometers south of Alexandria.

11. Shiʿa were those who supported ʿAlī Ibn Abī Ṭalib as the fourth caliph who was killed (A.D. 661) by Muʿawiya Ibn Abu Sufiyan, and later his son al-Husain was killed in Karbalā (A.D. 680). "The starting point of Shiʿism is defeat: the defeat of Ali and his house by the Umayyads. Its primary appeal is therefore the defeated and the oppressed. That is why it has so often been the rallying cry of the underdogs in the Muslim world. Central to Shiʿism's appeal, especially for the poor and dispossessed, is the theme of suffering and martyrdom" (Mortimer 1982, 44).

12. Also, she is believed to have a kinship relationship with the famous saint al-Sayyid al-Badawī (at Tanta).

13. One must mention that despite the fact that the descent line of the female saint is patrilineally traced to ʿAlī Ibn Abī Ṭalib, the people, motivated by high respect for the direct descent from the Prophet, have traced her to his daughter Faṭima al-Zahraʾ. As indicated in historical references (al-Ṭabarī 1960; Azdī 1967; al-Masʿudī 1965; Ibn al-Athīr 1929), the saint's father is ʿAlī al-Riḍā, son of Mousa, son of Jaʿfar, son of Muhammad, son of ʿAlī, son of al-Husain, son of ʿAlī, son of Abu Talib. When I pointed out the error that the name Abdullah had been written in the marble plaque, I was assured by both local religious leaders and those in charge of the shrine that they were aware of the error and the name of Abdullah should be replaced by that of Alī (known as ʿAli zain al-ʿĀbidin), son of al-Husain. ʿAlī al-Riḍa, who had five sons and one daughter (ʿAisha), was the eighth Imam of the Shi'ites and known for his outstanding knowledge, piety, and generosity. The period of his imamate coincided with that of the Abbasid caliphate (Hārūn al-Rashīd and then his sons, Amīn and Maʾmūn), whose policy toward the Shi'ites was very harsh. In an attempt to attract the Shi'ites and *ʿalawis* (supporters of ʿAlī Ibn Abī Ṭalib) to his side, Maʾmūn, then the caliphate, offered ʿAlī al-Riḍa to be his successor. ʿAlī reluctantly accepted the offer, but was later poisoned by Maʾmūn (Saunders 1965, 112). Among the people, ʿAlī al-Riḍa is so highly distinguished and deeply revered that when a person questions the arrogance of any individual claiming knowledge and prestige, he or she ironically asks *huwa anta ʿAlī al-Riḍa?* (Do you think you are ʿAlī al-Riḍa?).

14. Kamāl al-Munūfī (1978, 1980) has reached a similar conclusion regarding the acceptance of the notion of hierarchy among rural Egyptians.

15. Unlike as in Western societies, Muslims do not bury their dead individually in coffins, but rather wrap them in loose sheets of cloth and bury them in the tomb assigned to the deceased's family or kin group.

16. In a Tunisian village, Sidi Ameur, studied by Nadia Abu-Zahra (1982, 53–94), villagers use the word "*dār*" to refer to both extended and nuclear families; but unlike the people of el-Haddein who use *dār* to mean a descent group, those of Sidi Ameur refer to the descent group by using the word *ʿarsh* or *farīq*.

17. Although patriarchy is a dominant ideological force shaping both family structure and state politics (Sharabi 1988; Barakat 1993), other critical factors and, more specifically, values such as seniority or elderliness, religious knowledge, education, and wealth should be considered.

18. See al-Munufi's discussion (1978) of the economic, political, social, and religious dimensions of the notion of hierarchy among Egyptian peasants.

19. While it is true in certain social settings that "[u]pon marriage the Arab woman becomes *sitt el-bait*, or 'the lady of the home'—a term that stresses an autonomous managerial role" (El Guindi 1999, 82), it is not in all circumstances or social levels that a married woman is called the mistress of the house or plays a dominant role, especially when she lives in an extended family.

20. In his discussion of the meaning of *sharaf* in the Middle East, Michael Meeker (1976a, 246) says that "the sharaf of a clan is a totality of significance derived from acts accomplished by its ascendants."

21. Unlike Andalusian society wherein honor is conceived in terms of power or

authority by which people maintain their precedence and superiority (Pitt-Rivers 1974, 18–47), in rural Egypt, specifically in el-Haddein village, the concept of *sharaf* (honor) or *aṣl* (nobility) does not imply the notion of power or authority. *Al-aṣīl* or *ash-sharīf*, the noble person, is expected to refrain from showing or using his power. Moreover, people who do not have power might be considered *uṣalāʾ* (noble people) if their behavior meets villagers' expectations. In this context, Egyptian villagers' usage of the concept *aṣl* or *sharaf* resembles that of the Turkish where "'the powerful' may very well not have sharaf, while the 'powerless' are sometimes highly endowed with sharaf" (Meeker 1976a, 263). On the relationship between honor and social groups or tribes among the Bedouins (Awlad ʿAli) of Egypt, see Abou-Zeid (1966, 243–59).

22. Various studies have addressed the meaning of *aṣl* in the Arab world. In her study of marriage conditions in a Palestinian village (*arṭās*), Hilma Granqvist (1931, 65–66) refers briefly to the Arab usage of the word *aṣl*. Also, Lila Abu-Lughod (1986, 41–49) has discussed the meaning of *aṣl* among a Bedouin society in Egypt, while Lawrence Rosen (1988, 23, 24) has addressed the concept of "asel" as used by Moroccans.

23. This event was publicly commented on in the *al-Ahram* newspaper by Fahmy Huwaydy (no. 41,063, May 24, 1999).

24. El-Messiri (1978) discusses different meanings of the concept of *awlād al-balad* (*Ibn al-balad*) from the viewpoints of different Egyptian strata. However, el-Messiri tends to restrict the concept to folk people who live in Cairo. The concepts of *aṣl al-balad* (the origin of the village), *awlād al-balad* (sons of the country), and *ibn al-ḥitta* (a son of the locality) are frequently used by Egyptian villagers of el-Haddein in their daily life.

25. For a discussion of the cosmic meaning of the center of the heaven, see chapter 3.

26. Eickelman, in his study of Boujad, a Moroccan town (1976, 98), indicates that it is socially significant and important for each quarter to have one or more "big men" (*kubbār*). The quarter that lacks a big man might not be considered a quarter at all.

27. A similar conceptual division of the village is found in other villages in lower and upper Egypt. For example, Mush village (upper Egypt) "is divided (conceptually not visually) into two halves and a large and somewhat intermediate number of neighborhoods. The eastern and western halves of the village to some extent regard each other with suspicion and treat each other as political rivals" (Hopkins 1987, 35).

28. Mitchell (1988, 52), drawing on Bourdieu's account of the housing of Kabyle society, argues that "there is nothing, strictly speaking, in the North African house made to stand apart as a frame. Its order is not achieved by effecting an inert structure that contains and orders a contents." To support his argument, he refers to Ibn Khaldūn's work on *ʿumrān*, suggesting that the building "is an active, undetermined process, marked in cycles of abundance and decay, rather than simply the material realization of a predetermined 'plan'" (Mitchell 1988, 53). It must be noted that Mitchell (2000, 1–34) has recently restated his argument about the representation, plan, picture, text, scheme, and framework as related to colonialism and Western modernity.

29. Some of the most significant differences between these two folk houses are as

follows: 1) In the Emirates, the folk house is a single-story structure, while in Egypt it can consist of one-to-two stories, but is never three. 2) In Egypt, the courtyard is located behind the house, while in the Emirates it is located in front of or surrounding the house. 3) In the Emirates, the house contains a very spacious reception room, *majlis* (colloquially, *maylis*), used only for social gatherings, while in Egypt the house does not have such a big room. The living room, however, is used for social gatherings (el-Aswad 1996a, 67–73). For an assessment of the traditional architecture in Egypt, see Fathy (1989).

30. The implicit or embodied plan is a result of the work of *habitus* "systems of durable, transposable *disposition*, . . . that is, . . . principles of the generation and structuring of practices and representations which can be objectively 'regulated' and 'regular' without in any way being the product of obedience to rules" (Bourdieu 1977, 72 [emphasis in original]).

31. On the relationship between the internal structure of people's houses and their beliefs and social expectations, see Bourdieu (1977), Schwerdtfeger (1982), and Traube (1986).

32. From a cross-cultural point of view, the following example supports this statement. In its effort to implement the policy of resettlement of the Bedouins in the 1960s, the government of the Emirate of Abu Dhabi offered the locals free houses built on the modern Western model. Yet, because these houses were incompatible with the locals' social and cultural principles, they were rejected and deserted by the people. However, to solve this problem, the government applied two successful procedures: First, after consulting the locals and conducting social surveys, houses were changed to suit people's needs; and second, it allowed the owners to make necessary changes after consulting the government authorities of municipality and planning (el-Aswad 1996a, 22–23).

33. In his depiction of the spacing in premodern Cairo and in the village as well, Mitchell (1988, 54) maintains that the spacing was polarized "in many cases according to the direction of Mecca." There is no evidence in el-Haddein village indicating such orientation. North, not south (the direction of Mecca), is the direction toward which the village is oriented. This point is addressed in detail in chapter 3.

34. The notion that the house is a sanctuary (*ḥaram*) or a sacred thing is known in other areas in Egypt and is widely spread over Middle Eastern (rural and tribal) societies. Among the Bedouins of Egypt, the house "is often referred to as the *ḥaram* (sanctuary) and is regarded in this sense as a sacred thing. It is also *ḥarām* (taboo) and thus strangers are often forbidden to come near it without the permission of its members" (Abou-Zeid 1966, 253). Also, among the Kababish tribes of the Sudan, the "spot where the tent is pitched is known as the *dar*. This includes the area a little beyond the tent-pegs, the cooking-fire in front of the tent, and any adjacent trees and bushes used for suspending the water-skin and other possessions. A passer-by who is obliged to come closer to the *dar* should call out a greeting to the inmates of the tent even if no one is visible" (Asad 1970, 39).

35. The intricate relationship between the concepts of inhabitation and fullness has been addressed in the Middle Eastern context by Ibn Khaldūn (1320 A.D. [1981]) in his theory of the cycle of growth or rise and decline of civilization (el-Aswad 1996b), and by Bourdieu in his study of the Kabyle house (1977). See also Mitchell's insight-

ful study (1988, 53–54) in which he discusses both Ibn Khaldūn's and Bourdieu's notions of fullness and emptiness.

36. This point will be discussed in detail in chapter 3.

37. For further details, see chapters 3 and 4.

38. See chapter 4 for a discussion of the relationships among the person, society, and cosmos.

39. The notion of purity and its relation to "sanctity" is very important in articulating the social and religious domains of the community. See Mary Douglas (1966, 1970).

40. The cosmic arch of heaven is also replicated in the tomb structure.

41. Motivated by respect when a person finds a piece of bread on the ground or floor, he immediately removes it and puts it in a corner of the house or street. It is considered *ḥarām*, sinful or forbidden, to step on a piece of bread or on spilled milk.

42. Villagers contend that evil spirits, *jinn*, and *ʿafārīt* (living on dung) reside in the lavatory and stable, *zarībah*.

43. The Delta itself "is built of alluvial deposits with a clay cap 9-to-10 meters thick overlying coarser sand and gravel deposits that constitute the aquifer for groundwater. The cap, in general, has low permeability and contains its own groundwater. The coarser substrata are fully saturated with water" (Waterbury 1979, 132). The northeastern part of the western desert, east of Wadi el-Natrun, consists mostly of sand and gravel that, as it extends towards the east, becomes mixed with silt and clay (Hamdan 1980, 419).

44. In order to keep the soil rich and fertilized, peasants use a three-crop rotation system called *daura zirāʿīya* in which one crop, such as cotton, is planted once every three years in the same plot. As was stated earlier, one of the functions of the agricultural cooperative society is to ensure that peasants follow the three-crop rotation system. I will give an example showing how the *fallāḥīn* apply this system. The land is divided into three sections: A, B, and C, for example. In October (winter crops) short-term clover, *bersīm*, called *taḥrīsh*, is planted in section A. In section B long-term clover, which is cut four times at intervals of one month, is planted. Wheat is planted in section C. In February–March, peasants plant cotton in section A, while clover and wheat are still in sections B and C, respectively. In April or May the *fallāḥīn* harvest clover (section B) and plant maize or sorghum. In May they harvest wheat and leave the section (C) fallow until the following spring. They sometimes plant vegetables or clover in winter, but never plant any crop that takes a long time in the soil after harvesting the wheat so as to avoid exhaustion of the land. During the second or following winter, wheat is planted in section A and short-term clover in section B, while long-term clover or broad beans are put in section C. In summer, cotton is planted in section B, and sorghum in section C. *Nīlī* crops (July–August) such as cucumber and okra are also planted in section A (two months after harvesting the wheat). In the third year, in winter, peasants plant long-term clover in section A, wheat or barley in section B, and short-term clover in section C. In summer, section A is planted with sorghum, *mulūkhīyah* (which is picked three times, at intervals of one month), or peas. A *nīlī* crop of potato or pumpkin is planted in section B. This rotation method protects the land and is used where irrigation is possible, usually in the black and red or mixed soils. The *taḥmīl* method by contrast—planting more than

one crop in one plot at the same time—has negative effects on both the land and crops. The *fallāḥīn* use this method to take advantage of the long period needed for a specific crop to grow. For example, with taro, which remains eight to ten months in the ground, peasants plant peas and squash or cucumber. From the point of view of agronomists of the local cooperative society, the *taḥmīl* system might harm the fertility of land as well as the productivity of crops.

45. Regarding the perennial irrigation, there are two canals that irrigate almost 1,100 *feddāns*. The first canal, called *el-Nūbārīyah*, penetrates the southern half of the village and runs in a westerly direction. *El-Nūbārīyah* canal itself is a branch of *ar-rayyāḥ al-Beheirī*, which is connected directly with the Nile at the Delta barrages, fifty kilometers north of Cairo (Willcocks and Craig 1913, 2:636). *Ar-rayyāḥ al-Beheirī* (canal), which was completed in 1861 and that was "intended for the irrigation of the province of Behera, had its head situated on the left bank of Rosetta branch just upstream of the (Delta) Barrage" (Willcocks and Craig 1913, 2:635–36).

46. Timothy Mitchell has made a similar conclusion in his study of a rural community in southern Egypt. He observed that what is so-called capitalist agriculture, encouraged by the free-market reforms, is incompatible with the nature of capitalism. The market economy in a rural context cannot be depicted as a system of capitalists incorporated into a large capitalist economy. He concludes that "the free-market reforms produced results opposite from those their proponents anticipated. Instead of moving toward high-value export crops such as cotton and vegetables, farmers increased their production of staples such as wheat, maize, and rice" (Mitchell 1998, 31). Also see el-Aswad's review (2000).

47. See chapter 5 in which the metaphorical implications of watermelon as used by peasants are discussed.

48. The official economic definition of the *fallāḥ* (promulgated by Nasser in 1968 and adopted by Sadat in 1975) as a person who lives in the countryside and who owns or rents a maximum of 10 *feddāns* (1 *feddān* = 1.038 acres) and whose work (as well as his family's) is agriculture (*al-Ahrām* [June 5, 1968 and June 6, 1975]) does not correspond to the villagers' conception of the *fallāḥ*. This definition does not explicitly refer to peasants who do not own land. A *fallāḥ*, as villagers state, is the one whose work is agriculture and whose basic means for living is the hoe, whether he owns land or not. However, one frequently hears a landowner, official, or *shaikh* (man of religious learning) saying that he is a *fallāḥ* or son of a *fallāḥ* (*ibn fallāḥ*) to confirm his attachment to villagers' patterns of thought and behavior.

49. This male saint was originally a loyal servant of the honorable female saint Sit Raḍiyyah, who was *sharifa*—a descendant of the Prophet.

50. The phrase *yā sātir* (O, cover) is not exclusively used by men. Women also use it when approaching a house as an indication of good manners and respect of the other's privacy, even if males are not around.

51. For theoretical discussions of the peasant economy, see Bates (1978), Dalton (1967), Gamst (1974), Halperin and Dow (1977), Nash (1966), Potter, Diaz, and Foster (1967), Redfield (1960), and Wolf (1966). More specifically, Scott (1976) discusses the peasant moral economy, while Popkins (1979) addresses political theories of the peasant rational economy.

52. Through focusing on popular sayings as a source of documentation, al-Munūfī

(1978) shows that the Egyptian peasants have developed secular attitudes without giving up their religious outlook.

53. A similar assumption has been documented by Eickelman (1976, 127), who pointed out that "[p]rovisionality is the very essence of the cosmos" among Moroccan tribes.

54. See chapter 4, which discusses the cosmological meaning of *as-satr*.

55. In their everyday scenarios, villagers, though understanding the importance of budgeting and saving, contend that one can spend what one has (money in the pocket), anticipating that one will get what is for oneself from the unseen realm, *iṣrif mā fi al-jaib yā'tka ma fī al-ghaib*.

56. As happened in January 1977 when villagers, along with urbanites, reacted violently against the government's decision to reduce subsidies and raise prices on basic consumer goods including food items. The state in Middle Eastern societies, as Waterbury (1991) points out, has replaced local elites: "In the process peasant grievances have come to focus on the state itself, and because of increasingly blurred rural–urban lines of economic demarcation, resistance may take place in either environment. The point is that urban resistance should not be seen as driven purely by urban interests" (Waterbury 1991, 16–17).

57. The phrase *al-infitāḥ al-iqtiṣādī*, or "the open-door economic policy," appeared "for the first time on April 21, 1973, in a government statement. Initially, it referred to the role of Arab and foreign capital in the housing and construction sectors. In 1974, it acquired a high political sanction when the October Paper, issued by the president and approved in a referendum, adopted it" (Dessouki 1982a, 75). See also Richards (1980, 1984).

58. For further information on migrant laborers, *'ummāl at-traḥīl*, see el-Messiri (1983), Khafagy (1984), and Toth (1999).

59. See chapter 6 for further discussion of this point.

60. Elizabeth Taylor (1984, 4) says that "since the mid-1970s the migration of the agricultural laborer is blamed for a critical shortage of agricultural labor. The ministry of agriculture has called this one of the major crises facing Egyptian agriculture today." On migration in Egypt and the Arab World, see also Birks et al. (1983), Dessouki (1982b), Khafagy (1983), and Richards, Martin, and Nagaar (1983).

3

The Cosmos

the visible and the invisible

The Hierarachical Macrocosm

The cosmos, for villagers, is conceptually ordered in spatial and temporal terms and imbued with values of superiority and inferiority, the sacred and profane, strength and weakness, and benevolence and malevolence. It is more than it seems and is replete with hidden meanings related to the overarching axiom of the invisible, *al-ghaib*. Its apex is the conviction in the Ultimate Invisible Cosmic Being, Allah, who controls the entire universe as well as human destiny. The Arabic word *al-kaun*, the cosmos or universe, is derived from the root *k-u-n* that means *to be*, *to exist*, *to take place*, or *to happen*. It refers to the dynamic process of being and becoming as exclusively exercised by God Who "when He intends a thing, His command is, 'Be,' and it is!" (*Qur'an* 30:82).

Because rural Egyptian thought is holistic and accentuates the hierarchically interconnected relationship between body and spirit, the cosmos (*al-kaun*) or the world (*al-ʿālam*), is conceptualized as being composed of two different but inseparable and complementary domains: one knowable, visible, or natural, and the other unknowable, invisible, or supernatural. Two of the sacred names of Allah reveal that He encompasses the two opposites without any sense of contradiction: He is both the Visible, *Aẓ-Ẓāhir*, and the Invisible, *al-Bāṭin* or *al-ghaib*. About Himself, God says that He was a hidden treasure and desired to be known, hence He created the creation in order to be known (Ibn al-ʿArabi 1972). The invisible can be existent (*maujaūd*), present (*ḥāḍir*), and material in beings or entities as well as in discursive and nondiscursive actions. Ontologically, the invisible world consists of imperceptible beings such as spirits, souls, angels, *jinn*, *ʿafārīt*, and ghosts and includes such unseen powers as blessing (*baraka*), envy (*ḥasad*), and the eye (*al-ʿain*). The notion of invisibility here signifies *culture*, while that of visibility represents *nature*.

A vivid example indicating the coexistence of two differing worldviews is the sacred and well-known narration about how al-Khiḍr,[1] the Evergreen (cosmic) man, explained to the prophet Moses, through three exemplary events, the hidden or unseen but real dimension of life. In the story, al-Khiḍr expressed his concern that Moses would not be patient enough to understand his seemingly illogical deeds. If Moses were not able to show patience, trust, and understanding, al-Khiḍr would depart from him. To the surprise of Moses, al-Khiḍr scuttled a fishing boat owned by some poor fishermen, killed a young man, and then restored the fallen city wall of a corrupt community. Moses, overwhelmed and confused, questioned al-Khiḍr who, before his departure, provided this explanation: He scuttled the boat in order to save it from an unjust ruler who wished to posses all the good boats in the city. The young man was killed because he was not good to his pious parents and intended to commit a crime that would disgrace them. Finally, he restored the fallen wall because there was a treasure buried under it that belonged to two orphans who would suffer economic hardship in losing it. The lesson taught from this tale was that, beside the common-sense knowledge that depends on the logic of daily experience and observation, there is spiritual hidden knowledge guided by inner insight and revelation. Put differently, at the surface, literal, and visible level, al-Khiḍr's actions seemed to be illogical and evil, but at the deeper, symbolic, and hidden or invisible level they are not. In this context, al-Khiḍr represents a spiritual archetype of hidden knowledge that surpasses the normal.

Although the visible and invisible constitute two different worlds and are associated with different modes of thought, they form a unity that is the universe itself. Using Dumont's notion of hierarchical opposition, the visible and invisible components of the universe can be viewed as being hierarchically ordered in such a way that a highly valued idea contradicts and includes a lower valued idea: "The value of an entity is dependent upon or intimately related to a hierarchy of levels of experience in which that entity is situated" (Dumont 1986, 250). The visible and invisible worlds are not equivalent. For Egyptian peasants, the invisible or inward aspects of the world and of the person are more significant than the visible or outward aspects. This is a matter of the values attached to each domain of the world.

Most importantly, *al-ghaib*, as used in people's everyday lives, connotes different meanings in different contexts. It can denote what is absent, unseen, imperceptible, concealed, internal, and hidden. It can also refer to unforeseeable future events, as well as to mystic or divine knowledge, *ʿilm ladunī*, imparted by Allah through illumination. It is not uncommon to designate mysterious and supernatural events and beings that belong to the hidden sphere of reality as *ghaibīyyāt*. The invisible allows for possibility, a core concept in Egyptian peasants' thought, and renders the whole cosmos a dynamic structure. Anything is possible, because there is always room for the invisible to work. This explains their dynamic, open, and flexible worldview and attitude of alertness for any possible event, peculiar or normal, to occur. It is not then a mere naive belief in ghosts, *ʿafārīt*, *jinn*, blessing, or the eye that renders the peasants superstitious, irrational, or narrow-minded as some thinkers might suggest: It is the power of the imagined, socialized, internalized, and sanctified invisible within and through which these beliefs can be understood.

What makes the invisible, *al-ghaib*, a dominant theme is the fact that it is essentially a religiously grounded concept that refers to the belief in Allah, the angels, prophets, and holy books, as well as to such concepts as the hereafter and fate (Ibn Kathīr 1937). The invisible has a highest-order meaning founded upon "ultimate sacred postulates" that are "neither verifiable nor falsifiable but nevertheless taken to be unquestionable" (Rappaport 1979, 129). This religious meaning is a fundamental factor in maintaining and accentuating the concept of the invisible especially when it is applied to nonreligious spheres. When a cosmology is sanctified it "becomes something like an assertion, statement, description, or report of the way the world in fact *is*" (Rappaport 1999, 265 [emphasis in original]). Statements concerning ecological features as well as economic, political, and social activities may be sanctified by associating them with religious propositions (Rappaport 1979, 1984). Religious propositions, in accordance with which people conduct their lives, sanctify or certify their systems of understanding.

This explains the magnitude of Egyptians' belief in God's will, *irādat Allah* or *mashīʾat Allah*. It is God's will to create not only visible and invisible beings and forces, but also hidden and unknowable events that are beyond human sight and comprehension. The phrase *inshāʿ Allah* (When God wills) is commonly used by people in their daily lives when they wish for, anticipate, or promise some action or thing. For example, villagers believe that hard work in the field will not ensure a good harvest without God's willing. Past, present, and future are in the hands of God.[2]

In its totality, life encompasses material, personal, social, spiritual, and cosmological domains. It is not only the cosmos, but also the social world that is hierarchically divided and ordered through the dominant antithesis of visible/invisible. This dichotomy is correlated to other socially significant opposites related to the relationships between men and women. According to the sacred story of creation, Eve was encompassed or hidden in Adam's body. After creating Adam, Allah, in response to his complaint of loneliness, made Eve out of Adam's rib.

It is one thing to establish the visible and the invisible cosmologically as constituents of opposing sets—it is quite another to attribute social invisibility to women and exclude them from the public sphere and rituals on such grounds. In the social context, women are associated with the house, representing a sanctified invisible and private domain. The social invisibility of women, whether or not they are physically veiled,[3] is highly emphasized by men who use sacred scripture for such claims. Women are secrets of men and households and belong to the realm of the forbidden and should therefore be covered and unseen. However, it is difficult to accept Gilsenan's statement (1983, 172–73) that "peasant families are outside the honor scale as far as those above them are concerned, because they are peasants. . . . If they conceal their women as 'honorable' families do, they lose labor and income. . . . If they send the women to work, then, that is typical of the sort of life you expect peasants to lead. Their women are 'seen.'" Working outside and being physically seen by other does not nullify women or their families as far as their honor is maintained and protected by legally and socially acceptable work (el-Aswad 1994). The invisibility of women is still the main concern of men as far as this invisibility is understood more in social than in physical terms. Women are fully aware of this logic. Even when they walk in the street—a public domain—they are very careful not to make themselves visible or perform any action or signal that might attract attention, especially men's, otherwise their intention and behavior might be held in question. This does not imply that the vocabulary or social meaning of "veiling" is necessarily confined to the notion of controlling female sexuality or covering "sexual shame" (Abu-Lughod 1986, 159). Physically veiled women whose behavior is inconsistent with the moral standards of the community are the main targets of jokes, disrespect, and ridicule from both men and women who depict the veil as an ironic camouflage of their misconduct.

The social visibility of women, *inkishāf ʿala an-nās*, threatens the social position and moral visibility of men with whom these women are related. In such situations, men are either socially invisible or shamefully exposed, *mafḍūḥīn*. When women interact with one another in private gossip, men show great concern about the subsequent possible consequences in their private affairs that could result. Not only socially defined place, but also time imposes a division between men and women. In the village, it is not socially acceptable for women to go outside the house alone at night or in the dark. This deeply rooted logic is found in other Muslim societies where the "organization of the existence of the men and the women in accordance with different times and different places constitutes two interchangeable ways of securing separation and hierarchization of the male and female worlds" (Bourdieu 1977, 163).

The invisible domain with which women are associated does not hinder them from engaging in various sorts of economic activities outside the house, such as helping their husbands cultivate the fields, selling goods and domestic products in the local market, or holding a governmental job either as a clerk or an official. Social change resulting from the exposure of women to various kinds of work has not affected the image that both men and women have that women belong to the house or the interior world. It is not a matter of simple economic or political subordination of women to men—it *is* a matter of social values and religious orientation that give social, private, economic, and political scenarios themselves a subordinate position within the larger whole.

The Heavens and the Encompassing Space

The cosmos is viewed in spatial and temporal dimensions of being perceptible, conceivable, or imaginable. Unlimited cosmic space, *faḍāʾ*, goes beyond the world of humans to encompass other worlds inhabited with perceptible and imperceptible entities. Temporally, the heavens signify the far future, meaning that what they encompass is exclusively known to and predestined by Allah.

People's concepts of the visible and invisible components of the cosmos are rendered intelligible within the context of hierarchical but complementary relationships. In other words, cosmological entities have neither meaning nor existence when considered in isolation from one another or the space they occupy. The visible constituents of the universe, which are hierarchically ordered, are: sky or heaven (*as-samāʾ*), the sun (*ash-shams*), the moon (*al-qamar*), the stars (*an-nujūm*, sing. *najm*), the comets (*ash-shuhub*), and the earth (*al-arḍ*). As spatially conceived, the invisible components of the heavens consist of the upper or higher heavens and all unseen entities and forces that exist below, within, above, and beyond the visible sky.

For villagers, there are seven hierarchically structured heavens, leveled one above the other.[4] The only visible sky is the first heaven, *as-samāʾ al-ūlā*. The other heavens and their inhabitants are invisible. The opposition here is between the visible heaven and the invisible heavens. This macro-level

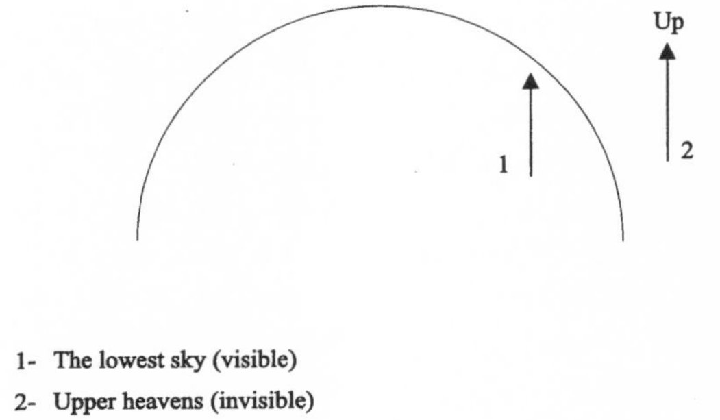

FIGURE 3.1 The visible and the invisible.

opposition is analogous to the micro-level opposition between the human body, which is visible, and the soul, which is invisible and enjoys a higher value than the body. Both the visible heaven and the space it occupies are viewed as being encompassed by the invisible but visualized levels of the higher heavens—the invisible contains the visible. The significance of the visible heaven lies in its ability to represent not only the unseen heavens, but also the omnipresent Invisible Force—Allah—that transcends them.

The first sky is also called *as-samāʾ ad-dunyā*, the lowest sky. The adjectival construction of the word *dunyā* implies two meanings associated with two different contexts:[5] first, as far as the relationship between the heavens and the earth is concerned, the lowest or first sky is the heaven nearest to people; and second, with regard to the relationship between the first sky and the other heavens, the first heaven is inferior or lower in order. This leads to another set of oppositions: lower/higher, near/far, and inferior/superior. Figure 3.1 illustrates the spatial dimensions of the universe represented in hierarchically structured oppositions. What is higher or superior encompasses the lower or inferior. It must be noted that the first sky, though lower in relation to the other invisible heavens, is higher in relation to the visible earth.

The first sky is described as being very high. It is conceived of as a large dome that rests on the earth.[6] The sky represents an encompassing space, though it is viewed from the center as a vertical line anchored in the horizontal dimension of the earth. The word *samāʾ* is used by villagers in the form of *samā* or *sumūw* to refer to that which is spatially and ethically very high, as represented in the values and attributes of nobility, honor, and social prestige. In order to sublimate himself or herself, a person must go beyond what is considered irrelevant or asocial such as fighting or arguing for something unworthy. People commonly use the word *samā*—sky—metaphorically with reference to superiority and authority. A person who disobeys his father or superior might be asked to look for another heaven, *irḥal ʿann samāyā*. Also, in a response showing the inability to fulfill someone's demands, a person metaphorically says, "This is the heaven and this is the earth" (*adī assam wa dī al-arḍ*), meaning that nothing is available.

A vernacular description of the sky is the "blue tent," *khīmah zargah* (*zarqāʾ*). One of the most popular names for Allah is *Abū Khīmah Zargah*, the "Owner of the Blue Tent" who watches over the universe and its occupants. The sky, visualized as a tent or dome, signifies *satr*, which in this context has the meanings of veil and protection. Within Muslim cosmic imagery the sky is viewed as a veil, in the sense that it hides what is beyond it. The sky is also a symbol of protection. The blue color of the sky is associated with the belief in the invincible power of blue amulets as a means of protection against evil forces, mainly the evil eye. All in all, the sky symbolizes the omnipotence of the Cosmic Sustainer and Protector, *As-Sattār*, or *Allah*. To cover something, which necessitates the existence of the protector, is to give it the value of being protected, because it is either precious or vulnerable. This logic is applicable to women. To express the need for men's protection, women, in daily social practice, say that man is the one who protects and covers, *ar-rājil satr wa ghaṭā*. Meanwhile, if faced with a disgracing misfortune related to financial or social misconduct, a person should hide or cover him- or herself by keeping it secret or he or she would be uncovered or shamefully exposed. In such a private scenario, one hears people, using folk sayings, utter, "If you are disgracefully afflicted [by a misfortune or misconduct] you should cover yourself" (*idhā ubtalaytum fa-istatirū*). In similar scenarios, one also hears them say, "Keep things covered" (*khally aṭṭābiq mastūr*) and "Cover or protect your candle to keep it lit" (*dārī ʿalā sham ʿitak tinawwar*).

Analogously, as a house has doors, the sky has *abwāb* (sing. *bāb*) or gates, the biggest one being in the center. These gates, however, are invisible. The highest point of the sky represents the center of the sky, *ṣurrat as-samā*. It is worth noting that the word *ṣurrah* also means a person's navel. Other meanings of the word *ṣurrah* include parcel, like the knotted handkerchief in which villagers keep their food or money. *Surrah* can also mean monetary savings or property. A rich person is described as having a "big savings" (*ṣurrah kabīrah*). In a word, the center of the heaven is associated with sacred origins as well as with future prosperity and good fortune. It is the knot that holds all together. The center, Eliade (1959, 17) maintains, "is preeminently the zone of the sacred, the zone of absolute reality." The sacred and celebrated night of the twenty-seventh of Ramadan in which the *Qurʾan* was revealed to the Prophet Mohammad, *lailat al-qadr*, is associated in villagers' beliefs with what they call "*ṭāgat lailat al-gadr*," meaning the opening that appears in the center of the heaven. Those who witness this opening are fortunate enough to be granted the fulfillment of their wishes. For Muslim scholars, such a belief is unacceptable. However, the peasants' belief is understood in the context of their views concerning the heavens as a whole. Livelihood or sustenance, *rizg* (*rizq*), as expressed by peasants, is made by Allah and comes through heaven.[7] It is also worth emphasizing that peasants depend mainly on irrigation in their agricultural activities, since rain is scarce. They therefore show great joy when it rains. Water, called *ghaith* (rescue), is associated more with life and with the sky than with the earth.

The center of the heaven recalls people's concepts of *waṣt al-balad*, the center of the village that symbolizes values of security, intimacy, and unity. As opposed to the periphery, the center is considered to be the heart or internal part of the village. Therefore the center is more highly valued than the peripheral parts. The center of the village represents and encompasses the entire community. Similarly, the center of the heaven represents and encompasses the entire visible heaven.

The center as well as the edge of the sky, which surrounds and overlays the earth, is circular. Analogously, the meal table (*ṭabliyyah*) is depicted by villagers as round, like the center of the sky itself. At mealtime, people place the main dish in the center of the meal table. Bread, or *al-ʿaish*, which means life, is also round and placed on the edge of the table. Round objects and numbers, such as the Arabic number five, *khamsah*, are taken to be symbols of good luck and protection. It is common to see villagers hang small plates and other round and curved objects on the doors of their houses to prevent the negative effect of the evil eye.

Cosmic entities such as stars (*nujūm*) or the lamps of the heavens (*maṣābīḥ as-samāʾ*) are considered to be manifestations or signs of the most Invisible Being, Allah. Some of these stars are comets (*shuhub*) and are believed to be arrows of fire thrown by angels to kill devils (*shayāṭīn*) and evil *jinn* who spy and try to gain some knowledge of that which is hidden. It is believed that the moon and *jinn* are the effective agents in magic. They help magicians by giving them secret information that, among other things, foretells people's futures. With the exception of God, invisible beings do not know the future; however, some mischievous *jinn* and devils are perceived as always attempting to unveil the mysteries in cosmic hidden knowledge.

Beyond the visible and known sky, there are invisible and unknown heavens that have been the object of imagination, speculation, and faith rather than observation. The imagined space of the invisible heavens is the world in which spirits, souls, and angels as well as human and natural entities, though different in many fundamental aspects from those existent on earth, reside. Between the second and the seventh heavens exist numerous angels, such as those who descend to earth to live on people's shoulders and record their good and bad deeds. According to their rank, the souls of deceased Muslims also reside in one of these heavens. Saints are able to move freely in the heavens. They share in the sacred space and are ascribed special power, being close to Allah, Who bestows His blessing upon them. The position of the saint in Egyptian peasants' cosmology depends fundamentally on the forces of life and death that are diffused in both the individual person and the world. Saints or blessed dead persons mediate between the social relations of the living with both nature's components such as heaven, earth, wind or water and supernatural or invisible forces or elements such as spirits, souls, and *karamāt* (miracles).[8]

In the eschatological realm, *ʿālam al-barzakh* (saints) are believed to continue performing miracles that support those who approach or call them for help. This image constitutes an imaginative and humanistic view that provides hope to those afflicted with illnesses. It is not then merely a naïve belief in the power of the dead to govern people's lives that causes polytheism and belittles God's power, as some scholars disapprovingly argue (ʿUways 1965, 1966). Rather, it is the participation of the saint in the hidden dimension of reality as well as his or her loyalty (*walīy*) or closeness to Allah that gives him or her the power to do extraordinary humanistic deeds. Saints are depicted as cosmic navigators who know the geography and traffic of the universe. Within this framework, people's belief in the ability of a living saint or mystic to be in different places or different periods of time simultaneously can be rendered understandable. This is also manifested in the image villagers have of the evergreen but invisible cosmic saint al-Khiḍr, or the "Pious Slave" (*al-ʿabd aṣ-ṣāliḥ*), upon whom Allah has bestowed divine hidden knowledge, *ʿilm ladunnī*, and who is believed to be alive and attentive to whomever mentions his name. It is within this cosmic imagery imbued with divine miracles that al-Khiḍr, like other revered saints, is able to be present, though invisibly, among those who recall his story.[9]

The other heavens and their inhabitants are beyond comprehension. However, there is a tendency among villagers to associate the invisible heavens with angels and other invisible beings and forces. Angels are important agents linking the spiritual world with the physical one. There is a strong connection between the remote heavens and the powerful angels and superior souls of the great prophets and messengers. For example, the most highly ranked angels exist in the seventh heaven. In the *Qur'an*, the angels are "classified into several categories in accordance with their functions and, thus, an angelic hierarchy [is] formed within the universal hierarchy of being" (Izutsu 1964, 16).

Above the seventh heaven there is *sidrat al-muntahā*,[10] the highest point beyond which paradise is located.[11] Near this point is the tree of creatures, *shajarat al-khalāʾiq*—a huge tree forever green with millions of leaves representing an archetype of imaginative universal human genealogy. Villagers connect this description of cosmology with the Prophet Muhammad's *miʿrāj*—his ascension to the highest horizon of the seventh heaven.[12]

Above all the heavens, *al-malakūt al-aʿlā*—in infinite time and endless space—there is *al-ʿarsh*, the Lord's throne that is carried by the most powerful angels. Around the throne there are angels who praise Allah day and night. The throne, for villagers, is identical with *al-kursī*, the chair.[13] Although it is conceived as being above all the heavens, the throne or the chair, which is beyond people's understanding, encompasses all the heavens and the earth. To protect their houses and properties as well as to feel secure, old people, before sleeping, recite the verse of *al-kursī* (*Qurʾan* 2:255). While reciting this verse they raise an index finger (keeping the other fingers connected with one another) and move it from right to left in a circular pattern. The direction of the index finger during the recitation coincides with the border of the house or any other property that needs to be protected. Children are very observant of what adults do or say. In the village, I heard a story about a female orphan child who used to hear her grandmother reciting the verse of *al-kursī* in bed immediately before sleeping. It happened that the grandmother spent a night with some female relatives for the purpose of condolence, leaving the granddaughter alone. Before sleeping, the girl tried to recite the same verse as her grandmother would do. However, because the child had not memorized it, she said, "*kursī, kursī, kursī, zayy* (*mithl*) *ma bitqūl sitti*" (Chair, chair, chair, as my grandmother says).

Taking all the heavens as constituting a whole, one finds that the structure is flexible. People sometimes place angels and souls of one heaven in another one. However, in hierarchical terms, the lowest heaven (*as-samāʾ ad-dunyā*) as well as the highest heaven (*as-samāʾ al-ʿulyā*) are more stable or changeless in their structures than the other heavens. Unlike the transitory entities of the first heaven, souls of deceased Muslims and other invisible beings and entities known only to Allah are eternal. This statement is represented by the following sets of oppositions: eternal/transitory and timeless/temporal. The cultural division between visible and invisible highlights other related opposite concepts such as outside/inside, concrete/abstract, natural/supernatural, and immediate place/limitless space.

The Earth and the Encompassed Space

Earth is often associated with mud or clay and is used as an allegory of the corporeal aspect of the creation of man. According to the sacred story of creation, Allah created Adam out of clay (*ṣalṣal*) and breathed into him, His Spirit rendering him superior to all other creatures.[14]

However, as there are seven heavens, there are also seven earths inhabited by various beings and entities. These seven earths are seen as inseparable layers that form the same entity. In other words, there is no space between these layers or earths. Unlike heaven, the earth is thought to be flat and encompassed. Although educated young people have learned that the earth is round, the older generation continues to view it as being flat. The first earth is the earth on which people, animals, and other animate and inanimate entities exist. Below this are the lower earths (*al-arḍ as-sufla*), in which such notorious creatures as *ʿafārīt* or *jinn* reside.

The heaven is a multivocal symbol of sanctity, patriarchy, masculinity, and protection, while the earth is an index of profanity, femininity, and vulnerability. In the social context, however, earth or land is highly valued in more than a monetary sense. To hold land, *arḍ*, is to have great honor. For villagers, the most distinctive feature of the land is mud, *ṭīn*. The word *ṭīn* is associated with arable soil as well as with people's values and views of the past and present. The *ṭīn* is precious and invaluable because it is, metaphorically, wet from the sweat of the ancestral landowners, *ʿaraq al-ajdād*. Landowners themselves are named after the land they own; a large landowner, for instance, is called *ṣāḥib aṭyān*. Socially, *ṭīn* is used in two opposite ways: A wealthy, well-mannered, and well-liked landowner is called *ṣāḥib ṭīn* or *ʿindahu ṭīn*, while the ill-mannered and disliked person, whether wealthy or not, is referred to as being coated with mud, *ʿalayh ṭīn*.

The second earth is believed to be a place of underground or stored water, which is especially important for villagers' agricultural activities located in the desert. The children of *jinn* and *ʿafārīt* are believed to reside in the subterranean water and springs of the second earth. Women are careful not to dump hot water on the ground without uttering certain protective words, for fear of hurting the *jinn* or their offspring. Alhough *jinn* are created of fire, which contradicts or opposes water, villagers believe that they can transform themselves to suit to any environment. Seas, rivers, and canals are believed to be inhabited by female *jinn*, known as *jinnīyāt al-baḥr* (sing. *jinnīyah*). This association of female *jinn* or *jinnīyāt* with seas and rivers might well be connected with the male villagers' habit of swimming in canals. Women do not swim in canals or rivers, though they might fetch water or wash clothes there. The point is that because men swim and sometimes drown in canals, villagers have developed a belief that the *jinnīyāt* admire or sexually desire them, seize them, and intentionally or unintentionally drown them. This belief is associated with the general assumption that men and women can have sexual relationships with *jinn*. A person who might be thought of as having this kind of relationship is called *mukhāwī*, meaning a companion of an invisible being or *jinn* (whose relationship is as intimate as that of a brother, *akh*). A socially isolated bachelor is often more likely to be suspected of having sexual relations with *jinniyyah* than an adult male who is sociable. This statement is also especially applicable to women who have been possessed by spirits.

Conceptually, the third earth is believed to be inhabited by various invisible beings. Hierarchically, however, demons and *ʿafārīt* residing in the fourth and fifth earths are stronger than those residing in the first, second, and third earths, but weaker than those of the sixth and seventh earths. The kingdom of *jinn* and *shayāṭīn* is in the seventh earth *sābiʿ arḍ*, where their monarch *Iblīs*, or Satan, resides. *Iblīs* is a fallen creature who has become associated with malevolent *jinn* and evil creatures that can possess and harm people. Nonetheless, of all the evil invisible creatures, only one, the *shaiṭān* or devil, tends to harm people by whispering or prompting them with evil and wicked temptations. He has the ability to penetrate people's minds or selves and run in their blood, driving them to do evil deeds or harm themselves. *Iblīs*, the most dominant and wicked devil, gives orders to his followers to do whatever is morally wrong. Devils and other evil spirits, called *sukkān al-arḍ* or *ahl al-arḍ* (the inhabitants of earth or the underworld), ascend to the surface of the earth and occupy deserted places, cemeteries, and impure areas. In daily life, when a villager threatens an enemy, he tells him that he will throw him into the seventh earth. Although *Iblīs* and other *jinn* or *ʿafārīt* are very powerful and dangerous, they cannot harm anybody who utters the name of God, *bismillah*. In terms of hierarchical oppositions, "good must contain evil while still being its contrary. In other words, real perfection is not the absence of evil but its perfect subordination" (Dumont 1986, 251).

When viewing villagers' concepts of the earth, there is a distinction made between what is apparent or visible (the surface of the earth) and what is hidden or invisible (underground). Nevertheless, the different earths are hierarchically related to each other. The first earth is believed to be less impure and less inferior than the second earth, and the second is less dangerous than the third. The seventh earth is *asfal*, the lowest and most dangerous place. This order is consistent, though differently, with that of the heavens, where the higher is more valued or sacred than the lower. The lowest (black) magic (*as-siḥr as-suflī*) is connected with *jinn* and other invisible creatures residing in the lower earths. In Egyptian cosmology the underworld is subordinate to the surface world, and both of them are subordinate to the heavenly, and more specifically to the invisible, world (see figure 3.2).

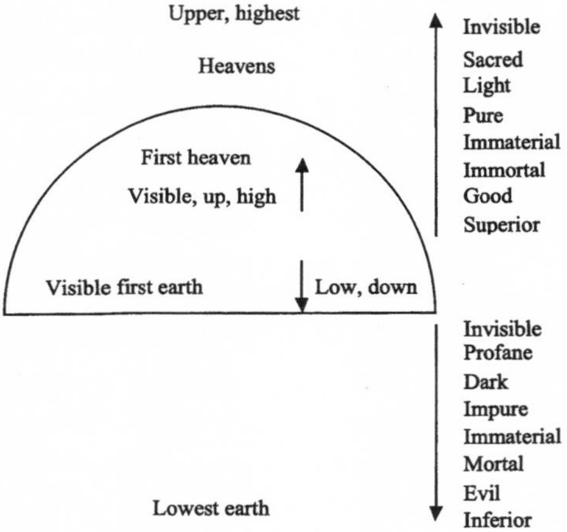

FIGURE 3.2 The visible and invisible components of the universe as conceived by villagers.

The Course of the Sun: The Identification with the East

The sun (*ash-shams*) is the dominant heavenly body in the sky during the daytime. The rising of the sun is the most significant and inspiring moment and serves as an inexhaustible metaphor in people's everyday lives. When a person, for example, is upset with a problem, it is common to hear the expression, "This is a day in which the sun does not rise" (*dā yaum maṭalaʿshī fīh shams*). The sun is associated with beliefs about cyclic growth and rebirth. When a boy loses a tooth, he throws it toward the sun's eye (*ʿain ash-shams*) in the early morning, saying, "Oh sun, take the ox's [or the donkey's] tooth and give me the bride's tooth" (*yā shams yā shammūsah khudhī sinnat al-faḥl* [or *al-ḥumār*] *wa hātī sinnat al-ʿarūsah*).

Agricultural work requires knowledge of weather conditions relative to specific months, the positions of celestial bodies, and types of soil, fertilizers, seeds, and so forth. Peasants carefully observe the courses of the sun and moon that impact their agricultural activities. The sun rises at the southeastern side of the village and, therefore, peasants plow the land and plant crops in a south–north direction so that the sunlight reaches the furrows. They differentiate between what they designate as the great sun (*ash-shams al-kabīrah*), which appears in autumn, and the small sun (*ash-shams aṣ-ṣaghīrah*), which begins to rise in February.[15]

In winter, the great sun appears large and close to the earth. Because of its apparent nearness, people say *ash-shams nazalat* (The sun has descended). According to the peasants' view, the sun maintains the balance of warmth during the cold winter months. The great sun (*ash-shams al-kabīrah*) is described as *shams ḥunaīynah*, a benign or kindly sun. The word *kabīrah* is a feminine form of the word *kabīr*, which connotes great, large, and elderly. A community without a big, influential man does not exist. Hierarchically, to be *kabīr* is to show benignity, mercy, and kindness to those who are young and dependent. In their daily social exchanges, people use the word *kabīr* with reference to the old and in association with kindness, order, love, and mercy. Winter is associated with elderliness, intimacy, and closeness. Although it is short, it renders family and social ties inside the house or interior world as warmer, stronger, or more intimate. Daytime becomes short and both indoor and outdoor activities seem to pass quickly, as represented in the folk saying, "Your morning is your evening and when you wake up, you prepare your supper" (*sabāḥak misāk tigūm* [*taqūm*] *min an-naum tiḥaḍḍar ʿashāk*). Warm food is prepared by women for the family members who gather together during long evenings to converse, watch television, or listen to stories told by the elderly.

In summer, the sun appears high and small in the sky but it is intense and of long seasonal duration, allowing for the cultivation of crops such as cotton, sorghum, wheat, watermelon, mangos, figs, and dates. Summer is the season during which the village becomes visible and open for social and economic activities. Wheat, watermelon, and cotton—the main capital crops—are readied and sold at the market. The resulting economic gain makes marriage ceremonies, among other social activities, possible and popular during this season.

The moon, associated with irrigation, also plays a part in people's daily lives. Most *fallāḥīn* prefer to irrigate the land when the moon is full, because crops irrigated by moonlight are supposed to be more abundant than those irrigated on dark nights. Also, the light of the moon is important for villagers who have to work in the fields at night. The moon becomes full on the night of the fourteenth day after its first appearance, *qamar lailat arabaʿ tāshar*. The new crescent moon (*hilāl*) is the symbol of the Arabic (Muslim) lunar month. The crescent is also identified with Islam at both the national and international levels.

Although the masculinity of the moon and femininity of the sun are not expressly defined, significant clues related to people's religious and social lives suggest this classification.[16] As stated above, the moon is central to the Muslim or Arabic calendar. Islamic religious feasts and rituals are arranged and performed in accordance with the lunar (Arabic) calendar. Therefore the moon becomes important and occupies a prominent place in people's religious worldview. Like a newly born male child, the crescent of each new Arabic month, especially that of Ramadan, is anticipated and received with great joy. Conversely, except for the regulation of daily prayers, the sun does not play a significant role in the arrangement of people's religious practices or rituals.

There are village beliefs about the moon and its eclipse that are not widely accepted by the literate or educated population. Village women believe that the moon, *al-qamar* (masculine name), attracts *banāt al-ḥūr* or *ḥūrī*, the black-eyed virgins of paradise who descend from the heavens to touch or possess the lowest sky. An eclipse is interpreted as a result of this activity. The women say "*al-qamar makhnūq*" (The moon is being suffocated). When it occurs, women and children are led around the village by a female leader who carries a drum (or a metal cane) and, beating it loudly, sings, "*yā banāt al-ḥūr khallī al-qamar yadūr*" (Oh virgins let the moon revolve). The chorus of women and children walk around the village singing the same song until the moon regains its normal light. Men do not participate in this ritual. Interestingly, villagers believe that both the moon and *ḥūrī* are created of light by Allah, while the sun is created of fire.

Undoubtedly, science confronts aspects of traditional outlook and ritual that are related to cosmic and natural phenomena. Young and old generations of both genders who are educated and exposed to scientific fact oppose some of these beliefs and practices. They do maintain, however, that the universe is full of secrets that cannot be completely comprehended by science. For example, when discussing the landing on the moon with both younger and older generation informants, a representative response was that although science had succeeded in this achievement, it has not been and will not be able to reveal the secrets of the universe that are known exclusively to God. To press their point, they asked whether science has or could put a man on the sun. For villagers, both scientific fact and local tradition seem to be encompassed by the overarching religious outlook.

The course of the sun is divided into main periods of time to which certain activities, qualities, and unseen beings and forces are attached.[17] These qualities are described in terms of the opposites visible/invisible, sunrise/sunset, light/dark, life/death, angel/demon, and good/bad. These periods of time regulate the rhythm of Muslim daily prayers.

The *dawn* (*al-fajr*) or *morning twilight* is favored for its spiritual quality. It is the time for all creatures to participate in the cosmic awakening. As an elder person awakes, he or she utters, "I began my day as a guest of Allah and Allah's guest is never mistreated" (*aṣbaḥtu li-llāhi ḍaifan wa ḍaifu Allah lā yuḍām*). During this time, the doors of heaven are opened for prayers and supplications. The spiritual dimension of the universe was confirmed by

Shaikha Badawiyya, who related the cries of birds and animals to the cosmic praising of God. Through mimeses she contended that the rooster's crow meant: "The Extolled, the All-Holy, the Lord of angels and the soul, praise Allah, O you negligent" (*subūḥ, qudūs Rabb al malā'ikati wa ar-rūḥ, udhkrū Allah yā ghāflīn*). Pigeons, to take another example, said, *waḥḥidū Rabbukum, u'budū Rabbukum*, meaning "O people, maintain that your Lord is one and worship Him." At dawn, men pray and prepare to go to the fields. Women wake earlier to prepare food for breakfast. It is believed that during this time harmful unseen creatures become less or cease to be active.

Morning (*aṣ-ṣubḥ*) or *sunrise* (*ash-shurūq*) is also highly praised: "The morning breathes" (*tanafath as-ṣabāh*) and "The morning is profitable" (*aṣ-ṣbāḥ rabāh*) are common phrases denoting that morning embodies blessing and prosperity. Newly produced items such as milk, eggs, or bread are depicted as *ṣābiḥ*, meaning that they are as fresh as the morning. When feeding chickens, women call *aṣ-ṣubḥ khair* (The morning is good). Social relationships inside and outside the house start with metaphorical morning greetings: *ṣabāh al-khair* (The morning is good); *ṣabāḥ an-nūr* (The morning is light [illuminated]); *ṣabāḥ al-ḥalīb* (The morning is as good as milk); *ṣabāḥ al-full* (The morning is like jasmine). The light of sunrise is believed to force evil spirits to retreat to their assigned locations underground. The villagers say "*ash-shams ṭala'it wa al-'afārīt rawwaḥit*" (The sun has risen and the ghosts have gone home).

Forenoon is divided into two periods during which villagers are occupied with their work. First is *aḍ-ḍuḥā*, which starts nearly two-and-a-half hours after sunrise. It is considered very late for people to wake up during this time. High forenoon (*aḍ-ḍuḥā al-'ālī*) starts nearly four hours after sunrise and lasts until noon. During this period people are generally at work.

Noon or *midday* (*aḍ-ḍuhr, aẓ-ẓuhr*) is the time for a light lunch (*al-ghadā*) prepared by women and carried to the fields. This period of rest (*qailūlah*) is generally very hot, especially in summer. The *fallāḥīn* perform the noon prayer and seek respite in the shadows of the trees or in their homes. However, during this period, *jinn* called *'afārīt al-qaiyālah* (*jinn* of the noontime) become active and dangerous.

Afternoon (*al-'aṣr*) is the period of time related to the course of the sun as it moves west. It is the time of conducting the afternoon prayers. Although villagers continue their work, they are not as active as they are in the morning. During this time, *jinn* and *'afārīt* are believed to become less troublesome and menacing.

Sunset (*al-maghrib*) is the time of quitting work and performing the sunset prayers. When the sun sets, villagers take their animals, leave the field, and head home. The words "west" (*gharb*) or "sunset" (*ghurūb*) have negative implications connoting darkness, lagging behind, disappearance, absence, and that which is alien. An outsider or foreigner is termed "*gharīb*." Opposing the word "*sharq*" (east), which implies light, happiness, home, or the right, is the word "*gharb*" (west), which connotes darkness, sadness, homelessness, and the left. A happy man is described as *mushriq al-wajh* (A man whose face is illuminated), similar to the earth when the sun rises. On the other hand, when a person dies or fails in achieving an important objective, it is common to hear people say "His sun has set" (*gharabat shamsu*). The most evil of spirits becomes active after sunset, as presented in the phrase, "The sun sets and the *ʿafārīt* appear" (*ash-shams gharabit* [*gharabat*] *wa al-ʿafārīt ṭalaʿat*).

Evening (*al-ʿishāʾ*) begins about two hours after sunset and lasts until dawn. It is darker and longer than the period of *al-maghrib*. *Al-ʿishāʾ* is the time of evening prayer (*ʿishāʾ*) as well as of supper. It is also a time for relaxing, visiting relatives and friends, and watching television.

There is an opposite relationship between the activities of people and those of evil invisible beings. The periods in which people are involved in their daily activities, especially in the morning and before noon, are those in which evil spirits cease to be active. Conversely, the periods in which people relax or work lightly (noon and night) are those in which evil invisible creatures are most active and dangerous. Laziness and idleness during working hours are considered a sort of *najāsah* (impurity), as represented in the phrase, "Contend that idle hands are unclean" (*al-yad al-baṭṭālah najisah*).

In summary, villagers demonstrate that they have different attitudes towards different periods of time. On the one hand, they relate what is right, blessed, high, resplendent, fruitful, and good to the period that extends from dawn to noon. On the other hand, they associate what is left, less sacred, less blessed, low, austere or ominous, behind, and less fruitful with the period that starts at noon and ends at dawn (see table 3.1).

Of the cardinal points, only two, east and west, are viewed as being related to the sun. While the east–west direction implies temporal dimensions, the north–south denotes ecological and spatial dimensions regulated by the Mediterranean Sea as well as by religious dimensions related to the *Kaʿbah* in Mecca. In brief, the temporal axis of the cosmic cardinal points runs from east to west, while the spatial axis runs from north to south. Of these cardinal directions, however, east and north constitute the most significant orientations for people. People of the village identify themselves with the north. A sense of cosmic significance is obtained though specific bodily orientations. When a person faces north, east will be to his right and west will be to his left. In this position, the course of the sun is from right to left (see figure 3.3). Within a cosmocentric context, east is right, light, and good,

TABLE 3.1
THE COURSE OF THE SUN AND THE VALUES ASSOCIATED WITH EACH PERIOD OF TIME

Dawn–Noon	*Noon–Dawn*
East	West
Light	Getting dark, dark
Angels	Devils, *jinn*
High	Low
Increase, ascend	Decline, descend
Awake	Rest, relax, sleep
Work, active	Less work, less active
Productive	Less productive

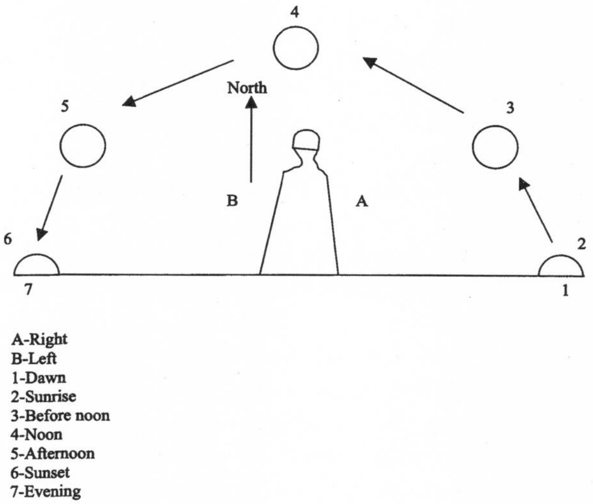

FIGURE 3.3 The course of the sun and a *fallāḥ* identifying himself with the north.

while west is left, dark, and evil or bad. As such, east is more highly valued than west—it encompasses the west. Thus it is a cosmological orientation rather than a political orientation that dominates people's concepts.

The south is referred to as *giblī* (*qiblī*) and not *janūb*, which has an actual referential meaning to the geographical direction of south. The word *qiblī* has reference to *al-qiblah* or the *Kaʿbah* in Mecca. This meaning is fundamentally related to religious practices. During prayer, Muslims direct their faces toward the *Kaʿbah* or *al-qiblah*, which, from the position of the village, is south. When they face south, the structural relationship among cardinal points is reversed; that is, the east is located to their left, the west is to their right side, and their backs are directed toward the north.[18]

This reversed structure becomes more comprehensible when we focus on villagers' attitudes toward *dār ad-dunyā*, the inferior abode or this worldly life, and *dār al-ākhīrah*, the afterlife or otherworldly life. In the secular domain of their life, east and north are predominant orientations, while in the religious domain, especially during prayer, the south, associated with the *Kaʿbah*, and west, associated with death, are eminent. In the ritual burial of the dead, the corpse is laid in the grave on its right side facing south, the *Kaʿbah*, while the head is oriented toward the west (el-Aswad 1987, 1994). The back and lower parts (legs) of the corpse are oriented toward the north and east, respectively (see table 3.2). "The worldly order is relativized as subordinated to absolute values" (Dumont 1985, 100).

Air, Wind, and the Primacy of the North

North is referred to as *baḥarī*, not *shamāl*. The word *shamāl* is used frequently by literate people who live in urban environments as well as by those who read classical or official Arabic. The local use of the word *baḥarī* is related to *baḥr* (sea), which in this context refers to the Mediterranean Sea located north of Egypt. By using the word *baḥarī* to denote north, villagers do not evoke the association of *shamāl*, which also means left. Left, *shamāl*, is associated with what is weak, inferior, erroneous, and impure.

As was previously mentioned, *baḥarī* or north is imbued with high value. It is also favored because of the cool breeze that blows from the north in hot weather. In the village, people prefer to build their houses directed northward. A man who has a house that faces north proudly says "*baitnā wajhitu baḥarī*" or "*dārnā wajhitha baḥarī*" (Our house is facing north). Housing development has spread noticeably northward in the village. A villager who wants to build a house north of a neighbor's house should ask permission first, discussing how to build the new house so that it does not block the old house's breeze.

TABLE 3.2

Hierarchically Reversed Cardinal Points and Body Orientations Related to Secular, Religious, and Death Contexts

Context	*Cardinal points of high value*	*Position of the body*	*Cardinal points of low value*	*Position of the body*
Secular context (mundane)	north	front—facing north	south	back
	east	right side	west	left side
Religious context (prayer)	south	front—facing south (*Ka'bah* or Mecca, the center of the universe)	north	back
	west	right side	east	left side
Death (burial) context influenced by religious beliefs	south	front—corpse is laid facing south (*Ka'bah*)	north	back of the corpse
	west	head towards west	east	lower extremities (legs) towards east

Villagers describe themselves as "people from the north or Lower Egypt," *nās* (*bitū'*) *baḥarī, baḥārwah* (sing. *baḥrāwī* or *biḥīri*), distinguishing from "people from the south or Upper Egypt," *nās* (*bitū'*) *giblī* (*qiblī*) *Ṣa'āydah* (sing. *Ṣa'īdī*). Moreover, villagers say that the Nile River runs north, while its legs or sources run south. Some marriage songs emphasize the *baḥarī* identification of both the bride and groom: *baḥarī, baḥarī, baḥarī, 'ārisnā rājil baḥarī wa 'ārūstuh wāḥadah min baḥarī*, which means "North, north, north, our groom is a man from the north and his bride is from the north."

The area between the sky and earth, *faḍā'*, means space or emptiness. Air, or *hawā'*, and wind, or *rīḥ*, occupy this space and are associated with life and other forms of visible and invisible beings. Like the visible celestial bodies such as the sun, moon, and stars, air is a link between the first heaven and the earth. Air, metaphorically speaking, mediates the high (above) and the low (below).[19] It is a vivid link without which life on earth would be impossible. Air is unseen but sensible. The sensibility of air can be recognized or felt by observing the movement of trees and plants as well as by, for example, breathing. The Arabic word "*rūḥ*" or soul also means breath or wind (Ibn Manẓūr 1966; D. MacDonald 1931; al-Jawzīyah 1984; el-Aswad 1987, 1999). For villagers, air is an unlimited gift given by Allah to His people and creatures. Unlike other critical elements that maintain life such as water and food that can be privately owned by individuals, air cannot be claimed as private property. Metaphorically, the Arabic word *hawāʾ* (air) is deeply associated with love and passion as far as it denotes the changeable emotional states that people in love have toward each other.

The Cosmos: Invisibility and Spirituality

The following points can be concluded about the cosmos. Ontologically, what is visible, *ẓāhir*, or present, *ḥāḍir*, is not the only substance that exists in the world. What is unseen or hidden, *bāṭin* or *ghāʾib* (absent) also exists. Metaphorically speaking, what is invisible or absent is *maḥjūb*, concealed, either by its very nature, such as a soul, or by something else, such as a veil. It is the cosmological context within which the problems of concealment, veil, cover, and secrecy can be understood. The universe is constructed on the relationships that exist between the opposites of visibility/invisibility or perceptibility/imperceptibility. Within both the first heaven and the earth exist visible, material, and invisible beings and entities; however, beings that belong to the invisible domains of the heavens are immaterial. This results in the opposition of material/immaterial.

Although what is behind the first sky and what is in the underworld (the seventh earth) are both invisible, the nature of invisibility differs in the two cases. Above the first heaven, all invisible beings and entities are made of light (*nūr*) by Allah. Moreover, behind the first heaven there is an eternal light that is unseen because of the *ḥijāb* or veil that, in this case, is the first sky itself. In this connection, the light is a unifying principle that renders as a unity the diversity of beings and entities that exist within the upper heavens. Meanwhile, the light seen on earth is cyclic and temporal, not eternal, as is that existing beyond the visible heaven.

As opposed to what is beyond the first heaven, which is *nūr*, light and divine, the invisible domain that exists in the earth is dark and profane. Here, another set of oppositions including light/dark and divine/profane is found. Both light and dark are considered as being invisible forces, *qūwā ghaibīyah.* Light is associated with benevolent forces, *qūwā al-khair*, represented mostly in the light of the Prophet Muhammad, while dark is connected with malevolent forces *qūwā ash-shar*, represented by Satan or the *shaiṭān.* Light contradicts and encompasses dark. The earth itself is transitory and, consequently, the dark within it is temporal and inferior. In this connection, the opposition between eternity and transience is implicit in the light and dark spheres of the cosmos. The ultimate source of the light of all the heavens and the earth, although invisible, is Allah. Villagers, in many different contexts, quote the verse of the *Qur'an*, *Allah nūr as-samāwāt wa al arḍ* (Allah is the Light of the heavens and of the earth) (*Qur'an* 24:35).

If the air is an invisible link between the first sky and the earth, then the saints, as represented by their sanctuaries, and angels are, respectively, visible and invisible links between the heavens and the earth. Angels, ordered by Allah, descend to the earth to undertake some specific work or deliver messages to men, then ascend to the heavens after completing their missions. On the other hand, all devils and non-Muslim *jinn* and their leader, Satan, *Iblīs* or *ash-shaiṭān ar-rajīm*, use their own knowledge for evil purposes. Here we have another set of oppositions, that between heavenly, divine, or productive knowledge (given by Allah) and earthly, profane, and destructive knowledge designed by the devil. This opposition can be reformulated as religion/magic, or *siḥrdīn*. Living people and saints known for possessing *baraka* or blessing become socially and religiously significant as immediate agents for achieving social cohesion, while magicians become representatives of malevolent and antireligious activities that endanger that social cohesion. *Iblīs* is known as being the enemy of God and the founder of magic. Angels, unlike *jinn*, do not eat or procreate. Although they are invisible, angels and *jinn* are created, respectively, of light and fire, which constitute different types of visible substances. Angels represent unity in so far as they are created of and identified with light (*nūr*), while *jinn* and devils represent diversity and disunity as far as they are created of fire and associated with winds. The point here is that light transcends fire in so far as it can exist without air—the opposition light/fire is further enhanced. *Jinn*, as mentioned earlier, are identified with *riyāḥ*, or strong winds, which are essential for keeping fires burning.

The invisible sphere is superior to and encompasses the visible sphere. Without the invisible domain, the visible world would be devoid of meaning. Peculiar events are rendered explainable by attributing their causes to invisible forces. In other words, the invisible beings and forces of the heavens are superior to or more powerful than the invisible beings and forces of the underworld. For example, demons attempting to ascend to the heavens are killed by angels using fire and shooting stars. Also, angels can penetrate the earth whenever they are ordered to do so by God.

Invisible beings, entities, and forces of both the heavens and the earth are approached or treated with great awe because of their potential danger. The name of Allah is often accompanied by one of His exalted attributes such as *al-ʿAẓīm* (The Most Exalted) or *ar-Raḥīm* (The Merciful). Souls and angels, for example, are addressed or mentioned with reverence. The word *shaiṭān* or the name of *Iblīs* is never mentioned without uttering words that seek Allah's protection. Furthermore, when villagers talk about *jinn* and *ʿafārīt*, they interject from time to time into their discussion the common phrase, “May our Lord make our talk [about *jinn*] light for their hearts [or acceptable to them]” (*Rabunā yajʿal kalāmunā khafīf ʿalā qalbuhum*). By uttering this phrase, villagers seek the pardon of *jinn* and the protection of Allah when they find themselves involved in a conversation that might, intentionally or unintentionally, upset the *jinn*. This statement leads to the fact that the invisible world (*ʿālam al-ghaib*) for villagers is both an unknowable and unquestionable reality. This invisible world belongs to a domain that transcends people's understanding in such a way that it is safe for them, as they believe, not to be involved in comprehending it.

All in all, Allah is the ultimate invisible and sacred being who dominates all spheres of the universe and all existing visible and invisible beings, entities, and forces. To confirm this belief, people refer to “a cosmos or universe organized or ordered by its Owner,” *kaun wa munaẓẓamuh ṣāḥbuh*. Villagers quote verses of the *Qur'an* in which Allah is described as *Aẓ-Ẓāhir wa al-Bāṭin* (The Visible and the Invisible) (*Qur'an* 57:3). The meaning of “Visible” refers to the fact that all visible beings and entities in the heavens and on the earth are signs of Allah's existence, omnipotence, and greatness. Other verses of the *Qur'an* are quoted, indicating that Allah has created everything and knows everything: “Say: O Allah the Creator of the heavens and the earth, who has the knowledge of the invisible and the visible!” (*ʿālim al-ghaib wa ash-shahādah*) (*Qur'an* 39:46).

Conclusion

This chapter has shown that the world is viewed by rural Egyptians as a place of visible and invisible dimensions. These dimensions necessitate two kinds of knowledge: One is related to the knowledge of everyday observation, the other to the knowledge of hidden reality, religious or otherwise. Neither the visible nor the invisible components of the cosmos have any value in and of themselves. They become meaningful when viewed within the hierarchical relationships that exist among them. The hierarchical scheme here is understood in terms of the oppositions between the above, complete, superior, and invisible on the one hand, and the below, fragmented, inferior, and visible on the other. Of these constituents, the invisible is the most significant because it represents the whole universe.

Because of the cryptic nature of the invisible, villagers tend to rely on what they can observe. In everyday practice, it is not uncommon to hear villagers say “If you had knowledge of the unknown, hidden, or invisible, you would choose the here-and-now” (*idhā iṭṭalaʿtum ʿalā al-ghaib laikhtartum al-wāqiʿ*). It is the face-to-face relationships that define the ways people choose to interact with one another. When these relations are rendered invisible, or when people are not in immediate contact, the relationships become uncertain and open to all kinds of possibilities.

As far as the universe as a whole is concerned, *al-ghaib*, the invisible or unseen domain, gives meaning to the visible world, *ʿālam ash-shahādah* or *Aẓ-Ẓāhir*. It is to be noted, however, that although the visible domain, including this world and the human body, is inferior to the invisible sphere, it is not denounced nor neglected. People show concern for the visible parts of the universe insofar as they are considered gifts given by God that should be maintained in good condition. This established cosmological order is viewed as an unquestioned reality. Although they calculate and work hard, *fallāḥīn* think and behave as if invisible forces, good or bad, interfere in the outcome of their deeds or actions. Good things are attributed to God, while bad things are due either to evil spirits and devils or the negative psychic forces of people.

Modern scientific knowledge is, of course, not denied; rather, it is highly valued and sought after by people who have the opportunity to pursue it. Villagers are not against science and technology. However, when science generates more problems than it solves as in the case of the endangered ibis, a bird known as "the friend of the *fallāḥ*" whose numbers are decreasing as a result of the use of insecticides, science is viewed as being counterproductive. Moreover, science is viewed as a secular means dealing with secular matters with both positive and negative consequences and is, therefore, disputable. The challenge villagers now face is how to incorporate the secular within the spiritual without questioning their deeply rooted religious outlook.

Notes

1. The narrative of al-Khiḍr is mentioned in the *Qur'an* (18:60–81). For further details on the place of al-Khiḍr in Muslim life, see A. J. Wensinck (1987).

2. Bourdieu (1966) and Eickelman (1976, 1977) found the same orientation among Algerian and Moroccan peasants and tribesmen, respectively.

3. The intricate phenomenon of "veil" or "veiling" has been extensively addressed and debated by scholars who, presenting different views, demonstrate its religious, moral, economic, and social (gender) implications in Muslim societies. For further information, see, for example, L. Abu-Lughod (1998b), Ahmad (1992), El-Guindi (1999), Hoffman-Ladd (1987), MacLeod (1993), and Zuhur (1992).

4. See, for example, the *Qur'an* (2:29, 164; 3:190; 14:32–34; 39:5; 67:3).

5. The word *dunyā* is related to the word *danā* (*dunūw*) that, in spatial terms, means to be near, close, or low.

6. The concept of the sky as a large dome or vault was recognized by ancient

Egyptians in their mythology whereby the Goddess Nut (Sky) was represented as a woman stretching her naked body over the earth or over her husband Geb. Geb appears as a recumbent man hoisting himself up on one elbow and bending a knee (el-Aswad 1997).

7. This belief is supported literally by the *Qur'an* (13:17; 51:22).

8. In his study of shamanism, Taussig (1987, 373) points out that the pagan dead mediate "the social relations of the living with nature's elements, with earth, wind and water, and beyond that."

9. Among saints themselves hierarchy also exists: "Saints are recognized as having a hierarchical worth or value exceeding that of ordinary believers, based very simply on the understanding that they have achieved a special closeness to God" (Smith and Haddad 1981, 184).

10. *Sidrat al-muntahā* is mentioned in the *Qur'an* (53:14). Some Muslim intellectuals describe *sidrat al-muntahā* as the lotus or tree whose leaves are as big as an elephant's ears (Ibn Kathīr 1937).

11. *Ash-shuhadā'* are martyrs who are believed to be alive in paradise where they can eat and drink. See the *Qur'an* (2:154–55; 3:169). Some Muslim intellectuals (al-Jawzīyah 1984, 129) state that the souls of martyrs are in vesicles of green birds that move freely in paradise.

12. On the night of the twenty-seventh of the Arabic month of Rajab (before the *Hijra*, the Prophet's migration from Mecca to Medina), the Prophet, mounted *al-burāq* and miraculously traveled from *al-masjid al-Ḥarām*, the sacred mosque at Mecca, to *al-masjid al-Aqṣā*, the farthest mosque at Jerusalem, where he led all prophets in a collective prayer. Then, accompanied by the archangel Jibrīl (Gabriel), he ascended to the highest point of the seventh heaven, passing through all the heavens. Only the Prophet was allowed to reach this highest point known as *sidrat al-muntahā*. During this heavenly journey, God assigned the five daily prayers to all Muslims. Some Muslim commentators interpret the *mi'rāj*, the Prophet's ascension to heaven literally, while others view it as a vision (Ibn Kathīr 1937, 2–24; Ibn Hishām 1978, 3–9; Younis 1967, 5–9).

13. Villagers have the concept of *al-kursī* as a throne. Some Muslim intellectuals, however, argue that the chair is a footstool (Heinen 1982, 77–81).

14. Clay as a substantive material from which man was created was a core theme in ancient Egyptian creation mythology, in which the god Khnum was portrayed as fashioning man on the potter's wheel (Ions 1968).

15. In their agricultural activities, Egyptian peasants still follow the Coptic calendar whose first month (Toot) begins on the tenth or eleventh of September. For more information, see Ammar (1966) and Ṣāliḥ (1971).

16. The association of sex with the sun and moon differs from one culture to another. Like Egyptians or Muslims, American Indians (Yuchi and Cherokee, for example) consider the sun a female (Leach 1972, 9–11). In Kedang, an Eastern Indonesian society, while the sun is a male, there is no clear idea of the sex of the moon. However, Barnes (1974, 111) states that "in so far as the moon stands in opposition to sun, it must be female."

17. For more information regarding the social significance of time in local com-

munities in the Middle East, see Bourdieu (1966, 1977) and Eickelman (1976, 1977, 1981).

18. Compare this with another context in which right and left are associated with south and north, respectively. Chelhod (1973, 239–62) argues that the location of the *Kaʿbah* affects or determines the values of these cardinal points. North of the *Kaʿbah* is called *shamāl*, which also means left, because it is located at the left side of the *Kaʿbah*. Moreover, the word *shamāl*, as Chelhod states, is related to the word "*shuʾm*," which means "misfortune" and "ill augury." Ancient Arabs called Syria "Sam," "which is unquestionably related in etymology to *shuʾm* . . . and *mashʾamat* which the Koran uses to designate the left" (1973, 247). On the other hand, Yemen, which is situated at the south of the *Kaʿbah* is so called because its location is at the right side of the *Kaʿbah*. The etymology of the word "Yemen" is derived from the root *y-m-n*, which refers to ideas of success and happiness and from it is derived the term "*yamīne*," which means right (Chelhod 1973, 247).

19. In archaic Egyptian cosmology, air was identified as the god Shu, who was depicted as holding up the sky, separating it from the earth (el-Aswad 1997).

4

The Hierarchical Microcosm

visible and invisible aspects of the person

As hierarchy orders the cosmic totality, it also constructs the totality of the person or individuality. The hierarchically ordered parallels between elements of the cosmology and constituents of the person are explicitly and implicitly reflected in Egyptian villagers' everyday scenarios, practices, and body language. The holistic view of personhood is studied in its relation to the hierarchically ordered universe that contains animate and inanimate and visible and invisible forces and entities (el-Aswad 1987, 1988, 1993, 1994, 1999).

Within broader cross-cultural frameworks, anthropologists (Dumont [1980, 1985, 1986], Hall [1983], Marsella [1985], and Showeder and Bourne [1984], among others) associate the following qualities and features of personhood with Western and non-Western societies respectively: independent/interdependent, individuated/unindividuated, monochronic/polychronic, autonomous/dependent or relational, bounded/unbounded, abstract/concrete, noncontextualized/contextualized, inworldly/outworldly, egocentric/sociocentric, and individualistic/holistic. However, this distinction of polar dichotomies that accentuates the Western dominant paradigm of individualism has been challenged by other studies (Hollan 1992; Holland and Kipnis 1994; McHugh 1989; Schwarz 1997; Spiro 1992). These studies purport, and I agree, that it is misleading to accept a mere grouping of peripheral characteristics associated with non-Western notions of personhood. This study attempts to demonstrate that Egyptian peasants have an autonomous sense of personhood that is distinct from, though attached to, both the society and cosmos. It is true that social relatedness is of a fundamental significance in Egyptian culture, yet this fact does not diminish the concept of the individual.

In Middle Eastern scholarship, classical literature that deals with the spiritual, mental, and emotional aspects of the person[1] is concerned with orthodox Islamic beliefs as reflected in the sacred texts of the *Qur'an* and *ḥadīth* and related exegeses of Muslim intellectuals overlooking local people's views and beliefs. Studies concerned with personhood and identity in the Middle Eastern context (Abu-Lughod 1986; Abu-Zahra 1970; Antoun 1968, 1989; Gilmore 1987; Meeker 1976a, b; Peristiany 1966) have focused on moral aspects of the person such as honor, shame, modesty, and so on separated from the holistic perspective of the person. The ethnography of rural folk is scanty when compared to the rich ethnography of the Bedouin personality.

The components of the person are associated in many significant aspects with those of the universe. Each basic component of the person is connected with either a visible or invisible area or domain, or both, which together constitute the universe. In other words, the constituents of the person, in their visible and invisible aspects, are associated with the heavens, earth, and underworld. The person as a microcosm synthesizes the most salient constituents of the world. It is unsound to detach the concept of personhood from people's social scenarios and philosophical orientations. In brief, personhood is comprehensible only when located within a total cosmology and a total pattern of thought and action. Within this holistic view of the person, it becomes inconsistent to consider the body per se as the existential ground of culture and self (Csordas 1990). The claim that "embodiment [is] an intermediate methodological field defined by perceptual experience and mode of presence and engagement in the world" (Csordas 1994, 12) overlooks domains of reflexive and discursive scenarios of human experience. However, this does not mean to abandon the body or embodiment as an analytic theme, but rather to incorporate it with other analytic units.

Parts and Wholes

It has been argued that "hierarchy is implicit in various aspects of people's cosmology and social life" (Dumont 1986, 8). Kluckhohn's statement (1963, 114) that "there is some notion of hierarchy among the components of a culture" can be of great help in understanding the concept of the person among rural Egyptians. Ethnographic material from the village shows that hierarchical and relational logic does not negate the distinctive character of a part or unit within the whole or system. This study utilizes the modality of proportioning that seeks to elicit the meaningful relationship between portions or parts of the whole person as well as between the components of that whole and those of the cosmos. Dumont's structural method that seeks to delineate hierarchies of relations within a whole or system is akin to the mode of comparison by "proportioning" that is elaborated on by Tambiah.[2] *Proportion* or the *act of proportioning* means "the relation as to magnitude, degree, quantity, or importance that exists *between portions, parts, a part and the whole, or different things*" (Tambiah 1990, 125–26 [emphasis in original]).

Peirce's social theory of the self maintains that man is a sign as well as a sign-interpreter—and self-knowledge is in principle the same as knowledge of the others (Peirce 1931–58, 5:314, 316). For Peirce, the locus, identity, and continuity of the self was not to be found in the individual organism. It was, rather, an "outreaching identity" that connected the feelings, thoughts, and actions of one individual with those of others through the process of symbolic communication. The self is thus both a product and an agent of semiotic communication and is therefore social and public (Singer 1984, 54–57; Short 1992, 124; Parmentier 1994, 16).

The concept of the person is never simply given, but is constructed and negotiated. The symbolic system of the person as constructed by rural Egyptians is not static nor symmetrical, but rather dynamic and asymmetrical. The hierarchical structure is diachronic and dynamic and contains, using Dumont's phrase (1986, 127), "a double relation of identity and contrariety." There is a distinction within identity, and there is an encompassment of the contrary. As far as the concept of the person is concerned, hierarchy is dealt with in two dimensions of distinction: First is the hierarchy within the whole, as in the case of the components of the person viewed as a whole. Second is the hierarchy of distinctions between persons as viewed on the basis of gender, age, rank, and other social characteristics.

The visible aspect of the universe is comparable to the visible structure of the person's body. Meanwhile, the invisible world is existentially constructed or divided into three worlds: the world of the spirit (*ar-rūḥ*); the world of angels (*al-malāʾikah*); and the world of *jinn*, *ʿafārīt*, and ghosts. These three invisible worlds bear semblance to some invisible components of the person; that is, the soul or spirit, the angels (residing on the shoulders), and the *ʿifrīt* or ghost that appears after death. In this analogical parallel is embedded the unity of both the universe and the individual.

In dealing with the constituents of the person, this study emphasizes that the whole is more than the sum of its parts. The person consists of components that are hierarchically ordered in terms of the opposition between invisible and visible. The invisible/visible dichotomy underlies such other hierarchical but complementary oppositions as soul/self, soul/body, mind/body, reason/emotion, transcendental/mundane, heavenly/earthly, immaterial/material, eternal/transient, and inside/outside.

Sacred and Spiritual Spheres

Local exegeses of the soul, *ar-rūḥ*, designate triple meanings.[3] First, it means the unseen, immaterial, and otherworldly entity that belongs to the heavenly and spiritual world, distinct from, though attached to, the earthly world. The soul is the sacred life-force and the unifying principle that unites the multiple aspects of the person together into one living unit. It belongs to the invisible and sacred world, *ʿālam al-ghaib*, and exists before birth and continues after death.[4] Second, it refers to the psychological spheres of the person. And third, the soul is associated with the social and ethical qualities of the person.

The soul is depicted as a divine secret (*sirr ilāhī*) made of the light of God,[5] *qabas min nūr Allah*. Humans participate in the invisible, transcendental, secret, and divine qualities of the cosmos through the participation of their souls with the divine world. In other words, people assert their relationship with the unseen and spiritual world through participation with invisible entities and forces such as souls, angels, and intermediary holy persons or saints.

Although communication between humans and invisible entities necessitates certain discursive and nondiscursive actions, communication directly from invisible beings can be made without either intention or specific means from humans. As being part of the spiritual world, a person's soul can communicate with other living and dead people in different ways. The soul manifests itself in such multiple spheres of life as dreams, motions of the body, miracles, and the mysterious influence of certain events. There is debate among people concerning the reliability of dreams as a source of information about the soul or the unseen realm. Two major kinds of dreams are recognized: First is the *dream vision* (*ruʾiyah*) that is experienced repeatedly, carrying certain messages from the spirits or souls of ancestors, relatives, friends, saints, or prophets. A leading *shaikh*, drawing on what he believed to be part of the Prophet's tradition, contended that if a person experienced the same dream conveying the same message forty times consecutively or without interruption, that dream is a reliable and true vision.[6] The second category includes *regular dreams* (*aḥlām*, sing. *ḥulm*) caused by the communication of the soul with the invisible realm. These dreams, however, are subject to different interpretations depending on the knowledge, experience, purity, and religiosity of interpreters.

In dream visions, as in ordinary dreams, souls have glimpses of and receive messages from *ʿālam al-ghaib*, the unseen and unknowable world. However, villagers concede that the *dream vision* is sharper, stronger, more veracious, and higher in dignity than other kinds of dreams. Dreams are interpreted as being related to the activity of a person's soul (not self). It is the material shackles of the body that hinder the soul from moving freely in the universe. Through dreams people contact with other people, whether alive or dead. Symbolic features of dreams make them interpretable according to specific signs. Dreams themselves are signs of the unseen world in which the soul can penetrate and transform dramatic events into symbols that affect them mentally and emotionally.

Dreams are not considered mere fantasy, but are treated with respect and sometimes awe. The social significance of dreams is that they are interpreted as messages coming from people, dead or alive, seeking or demanding certain things. The dreams that were recounted to me by villagers were never doubted nor questioned. For instance, a middle-aged man was angry with his married sister and hence severed his relationship with her because she had convinced her dying mother to sign a document giving her the right to possess their house. After almost a year of estrangement and dispute with his sister, the man started seeing his mother in his dreams asking him to restore his relationship with the sister. He contended that his mother was "haunting" him every night and showing great pains in asking him to forgive them. When the man went to visit his sister he was surprised to hear that she also had seen their mother in her dreams asking her to compensate her brother, which she did.

The existence of the soul after death can be proven or explained through the occurrence of wonders or miracles, *karāmāt*. In a story that was retold to me by different speakers, a dead man from a nearby village was being carried to his grave when his bier unexpectedly changed direction and led the procession to a spot where it stopped. People tried unsuccessfully to move the stubborn bier. This caused a heated debate between the relatives of the dead man and the owners of the land on which the bier lay. Eventually, and after investigation by the authorities, the bier was understood as a sign (*ʿalāmah*) of the invincible power of the soul of the blessed deceased. Consequently, the event ended with the building of his tomb at that spot. It was subsequently recounted that this piece of land had been seized by force from his father. Of this unexpected public event individuals concluded the following: First, the existence and effect of spiritual power should not be underestimated; and second, justice will inevitably be attained by a higher power, that of Allah, if the mundane power fails. Before death, the man had fought to restore the land, but failed. It made people wonder and speculate that in his death, the man managed to achieve what he could not in life. The soul or spirit gives the per-

TABLE 4.1

THE STATES OF A PERSON'S SOUL DURING EVERYDAY ACTIONS, SLEEP, AND DEATH

Everyday action	*Sleep*	*Death*
understanding	consciousness	illumination
regular vision	sharp vision	sharper vision
encompassing	partly free	completely free
heavy	partly light	fully light
this world	this/other worlds	other worlds
intuition	signs/foresight	signs/foresight

son mystical powers over others.[7] From the people's point of view, this was not a mere fantasy or fiction but a faithfully conceded actual and natural event. Interestingly, it is not the body or the self through which this phenomenon was explained, but rather the soul, which exists independently and gives the person autonomous character even after death (see table 4.1).

The soul undergoes profound changes but never loses its divine and transcendental qualities. It lives in corporeal form in this present life, in noncorporeal form in the tomb, and again in corporeal form—though different from that of this worldly life—in the hereafter.

Religious knowledge and spiritual experience such as praying, fasting, and reading the *Qu'ran* strengthen the soul and enhance its potential power of inspiration. However, people's souls differ depending on their age and gender. Souls of men are believed to be stronger than those of women. Because of the weakness of their souls, women are believed to be more susceptible to spirit-possession than men. Likewise, children are believed to have such immature souls that they are vulnerable and in need of protection against the psychic power of the evil eye as well as invisible evil beings and forces.

The Body: Cosmic Embodiment

It is important to mention at the outset that of the nine constituents of the person discussed in this chapter, only one component, the body, is visible. This visible component is the manifest dimension of the invisible cosmology. It is

> the countless acts of diffuse inculcation through which the body and the world tend to be set in order, by means of a symbolic manipulation of the relation to the body and to the world aiming to impose what has to be called . . . a "body geography," a particular case of geography, or better *cosmology*. (Bourdieu 1977, 92–93 [emphasis added])

The relationship between the body or the living person and the soul can be viewed through linguistic evidence and everyday discourse or activity. The plural form of the Arabic word *rīḥ* (wind) is *aryāḥ* or *arwāḥ*, which is the same plural form of the word *rūh* (soul). Like wind, air, and breath,[8] the soul is always in motion. Neither the soul nor the wind can be seen by individuals; however, they can be felt through the motion of the body. A faint or unconscious person is depicted as *mirawḥan*—having a weakened or dizzy spirit. Moreover, anything dead is recognized as being without a soul, *lā rūḥ fīh, mā fīh rūḥ*. An intelligent, amiable, and sociable person is metaphorically described as having a light soul, "*rūḥ khafīfah*," as opposed to a stupid, bulky, and disagreeable person, known as having "*rūḥ thaqīlah*," a heavy spirit. The body, *al-jism*, *al-badan*, or *al-jasad*, is inhabited by the spirit or soul as well as other invisible forces. In the sacred scenario of creation, the body was created of clay (*ṣalṣāl*) or mud (*ṭīn*). Simply put, both the body and the earth share the fundamental common quality of being transient. The belief that the body is earthly is connected not only with creation, but also with death, where the body, except for the large bones, is thought to disintegrate and become dust. Prayers for the deceased, including recitations of the *Qur'an*, are performed on behalf of the soul—not the self or the body. The living body participates with earth in the material quality although it is connected to heaven through the soul. The soul is deemed to surpass, as well as to oppose and encompass, the earthly body.

The relationship between the body or the person and the society and the cosmos can be explored by the way people symbolically utilize certain tangible parts of their socially informed bodies (Bourdieu 1977, 124; Lambek 1998). The social skin of the body, Terence Turner (1995, 149) maintains, is a social skin of signs and meanings that represent the socialized self by mediating its relations to the social world. Symbolization is an act that calls something to exist, and the symbolizing is part of the symbolized (Todorov 1982, 119–21). In this context, it is insufficient to accept Mitchell's claims that in the traditional world of the Middle East there is nothing symbolic and nothing stands for something else. Rather, he alludes, there are "the necessary relations at work in a world where nothing occurs except as something that resembles, differs from, duplicates, or re-enacts something else" (Mitchell 1988, 61).

The bodily symbols used consistently in the village are the hand (*al-kaff* or *al-yad*) and the eye (*al-ʿain*), representing notions of blessing and envy, respectively. Hidden or invisible forces are aptly typified as arising from the glance of the eye as well as from the touch of the hand. Both the hand and the eye are vital parts of a person's body that, physically and symbolically, connect that person with the outside world, including other people, without losing his sense of autonomous self-hood or identity. In a word, they are crucial means of communication. However, for the villagers, the hand and the eye are used differently in the communication process.

The hand is an embodied symbol of the benevolent invisible (cosmic-heavenly) force that displays itself through touch. The hand is associated with touch, which is an important means for establishing good relationships with others. When they salute one another, villagers insist on firmly shaking or clasping their hands. The good hand of the people of *baraka* is called the "white hand"[9] (*yad baiḍā*). For villagers, the color white signifies purity, goodness, and health.

Eye contact is also very important in the process of communication among individuals. However, people avoid gazing or staring at one another. Rather, they make very short eye contacts. Gazing or staring is interpreted either as *baḥlaga*—a complex concept that signifies fear, anger, and disgust—or as *naẓra*, meaning a strange and envious look. The eye is the mirror that instantly reflects the hidden spheres of a person. In an argument, I heard a person questioning the credibility of a story told by his neighbor, saying "I know the truth from your eye, not from your tongue."

Two types of the eye associated with two states of both the cosmos and the person are acknowledged: On the one hand, there is the *cool eye* (*ʿain bārda*), which is harmless, and on the other there is the *hot eye* (*ʿain ḥārra*), which is evil or destructive (*ʿain radiya*). To display good intention when admiring someone, a person utters: "May my eye be cool and cause you no harm" (*ʿainy ʿalaik bārda*). Because it causes *al-ḥasad* (envy), this second kind of eye is called the *envious eye* (*ʿain al-ḥasūd*). It is depicted as either the blue eye (*ʿain zargah*) or the yellow eye (*ʿain ṣafrah*). An envious person is described as the one who has a yellow eye, *abū ʿain ṣafra*. The color yellow denotes sickness, weakness, dryness, and impurity and is colloquially used by peasants to mean excrement. There is an anomaly regarding the color blue: for villagers, blue denotes simultaneously both destructive and protective powers. On the one hand, as far as blue is associated with people, it signifies destruction, death, or viciousness as expressed in the phrase "The blue bone" (*ʿaḍma zārga*). Moreover, the corpse is described as being blue, and bereaved women dye their clothes with indigo (*nīlah*) as a sign of grief. On the other hand, blue is cosmologically associated with heaven, particularly during the daytime, and symbolizes protection. In this connection, peasants use blue amulets to protect themselves and their property from the envious eye.

The psychic force causing envy is believed to be so strong that it can destroy solid stone or kill a large camel immediately.[10] The presence of the psychic force of the malicious self is mediated through the indexicality of the eye (*al-ʿain*) or the inhaled breath of air or gasp (*shahqa*). Women and children are vulnerable to the other's dangerous self. To avoid the effect of the wicked self, women deliberately cover themselves and their children or neglect their children's appearance.[11] Women who cover themselves are motivated to do so not merely by notions of modesty and honor, but also by fear of an envious person, *al-ḥasūd*.

The hidden feelings of jealousy one might have toward another person are reflected in the eye. The first sign that a sick person has been the victim of coveting is when he yawns—opens his mouth widely and inhales deeply. Such a case generates an action by which people say, "This is the psyche or self" (*dī nafs*) and "This is the look or glance" (*dī naẓrah*). A vulnerable person is called *ibn naẓrah* (The victim of the glance). The eye becomes the agent when the *nafs* (self) of the envious person hits or penetrates the body of the victim through his or her glance. A sick or coveted person is described as being stricken, attacked, or afflicted by the envious eye, *al-ʿain ṣābituh*. Although the notion of envy reflects unhealthy relationships among members of the community, the envious eye as a negative psychic force goes beyond the social reality and imposes itself as an existing phenomenon. Through an envious eye, a person can destroy himself as well as his property. In such cases, people say "Money [asset] is not to be envied by anybody but its owners" (*mā yaḥsid al-māl illā aṣḥābuh*).

The eye, which is viewed as an embodied symbol of the malevolent, invisible cosmic-psychic force exercising its destructive effects through the glance, is primarily counteracted through two symbolic bodily devices, the eye and the hand. The eye is used as a symbol of protection against the malevolent invisible forces dispersed in the cosmos. It is believed to watch not only the visible world as defined by culture, but also the invisible or hidden world that exists beyond human control. In a word, the eye has magical power that is simultaneously connected to psychological and cosmological spheres (see table 4.2).

As a symbol of unseen protective power and blessing, the hand is used as an amulet for warding off the envious eye. On walls of houses and other buildings are pictures, paintings, and drawings of the hand (*al-kaff*) made by villagers—not to decorate their houses but to protect themselves and their property from the envious eye.[12]

For the purposes of protection, women of different ages carry or wear on their clothes or around their necks little amulets in the shape of the eye and hand (*khamsah wa khamīsah*), showing the five fingers encompassing an eye. Fingers are believed to oppose the eye and destroy it. According to the principle of similarity whereby like affects like, the symbol of eye averts the envious eye (*ʿain al-ḥasūd*) and protects people from its danger. Likewise, the symbol or the amulet of the hand, according to the principle of opposition, destroys the envious eye. Both symbols or icons of the eye and the hand

TABLE 4.2

THE CULTURAL AND COSMIC SIGNIFICANCE OF THE BODY REPRESENTED IN THE DISTINCTION OF THE HAND AND EYE

Hand (baraka) blessing	*Envious eye (ḥasad)*
benevolent invisible force	malevolent invisible force
cosmic/spiritual (holy)	cosmic/psychic
public/private	individualistic
given and maintained by God	activated by the *nafs* or self
superior	inferior
collective or social cohesion	conflict, self-interest
healing power	affliction
its symbol is the hand	its symbol is the eye
its medium is "touch"	its medium is the "glance"
associated with "white"	associated with "yellow"

that represent parts of the body coexist in one iconic sign and serve as means of protection.

As opposed to the envious eye, believed to be possessed by vicious persons described as being friends of the devil, the hand indicates *baraka*, which is thought of as being possessed by blessed people such as prophets, saints, people of piety, or *shaikhs*. In the village, the head of the Ghanim family, widely known and acknowledged for the *baraka* (power of blessing) inherent in his hand and saliva, helped those who suffered from illnesses. The blessed man rubbed the bodies of the sick persons with his right hand in order to heal them. The hand represents the blessed person as a whole and is believed to have had a curative effect on the sick.

While the *baraka* of a good person is believed to be efficacious both before and after death, the evil eye is confined to the malevolent person's self and ceases to be effective after death. As representing a benevolent force, the right hand especially encompasses the eye, which denotes an evil, hidden force. Both the hand and the eye are indices that refer, respectively, to invisible benevolent and malevolent forces existent in the person as well as in the universe, which are hierarchical (Dumont 1986, 230).

The Soul and Self

In the public sphere, specifically during Friday sermons, religious leaders, like religious reformers in other Muslim countries (Eickelman 1976; Rosen 1984), address the relationship between reason (*ʿaql*) and self (*nafs*), indicating the tension between rationality and egoistic desire. They also address the relationship between the soul (*rūḥ*) and self, referring to the tension between religious ethics and individual self-interest. The relationship between the soul and the self is profoundly complicated and necessitates special attention. In specific contexts, the *rūḥ* is referred to as *nafs*, causing confusion among individuals. *Nafs* means self, ego, spirit, or soul in so far as it is attached to the body. Both terms share a common quality related to wind or air. When facing the crisis of death, one hears the common phrase that "Each person has a definite number of breaths in specific places" (*anfās maʿdūda fī amākin maḥdūdā*), and that each breath taken reduces the span of life (el-Aswad 1987, 213).

The *self* is a concept attached to the agent or the physical condition of the autonomous living person and vanishes immediately after death. Although people use the terms *self* (*nafs*) and *soul* (*rūḥ*) interchangeably, they attach to each one specific connotations. It is true that in their daily actions people use the term *self* more frequently than the term *soul* with reference to living persons, yet the soul is still imbued with significant qualities as both the true source of life and metaphor of social relationships. For example, each self—not the soul—is destined to experience death, *kull nafsin dhāiqat al-maut*. Furthermore, when a person dies, his soul, *rūḥ*—not self, *nafs*—"comes out," *tiṭlaʿ*. Socially, it is the soul that meets and joins the aggregation of souls belonging to both social-local and global Muslim communities. In this context, a hierarchical opposition of soul/self exists in which the first component is more highly valued than the second and therefore encompasses it. Differences, Dumont points out (1986, 266), are acknowledged, but they are subordinated to and encompassed in one unity.

Although all individuals have selves (*anfus*), these selves differ according to gender and age. Women's selves are believed to be weaker and less assertive than those of men, especially in the public domain. Children's selves are vulnerable and in need of the protection of adults. The qualities of a person's selves depend on the moral values to which he or she adheres as well as on the psychic power he or she possesses. The self, like the soul, grows as the person grows, yet, unlike the soul, the self is mortal.

The self (*an-nafs*) or ego (*dhāt*) is represented in the existential "I" or *anā*. It refers to egoistic, private, and individualistic aspects of the person that might conflict with the collective interest of the family or community. In particular private contexts, however, both concepts of soul and self are semantically equivalent and used to connote a desire or wish. The phrase "*anā rūḥī fīh*" or "*anā nafsī fīh*" literally means "I am [my soul is] in it" or "I am [my self is] in it"; it cannot be translated into English without stripping it of its intended meaning, "I want it" or "I am dying for it." Nevertheless, the word *soul* is more expressive than the word *self*, because it is loaded less with selfish and egoistic connotations, and more with religious and cosmic meanings.[13] These two words are not used by English-speaking people in the same way or for the same purposes as they are used by rural Egyptians (el-Aswad 1999).

An independent sense of self-hood is emphasized through using the first-person pronoun "I." In certain social contexts it is acceptable to keep a low profile without losing the sense of autonomy. In such contexts, one hears a person in a situation say, "The self is the cause of all evil" (*an nafs sabab kulli sharr*) and "God save me from saying I" (*a'audhu bi-Allah men qual ana*). As aforementioned, the *self* (*an-nafs*), not the *soul* (*ar-rūḥ*), is believed to have potential negative effects on people and objects through envy and can intentionally or unintentionally destroy them. The autonomous sense of self-hood is represented in the invisible destructive power of a person implicit in the psychic phenomenon of envy that reveals his malevolent intention. The envious person rejoices on hearing about people's misfortunes. This personal or psychic attribute can be controlled or developed by the person himself. Controlling the negative spheres of the person through sincere and proper intention and action is the main concern of both private and public discourses.

It is true that the concept of privacy among Arabs, as El-Guindi points out (1999), does not connote meanings of individualism and seclusion as in Western culture. However, Arab privacy neither eliminates the notion of secrecy nor is confined only to "two core spheres—women and the family," as El-Guindi (1999, 82) argues. At both individual and collective levels, privacy and secrecy are associated more with the notion of avoiding the risk of unveiling what is covered (*faḍḥ al-mastūr*) or eliminating the danger of being publicly and negatively exposed. It is not uncommon to hear a person say in daily conversation or activity, "May our Lord protect us from the evil of people" (*rabbunā yakfīnā sharr an-nās*). The most common response to such an utterance is: "Those people are our selves" (*an-nās hum anfusunā*). In this sense, secrecy (*sirr* or *katmān*) is highly recommended for those who want their plans to be accomplished or property to be maintained without the unwelcome interference or intrusion of other people. In many different private and social situations I heard people say, "In order to get your things or needs met, uphold them in secrecy" (*ista'īnū 'alā qaḍā' ḥājatakum bil-kitmān*). Even in the moment of frustration and disappointment, a person should show steadfastness and independence as expressed in the maxim, "To be patient with myself is much better than asking people to be patient with me" (*ṣabrī 'alā nafsy wa lā ṣabr an-nās 'alay*).

In conclusion, this meaning of *self* (*nafs*) is reflected in both public and private zones—that is, the *nafs* of a person is recognized according to the ways he or she behaves or interacts with people. A person who is socially recognized as honorable is one who enjoys a venerable identity or noble self, *nafs ʿazīza*. On the contrary, a person depicted as having a wicked or vicious self (*nafs laʾīmah* or *khabīthah*) demonstrates misconduct, betrays people, or envies them through what is locally known as *naqq* or *garr*—vicious gossip. To be a person is, first of all, to respect yourself, *iḥtrām an-nafs* or *iḥtrām adh-dhāt*, and to be aware of other people's rights in dealing with them privately or publicly with respect.

Within the social environment, a person is visible through symbols and signs of physical fitness, reproduction, family ties, accomplishments in work or harvest, and the ability to interact with others as well as with the universe. Privately and socially, a successful person interprets his success as a result not only of hard work and good luck but also of his parents' invocation that causes the *baraka*—blessing of his health, property, work, and offspring. An indigenous person must move easily and carefully within the multidimensional aspects of identity, with its personal, social, and cosmological meanings. It is questionable, then, to say that in non-Western cultures that are characterized by holistic worldviews, the person is viewed as being sociocentric or dependent on social relationships rather than having his autonomous sense of personhood (Showeder and Bourne 1984).

Reason and Emotion

The relation between reason and emotion constitutes a major arena for discussing the personal, social, and cosmological spheres. Although the mind is highly valued and considered to be the measure by which individuals are evaluated as rational or irrational, it is viewed as being earthly and effected by the physical condition of the body,[14] as represented in the saying, "The healthy mind exists in the healthy body" (*al-ʿagl as-salīm fī al jism as-salīm*). Reason is a multimeaning concept denoting such diverse mental activities as reasoning (*taʿaqqul*), thought (*tafkīr*), distinction (*tamyīz*), understanding (*fahm*), abstraction (*tagrrīd*), wisdom (*ḥikmah*), rationalization (*tabrīr*), reflection (*taʾammul*), and imagination (*takhayyul*), among other things. However, the most distinctive quality of the mind is its quickness in discerning the relationship among things and/or ideas. For example, a villager tried to convince a government official to fund a local project that would serve the local community. Within his speech he frequently interjected a phrase that is used extensively by villagers in their arguments in both the private and public spheres, emphasizing the value placed on the keen use of the faculty of rational thought, saying, "We have not seen our Lord, *rabbunā*, we know Him through reason, *bi-al ʿagl*." When the official, in an attempt to dissipate or dissolve the dispute, replied, "We know our Lord by faith, *imān*," the villager immediately said, "Yes, but first by the reason otherwise you would have a shaky faith and we would have a shaky project," to which they all laughed. Reason, then, is public and renders subjective or inward thought visible and social so as to be shared or commonly recognized.

As opposed to angels who are created of light, have pure minds, and submit themselves ultimately to God through unconditional praying, humans are made of two opposing components: one is spiritual and rational, the other is bodily and instinctual. Man is thus located between angels (reason) and animals (instinct). However, man surpasses both in value because he has the ability to choose among alternatives and therefore holds responsibility for his intentions and actions. What makes the mind, *ʿagl* (*ʿaql*) so crucial for humans is that it faces challenges from different directions. One of these is the ability to maintain the balance among bodily desires, especially in time of deprivation; others involve intellectual, spiritual, and social demands.

A wise, reasonable, or intelligent person is depicted as having a large brain, *mukh kabīr*. People's minds differ depending on their age, gender, and temper. Although physical development contributes to the growth of intelligence, experience and accumulated knowledge are necessary for the maturation and integration of reason. Men view themselves as superior to women in mental and emotional characteristics. Due to the emotionality of their reactions and inclination to gossip, women's minds are depicted by men as being incomplete, *nāqiṣ*. Such a view is rejected by women, who contend that it is lack of experience due to social conditions—not intelligence—that renders them naïve in men's eyes. For both men and women, children are ignorant, *jāhilīn* (*jāhil*) and have little minds (*ʿuqūl ṣaghīrah*) that are not able to think or distinguish clearly among things.

Although reason is essential for their daily lives, individuals within rural Egyptian society, unlike in Western culture, do not separate it from the heart or emotion. In specific social and humanitarian contexts, they consider the heart to be the faculty for both feeling and thought.[15] The heart is the principal factor in driving people's social actions insofar as it is interconnected with intention and conscience. *Mind without heart* is rendered to a mere abstract calculation, while *heart without mind* is relegated to a type of insignificance and foolishness.[16] Heart is not confined to feelings or emotions, but rather encompasses values and ideas as well. An honorable man is metaphorically referred to as having not only a big mind but also a big heart. When a person has to choose between mind and heart, he or she chooses the heart for the reason that feelings and emotions imply ideas and images about other peoples and things.[17]

It would be a mistake, however, to argue that Egyptians are more emotional than intellectual or are inclined to deal with tangible rather than abstract problems. Simply put, they evaluate the heart over the mind when the heart is simultaneously guided not merely by emotions but by ideas, values, and feelings. For Egyptians, a person with a big heart is not an individual controlled by emotions, but is a wise, loving, caring, and rational person. The one who is dominated by emotions is depicted as being thoughtless (*ahwaj*), empty-headed, or flippant (*arʿan*). Of the two spoken phrases, *ʿaqly dalīly* (My mind is my guidance) and *qalby dalīly* (My heart is my guidance), the latter one indicates that the heart implies ideas, intuition, transparency (*shafāfīya*), and feelings, while the former one implies only reasoning or thinking. As Bateson (1972, 464) maintains, "The reasonings of the heart . . . are accompanied by sensations of joy and grief." Only the soul and heart are associated with intuition and hidden knowledge that go beyond everyday thinking. The heart then encompasses the mind and, as the seat of insight and intuition, orients rationality. When faced with a complicated problem that cannot be easily resolved, it is common to hear villagers say *istaftī qalbak* (Consult or think with your heart).

According to the Egyptians' view, everything animate or inanimate has a heart or center that is hidden or invisible. Likewise, the heart is the kernel of the person. The heart is related to both the soul and the body insofar as it serves as an index of the living person. An active or energetic person is described as one who has a beating or pulsating heart, *galb nābiḍ*. Nevertheless, the heart is hidden or inward (*bāṭin*), as being the seat of intent (*niyyah*) that implies an inner awareness of an autonomous self or identity in thinking and behaving.[18] In this sense, the theme of *bāṭin* (inward) and that of its opposite, *ẓāhir* (outward or visible) have important meanings in the context of people's interactions with one another. Except for God, nobody can directly tell, predict, or know what other people have hidden in their hearts.

The heart maintains the relationships between the individual and the community. However, a person is not perfect or self-sufficient as far as his physical, moral, emotional, social, and economic conditions affect his action and identity. Whatever a person does, it is hard for him to meet the expectations of the members of the community. Therefore, what a person is or should be concerned with is *raḥat sirr* (peace of mind and well-being), because otherwise life would be unbearable and meaningless. It is common to hear people say *raḥat as-sirr birr*, meaning that peace of mind or calmness of heart is a piety. The word *sirr* (secret) is associated here with the *bāṭin* (heart or inward state), which should be maintained in harmony with the *ẓāhir* (visible or outward state): "For the attainment of grace, the reasons of the heart must be integrated with the reasons of the reason" (Bateson 1972, 129).

It is not only the society that cannot meet its members' needs, but also the person who cannot meet society's expectations. In this context, people rely on patience (*ṣabr*) to overcome the tension between reason and emotion, as well as the imperfection of both the self and society. Therefore, patience is portrayed not only as sweet (*ḥulw*) or beautiful (*gamīl*), but also as being half of faith, *niṣf al-īmān*. Patience is not thought of as merely a passive attitude toward frustrating and conflicting events. The Arabic word *ṣābir* connotes neither passivity nor indifference, nor does it refer to a sick person as the English word "patient" does. A person might be sick but not patient, and conversely, a person might be patient but not sick. *Patience* refers to the ability to undertake and tirelessly endure arduous activities without complaining as well as the ability of willingly and actively avoiding what is unacceptable or forbidden.[19] Although "self-control" is the focal point of patience, the person is not expected to be fully independent, but may rely on those people around him. Patience or controlled emotion renders values of dependence and relatedness acceptable. Dependence is not viewed as an inferior quality, but as an attribute regulated by the local logic of the hierarchical tension between the powerless and powerful as reflected in the maxim of the power relationships: "Pretend to be weak until you hold the power" (*itmaskin lammā titmakkin*). Individuals not only ask those who are in power for protection or for securing their interests, but also use them to attain power.

Multiple Invisible Spheres

Certain concepts related to the cosmos and the person have a historical-religious background as represented in Muslim classical writings and exegeses of the *Qur'an* and tradition; however, these concepts are not fixed in scripture, but rather have different meanings for different people in different ethnographical settings. Some of these concepts can be found elsewhere in Muslim societies although their meanings may vary in different social contexts. My major concern here is with rural Egyptians' own views of such concepts as actualized in their daily activities.

Previous sections have discussed the notion that inside everyone there are benevolent and malevolent unseen forces, represented in notions of the soul and self, that empower people and allow them to do certain things. However, ethnographic material suggests that there are other multiple invisible forces embedded in the concept of "personhood." These concepts include the double, invisible brother/sister, ghosts, and angels.

The double (*qarīn*) is what can be labeled as the "invisible iconic double." The Arabic word *qarīn* is derived from the root "*q-r-n*," meaning to tie or compare something with something else. In daily life, a friend or spouse is known as *qarīn* (fem. *qarīnah*). Although the nature of the invisible double is portrayed differently by individuals in various contexts, there are some common attributes ascribed to it. On the one hand, the double (*qarīn*) is identical to the person in every aspect, including gender and temper, except that it is invisible. It represents the mimetic image or unseen replica of the body or person.[20] On the other hand, the double is not just an imagined iconic figure, but rather is an invisible constituent of the living person that metaphorically resembles the image or reflection of that person within a mirror. Physical, moral, and social attributes of the person are refracted in the double. If a person is left-handed or one-eyed, his or her double would be the same. Another view implies that the double is associated with the convention that everything animate or inanimate, except for *jinn*, has a shadow. The double is viewed as an invisible shadow or image that can make itself visible. Like a shadow, the double accompanies the person wherever he or she goes.[21] The double is born with the person and feels, thinks, and does whatever the person does. It dies immediately after the person's death and is resurrected with the person on the Day of Judgment, where it will serve as a critical witness confirming or denying the person's claims about him- or herself.

Exceptional attributes of a person are also believed to exist in the double. The concept of *qarīn*, as some villagers maintain, explains the widespread belief of *badal* (pl. *abdāl*), substitution, explaining changeable qualities of the same person or body. According to that belief, a pious person known for his miracles (*karāmāt*) can be seen in two different places simultaneously where the *qarīn* or *badal* (substitution) reveals itself materially instead of maintaining its invisibility.

If the *qarīn* is the invisible iconic image or double of the person, the *ukht* and the *akh* are invisible gendered siblings of that person; that is, each person has an invisible sister (*ukht*) and invisible brother (*akh*) who live underground and come to visit and care for the person in times of need. The concepts of brother and sister emphasize the villagers' awareness of the importance of kin or family ties, particularly those of siblings. For instance, when a person, male or female, makes a mistake or forgets to do certain things, he or she, after recognizing the mistake, exclaims *akh!*—"O brother!"

In everyday life the brother holds certain responsibilities toward his sister, even after her marriage. Similarly, the relationship between a man and his invisible opposite sister is thought to be stronger or more intimate than that between him and his invisible brother. Similarly, the relationship between a woman and her invisible brother is stronger than her relationship with her invisible sister. The invisible sister is always alert and watches over her visible brother. It is common to hear a woman or mother, after seeing her son fall down on the ground, say, "May the name of Allah protect you and your sister" (*ismallah ʿalaik wa ʿalā ukhtak*), hoping that the boy (and his invisible sister) will not be hurt. This phrase reflects the loving and intimate relationship between cross-sexual siblings as well as between siblings of the same sex. Children are very aware of such utterances, internalizing them and related beliefs at a very early age.

Children are socialized and indirectly taught by their parents, siblings, relatives, and neighbors that their behavior is being observed by two angels, *malakān*, residing on their shoulders. Being depicted as links between the heavens and the person, the two angels serve as unbiased observers who record all the deeds and doings of the person to be judged in the hereafter. On the right shoulder resides the angel responsible for counting and recording all the good deeds done by the person in everyday life. On the left shoulder resides the angel responsible for counting and recording all the bad deeds done by that person.[22] These recordings will be used as evidence upon which the person will be judged in the afterlife. The social significance of the two angels is that they are important imaginary cultural devices or agents in sustaining individuals' conscience and awareness of what is right and wrong. Both angels survive after the person's death and return to their place in the heaven, waiting for the moment of death and resurrection. The belief in the two angels is connected to the rhetoric of angelic presence and guardianship. For instance, when people talk about someone who is absent, they say, "He is absent but his angels are present" (*huwa ghāib wa lākin malāktu* [*malāʾkatahu*] *ḥāḍirah*), meaning that the unseen angels will witness what people say about the person whom they guard.

In addition to these unseen spheres of the person, there is an anomalous invisible component, the *ʿifrīt*, about which I have heard various accounts. Villagers distinguish between two kinds of *ʿifrīt*. On the one hand, *ʿifrīt* is one of the evil or dangerous *jinn* whose nature and behavior are completely different from that of human beings.[23] This type of *ʿifrīt* is not considered to be one of the components of the person. In certain contexts in which children or even adults show fear of the *ʿifrīt*, they are assured that such entities do not exist, saying, "There is no *ʿifrīt*, but children of Adam" (*ma ʿifrīt illā bany ādam*). On the other hand, *ʿifrīt* is considered to be a component of the person insofar as it refers to the ghost of the dead person. The ghost is most often described in negative terms, depending on how the person died. A person who died naturally does not have an active or dangerous *ʿifrīt*. People who are killed, however, are believed to have very dangerous and active *ʿafārī*. In short, the *ʿifrīt* leaves the body at death; however, it is mortal until resurrection. After the person's death, his or her *ʿifrīt* lives in the cemetery or, if the person was killed, wanders in the street and around places where the dead person used to frequent. Other perspectives suggest that the *ʿifrīt* is the frustrated double (*qarīn*), whose image is identical to that of the victim at the moment of death. It is worth noting that people metaphorically associate a person's bad emotional temper with that of the *ʿifrīt*. I heard *Shaikh* ʿIsā, a prominent medicine man known for his power of blessing, say that the violent and agitated mood of the self renders the person vulnerable to evil *jinn* to ride him (*yarkabu*) but not to possess him. Intense and disruptive emotions

TABLE 4.3

CONSTITUENTS OF THE PERSON AND THEIR ASSOCIATIONS WITH THOSE OF THE COSMOS

Heavenly	*Earthly*	*Underground*	*Function*	*Attribute*
soul (*rūḥ*)			life force	invisible, immortal, immaterial
the two angels			observing, recording	invisible, mortal, immaterial
	self (*nafs*)		psyche, self-interest	invisible, mortal, immaterial
	heart (*qalb*)		insight, passion, balance	invisible, mortal, material
	mind (*ʿaql*)		reasoning	invisible, mortal, immaterial
	body (*jasad*)		life enactment	visible, mortal, material
		double (*qarīn*)	mimesis	invisible, mortal, immaterial
		brother (*akh*) sister (*ukht*)	protection	invisible, mortal, immaterial
		ghost (*ʿifrīt*)	nonspecified	invisible, mortal, immaterial

generated by an inflamed self suggest that the fire (*nār*) of which the *ʿifrīt* is made is metaphorically used to depict the destructive aspect of the person. For instance, when a person becomes angry with somebody else, he usually threatens or warns him or her by saying, "Do not let me unleash my *ʿifrīt*" (*aṭṭallaʿ ʿifrītī ʿalayk*) or "My *ʿifrīt* is coming out" (*ʿifrītī ṭāhiʿ*). Moreover, an energetic, sometimes troublesome person is depicted as *ʿifrīt* (see table 4.3).

Conclusion

The thesis of this chapter has been to demonstrate that the cosmos is replicated on a small scale within the person or microcosm. The parallel between the universe and the individual is explicitly shown in villagers' beliefs and scenarios concerning life, death, and the world to come. Egyptian peasants show a deep concern with the person within the context of life in its totality or in its visible, sensory, practical, phenomenal, and transitory as well as invisible, abstract, spiritual, and eternal aspects. These different and seemingly contradictory domains represented in the oppositions of social/individual, public/private, body/mind, emotional/rational, material/immaterial, corporeal/spiritual, and mortal/immortal constitute complementary dimensions of both the cosmos and the person. The Egyptian holistic view of self-hood with its hierarchical implications does not necessarily result in the lack of the autonomous or independent sense of personhood. Among rural Egyptians, the word *shakhṣīyah* (personality) refers to a holistic, autonomous, and independent sense of individuality as having a distinctive character. A powerful personality (*shakhṣīyah qawīyah*) is expected to be found among both men and women regardless of social, economic, or occupational status. Also, an autonomous sense of self-hood is shown in the claim made by a person that he or she submits him- or herself to nobody but God. Egyptian peasants emphasize such attributes of the self as self-awareness, self-respect, self-control, self-assertion, self-confidence, and self-help—all of which are observable in their actions. Men and women as well are very careful to socialize their children to act according to these values or characters.

However, the invisible domain in Egyptian cosmology seems to be overwhelmingly dominant, where eight of the person's nine constituents are unseen, invisible, or hidden, while only one, the body, is apparent or visible. Invisible spheres are not to be considered inconsistent or irrational manifestations of a premodern or prelogical mentality as some intellectuals might suggest, but rather they constitute generative factors in an imaginary cosmological system shaping and being shaped by folk culture and the experiences of both individuals and collectivities. Without the invisible domain, the visible world would be devoid of meaning.

The visible aspect of the universe is comparable to the visible structure of the person's body. Meanwhile, the invisible world is existentially comparable with that of the person. Put differently, if the invisible universe is composed of three worlds—the world of the spirit (*ar-rūḥ*), the world of angels (*al-malā'ikah*), and the world of *jinn*, *'afārīt*, and ghosts—these three invisible components are also comparable to some invisible constituents of the person; that is, the soul or spirit, the angels (residing on the shoulders), and the *'ifrīt* or ghost that appears after death. In this analogical parallel is embedded the unity of both the universe and the individual. As a cultural construct, the cosmological scheme renders the person a *homo-cosmos* and helps him or her understand the unique blend of characteristics that builds his or her personality. The relational or interdependent sense of self as represented in peoples' relationships with others (society) as well as with other visible and invisible entities (cosmos) coexists with their autonomous sense of self. In brief, personal, social, and cosmological dimensions are fused in the person as symbolically and hierarchically constructed by Egyptian culture. In this sense, cosmology serves as an effective personal and collective coping mechanism, helping individuals get along better with themselves as well as with other people.

Notes

1. Calverley (1938, 1943), al-Jawzīyah (1984), MacDonald (1931), Rahman (1960), Tritton (1938, 1971), Smith (1979), among others.

2. Levy-Bruhl, Maurice Lienhardt, and Suzan Langer, as Tambiah (1990, 106) points out, were speaking of a holistic and configurational grasping of totalities as being integral to aesthetic enjoyment and mystic awareness.

3. For the etymology and lexical meaning of the word *rūḥ*, see, for example, Ibn Manẓūr 1966), Rāghib al-Aṣbahānī (1970, 299–300), and MacDonald (1931, 307–8).

4. The real nature or mystery of the soul is known to nobody but Allah (*Qur'an* 17:85).

5. Although the light of the Prophet Muhammad is widely acknowledged in the local Egyptian community as a divine universal fact, there is no direct connection between components of the person and the light of Muhammad as held by the Muslims of Gayo in Indonesia. According to the Gayo's views (Bowen 1993, 116), "Muhammad's light is first manifested in each human body (and in other sentient beings) as a 'white image.' . . . Each white image has a corresponding 'black image' . . . which also derives from Muhammad." This black image "is the basis of destructive conduct" (Bowen 1993, 116). Such ideas are neither found nor are accepted by both the shaikhs and ordinary people of el-Haddein village.

6. There is an analogy here between sleep and death, where the spirit is believed to be able to move freely without the shackles of the body. Muslim intellectuals such as Abū Ḥāmid al-Ghazālī (1979, 488) and Ibn Khaldūn (1981, 81) state that because of its spirituality, the dream vision is defined by the Prophet Muhammad as being the forty-sixth part of the prophecy. Al-Ghazālī (1979, 488–94) presents a full discussion of dreams as effective means of communication between the dead and the living.

7. See Abu-Lughod (1993, 195). In Avatip religious thought the spirit is conceived as the source not only of growth and health but also of self-assertion and mystical powers over others (Harrison 1985, 117).

8. For further discussion of the sacred breath and its connection with the soul and wind in Muslim tradition, see Isutzu (1956, 27–34).

9. The "white hand" is religiously significant for Muslims who recount the miracle of the Prophet Moses when he displayed his hand that turned as white as light when he took it out from his garment. Also the hand of Fāṭima, daughter of the Prophet, is recalled as a proof of the sanctity of the hand in Muslim tradition.

10. This belief is not confined to Middle Eastern societies; rather, it is found among other Western and non-Western cultures, as well as among some individuals involved in religious activities. "Famous people as well as folk are thought capable

of casting the evil eye. According to Edward S. Gifford, Jr., Pope Pius IX (1792–1878) was widely believed to be able to do so" (Georges 1998, 193). For example, there is the story of a baby who fell from its nurse's arms through an open window to the pavement below and was killed just as the pope was driving by on a Roman street (Georges 1998, 193).

11. Blackman (1927) observed similar beliefs in her study of the *Fellāhīn* of Upper Egypt.

12. For further discussion of the cosmological significance of such practices, see chapter 5.

13. Lienhardt points out that the concept of "self" is viewed by the Dinka as being simultaneously apart or separate from others and as self-interested or self-indulgent. Also, the "self" is defined by outside references to tribes or clans and divinities (plants, animals, natural forms, and so forth) that subjoin to their individuality (Lienhardt 1985, 154–55).

14. Surprisingly, a reductionist trend has recently emerged among social scientists who argue that consciousness, metaphors, and conceptual structures consist of neural structures in the brain, stripping reason or mind from its cultural context. For further evaluation of the neuroreductionism, see Martin (2000, 569–90) and Quinn (1991). In her criticism of this trend, Martin (p. 572) points out that the postulation of universal physical experience can be seriously undermined and refuted when we take cultural variations seriously.

15. Geertz maintains that "neither thought nor feeling is, at least among humans, autonomous, a self-contained stream of subjectivity, but each is inescapably dependent upon the utilization by individuals of socially available 'system of significance,' cultural constructs embodied in . . . symbols" (Geertz 1968, 18–19). Also, see Wierzbicka's studies (1989, 1999) that discuss the relationship between reason and emotion.

16. The separation of the intellect from the emotion reflected in Western culture is dangerous (Bateson 1981, 464) and forms a dualism devoid of religious, social, and moral dimensions and outweighs rational thinking over other domains of human experience.

17. On the relationship between folk thought (mind) and feelings people attribute to other people as well as to themselves, see D'Andrade (1987, 1989), Wainwright (1995), and Wierzbicka (1999).

18. See Bowen's (1993) discussion of intent in Gayo Muslim society, and Rosen's (1984, 49–56) analysis of the same concept in a Moroccan context.

19. For a detailed discussion of the theme of patience in Egyptian society, see el-Aswad (1990a).

20. See Taussig's insightful discussion of mimesis as related to both the visible and invisible realms, especially of the notions of spiritual copies of the physical body (1993, 20, 101).

21. Both concepts of the *double* and the *soul*, in certain aspects, are respectively similar to ancient Egyptians' concepts of *ka*, which was believed to come to existence with the birth of a person, and *ba* (vital force), which was represented as a bird with a human head and believed to reside in heaven after the person's death. Also, the *ba* was believed to enter a person's body with the breath of life, and leaves at the time of death. It can return to its tomb on earth so as to receive offerings (Ions 1968; Moret

1972; Morenz 1973). It is important to state that *ka* is "the other personality of the individual. . . . The concept of *ka* has something of the alter ego in it and something of the guardian spirit with the protected arms" (Wilson 1946, 53).

22. According to Muslim tradition, the first angel who resides on the right shoulder is called *raqīb*, the supervisor, while the second one who resides on the left shoulder is called *ʿatīd*, the prepared. However, the names of these angels are not equally known to villagers.

23. With reference to the Dinka, Lienhardt (1961, 153) states: "[G]hosts are to be understood as reflections of a kind of experience, not as a class of 'beings.'"

5

Symbolic Exchange, Gender, and Cosmological Forces

Cosmology and the Gift Economy

Symbolic or gift exchange, an absolute social fact (Mauss 1967), is a basic element in understanding participation and reciprocity and suggests the profound unity of visible and invisible things, forces, and entities. It is used here as a cultural medium that encompasses the personal, social, and cosmic spheres, going beyond the mere exchange of gifts, to include the ongoing reciprocity of material and immaterial symbols such as words, prayers, songs, or incantations. As Mauss observed, not only are people involved in the exchange process, but also God and invisible beings "are there to give a considerable thing in the place of a small one" (Mauss 1990, 17). Symbolic exchange is essential to cosmic structure in the sense that it regulates the relationship between entities and beings, humans and nonhumans. A failure in gift exchange or reciprocity is a violation in the order constituting the world or cosmos.

Symbolic exchange is both a public and private event that establishes the social bonds necessary for maintaining basic community relationships. It strengthens social relationships, facilitates communication between individuals, and deepens alliances and solidarity (Mauss 1990, 9–12; Sahlins 1972, 169; Strathern 1988, 1992). Bourdieu states: "One function of symbolic exchange such as feasts and ceremonies being to favor the circular reinforcement which is the foundation of *collective belief*" (1977, 167 [emphasis in original]). Put differently, "[b]ecause, as in gift exchange, the exchange is an end in itself, the tribute demanded by the group generally comes down to a matter of trifles, that is, to symbolic rituals (rites of passage, the ceremonials of etiquette, etc.), formalities and formalism" (Bourdieu 1977, 95). Although symbolic exchange can make the invisible visible and the private public, it is the visible, public, and social activities that bind people together.

In its local context of the community under study, symbolic exchange[1] occurs on occasions that can be classified into three major categories, implying both gender and generation hierarchy: *religious*, *mundane*, and *mystical* or *magical*. The *religious* category includes the Muslim feasts and rituals of *ʿīd al-fiṭr* (*al-ʿīd aṣ-ṣghīr*), the breaking of the fast of Ramandan, *ʿīd al-aḍḥa* (*al-ʿīd al-kabīr*), the feast of sacrifice, *maulid an-nabī*, the birthday of the Prophet Muhammad, and *al-israʾ wa al-miʿrāj*, the Prophet's ascension to heaven. Specific prayers and rituals, including the *zikr*, are performed or offered during these religious occasions. The *mundane* occasions of symbolic exchange are associated with the cycles of life or, more specifically, with the rites of passage of birth, marriage, and death (Van Gennep 1960). Villagers are more concerned with such landmark events than with people's annual birthday celebrations. *Mystical* or *magical* symbolic exchange includes, for example, magical performances such as the *zār* cult that will be compared with the religious ritual of the *zikr*. In everyday life, these three domains interface and are inseparably interconnected.

During the first two Muslim feasts mentioned above, *ʿīd al-fiṭr* and *ʿīd al-aḍḥa*, parents and relatives offer women and youngsters gifts, sometimes in the form of money, referred to as *ʿīdīyah*. The word *ʿīdīyah*, a derivative of the word *ʿīd* or feast, is used to mean a gift given on these religious occasions. A newly married woman also receives a gift (*ʿīdīyah*) from her husband and her father or elder brother on the feast that immediately follows her marriage (el-Aswad 1993). The two religious feasts are good occasions for maintaining, through offerings, the relationship not only with the living but also with the dead. After performing the prayer of the feast, or the prayer of the sunrise, *ṣalāt al-ʿīd* (*ṣalat aṣ-ṣubḥ*), men go to the cemetery to visit to their deceased relatives as well as to recite verses of the *Qurʾan* on behalf of their souls. Meanwhile, women are careful to go to the cemetery earlier than men. It is interesting to observe that while women receive gifts from men, they distribute a different kind of offering to others for the sake of the dead. Women distribute money and food (bread, doughnut-like rolls, and round dried cakes) to the poor and to *fuqahā*, reciters of the *Qur'an*, who gather around the graves waiting for gifts and offerings. With these gifts, known as *raḥmah* (mercy), the women say, *raḥmah ʿalā rūḥ al-maiyt* (This [mercy] is for the soul of the dead), mentioning the name of the deceased for whom they are asking mercy. This food is eaten by the poor in the name of the deceased (el-Aswad 1987). Offerings are gifts given by the living to the dead not only to express their love and gratitude or to repay a debt (Mauss 1990, 16; Godelier 1999, 186–88), but also to maintain a peaceful relationship with them.

Within the context of the lifecycle, newlyweds receive gifts (*ṣabāḥīyah*) from relatives and friends[2] on the first day or morning following their wedding. A cosmologically loaded metaphor, *ṣabāḥīyah*, is derived from the word *ṣabah*, meaning sunrise or morning. In offering gifts, people, directing their speech to the bride, say *ṣabāḥīyah mubārakah yā ʿarūsah* (A blessed morning for a blessed bride). They also address the groom (*ʿarīs*) with the same phrase, changing the feminine form of *yā ʿarūsah* into the masculine form *yā ʿarīs*. The couple, in turn, offers the visitors such symbolic gifts as colorful scarves, handkerchiefs, and candy.[3]

During marriage ceremonies, people give what they call *nugṭah* (*nuqṭah*), literally a drop of rain or any other liquid, as a kind of symbolic exchange or gift. If *ṣabāḥīyah* denotes a cosmic wake, *nugṭah* indicates cosmic reproduction in the sense that drops of water are necessary for irrigating and fertilizing the land. The cognates of the verb *yanaggaṭ* include "to rain or shower," "to drop," and "to give a present." It is also used to refer to men's semen. In some specific perspectives, the giving of *nugṭah* resembles the giving of gifts during the bridal or baby shower in North American culture. The common elements implicitly being in the giving of water (*nugṭah* or shower) collectively for regeneration. The *nugṭah*, although it is possible to be in various forms, is most frequently given in the form of money so as to give the recipients a chance to use the gift or money freely depending on their needs (el-Aswad 1993).

Symbolic exchange, accentuating gender hierarchy, continues as the lifecycle goes on. On the seventh day following the birth of a baby, a celebration or *subūʿ*, derived from the word *sabaʿa* (seven), is held in honor of the mother and child. Relatives, neighbors, and friends are invited. The most meaningful gift in this celebration is that which is given to guests by the mother's family. This gift, also called *subūʿ*, consists of a small box made of clay, ceramic, or glass, containing pieces of candy, almonds, roasted chick peas, and peanuts. If the infant is male, relatives of the nursing woman's family decorate a spouted clay pitcher (*ibrīq*), symbolizing maleness. For the girl, members of the family decorate a clay jug (*qullah*) without a spout, but with a large opening symbolizing femaleness.[4] Meanwhile, the mother lays her infant on a large wooden-rimmed sieve (*ghurbāl*) and places both on the ground next to the decorated container. Then, while incense is burning, the mother stands and, stretching her right foot forward, steps over the child seven times. During the *subūʿ* ritual, women and children carrying candles perform a procession inside the house. While the children sing, a female relative beats a copper mortar with a pestle. Women gather around the nursing mother and, addressing the male child, say loudly, "Grow up and behave like your father, not your mother" (*iṭlaʿ l-abūk mātiṭlaʿsh l-ummak*) or "Listen to your father, not to your mother" (*ismaʿ kalām abūk mā tismaʿsh kalā ummak*).[5] If the child is female, women advise her to listen to her father and behave like her good mother. These words and utterances imply a deeply rooted gender division.

Mediation and Mystical Exchange

Mystical and mundane forms of symbolic exchange occur in different contexts. The mystical form is represented in the notion of *nadr* (*nadhr*), or vow, in which a promise for an offering or an action (such as a sacrifice) is given to a spirit or saint in exchange for some form of requested intervention. Although *nadr* can be pledged by anyone, women tend to do so more than men. The value of *nadr* ranges from, for example, a handful of money paid to or a dozen candles lit in the shrine of the saint, to a sacrifice of a goat or calf whose meat is distributed among the poor and those who watch over the shrine. As *nadr* differs in size and value, depending on the seriousness of the demands or objectives, saints also differ in weight and dignity. For example, barren women wishing to have children may visit the local shrine of *Sit* Raḍīyah, or that of the saint al-Badawī in Tanta, to make a vow to the saint promising to light the shrine with candles or sacrifice a sheep if the wish can be granted. It is both dangerous and dreadful for someone not to fulfill or carry out the *nadr*, especially if the matter requested has been accomplished through the help (or *baraka*) of the saint. Any fatal disease or disaster that happens to a person or collectivity might very well be interpreted within the framework of whether the *nadr* was fulfilled or undertaken. "The negative value placed upon the failure to fulfill reciprocal obligations follows from the assumption that reciprocity is fundamental to cosmic structure" (Rappaport 1999, 264).

Although material aspects are involved in this sort of mystical exchange, the relationship between the person and the saint is not a business deal, but rather a spiritual appeal, at least from the person's point of view, in which the saint, because of his or her closeness to God, intervenes on behalf of the person. This relationship is understood within the concept of *shafāʿah*—mediation or intervention.[6] The preceding example shows that invisible forces and beings, human or supernatural, as materialized in symbolic forms represented in offerings, are inseparable from the social reality. They constitute integral parts of the totality.

Another kind of mediation, *wāsṭah*, is the mundane or secular means by which people seek to gain benefits or privileges by manipulating people who are believed to have the power to actualize those privileges. Although two words, *shafāʿah* and *wāsṭah*, are used interchangeably to mean mediation, *wāsṭah* is used more frequently with reference to secular experiences in which people and not invisible forces or agents are involved. Mundane mediation (*wāsṭah*) can be facilitated through gifts or other kinds of symbolic exchange. Villagers use symbols and metaphors intensively to communicate the idea of mediation among themselves. A common metaphor used by the *fallāḥīn* to mean *wāsṭah*, is *kūsah*, or zucchini.

For villagers, *kūsah* refers to a relationship in which one person seeks a benefit and the other either fulfills it or works as a mediator to fulfill it. A person is described as having *kūsah* if either he or his family has a relationship with a powerful person who can and is willing to help him in achieving his goals. This relationship defines the boundaries of "us" in relation to "others." The metaphorical usage of *kūsah* is based on the analogy of the limbs or branches of the zucchini plant, which are interconnected and support one another. According to this analogy, the mediator or powerful person should help and support his relatives, neighbors, or friends. Politically, the strong person or mediator who protects his relatives' interests is called *ḍahr* (*ẓahr*), or "back." In this context, one hears the proverb, *illī lahu ḍahr mā yanḍarabsh ʿalā baṭnuh*, meaning that the one who has a *ḍahr* (a strong protective person) will never be beaten on his stomach. Mediation, on the one hand, generates differences and hierarchies between those who offer gifts or favors (*jamīyl*) and those who seek or accept them. On the other hand, mediation is associated with the popular concept of *al-ʿasham*, a word used in the vernacular to mean the moral or positive expectations someone has toward another person and that might be used as grounds for demanding benefits from that person. The intensity of *al-ʿasham* depends on the degree of closeness between people in such a way that it becomes very strong among close relatives or friends. The meaning of the positive expectation (*al-ʿasham*) is extended to encompass people's relationships with both God and saints.

When a mediator fails to support his relatives or friends, he causes the loss of *ʿasham* (their moral and positive expectations toward him) and is publicly denounced and abandoned. In such a context, those who are injured say, "*ash-shajarah illī mā tiḍallil* (*tiẓallil*) *ʿalā ahlihā yaḥil gaṭʿahā*" (The tree that does not provide shade for its people should be uprooted). Also, if the mediator crosses the boundaries between "us" and "others" by supporting other people instead of helping his relatives and friends, he becomes not a *kūsah* or *ḍahr* but a *garʿ* (*qarʿ*)—pumpkin, which extends its limbs outside its own boundaries, *yamid libarrah.* Although pumpkins, like zucchini, have extending limbs or branches, villagers think that they are less useful and nutritious than zucchini. The word *qarʿ* is used as a noun and verb for expressing social mistrust and worthlessness. This feature of exposure, a very important local metaphor, implies weakness, because the person is no longer attached to his kin group—he belongs to nobody. Metaphorically speaking, as far as a person does not "cover," help, or serve his kinsmen (*yakhdim ahlahu*), he is publicly and shamefully exposed and will not be covered by them. This uncovered person, on accepting money for his services, is accused of accepting bribes (*rishāwah*) and is depicted as the one whose conscience is dead, *ḍamīru māt.*

As zucchini differ in size and weight, mediators also differ in influence and position. *Kūsah kabīrah* (big zucchini) is a phrase used by the *fallāḥīn* to denote a very influential person or high-ranking official. *Kūsah* is associated with notions of hierarchy and power in the sense that those who are relatives of or have connections with big men have *kūsah kabīrah* and are more privileged than others who do not. Politically motivated peasants think that it is good to have *kūsah*, as far as they gain benefits without harming anyone. Although the mediation is a private matter between the persons involved, it is publicly recognized and commented on. Villagers support this view by saying *al-balad kullahā kūsah*, which literally means that "the entire country is zucchini." The majority of the population, including politicians, understands the notion of mediation (*wāsṭah* or *kūsah*), which implies the manipulation of power, and therefore they deal with one another accordingly. However, other persons think that it is not good or moral to have such mediation, because it encourages favoritism (*maḥsūbīyah*) and threatens the values of equality, hard work, and personal talents and abilities. Although *kūsah*—zucchini as a metaphor denoting the concept of mediation—is used in daily life, villagers tend to use it more frequently in their relations with state and government bureaucracies.

Symbolic Exchange, Hierarchy, and Gender Relationship

Hierarchy is implicit in various domains of people's social and political relationships as well as in their cosmology. Linguistic evidence emphasizing hierarchical relationships is abundant. It is common to hear villagers say *an-nās darajāt*, meaning that people are ranked. The word *darajāt* is a plural form of the word *darajah*, which means a step of a stair or ladder. It is also used with reference to rank or class. Relatives or members of the same descent group recognize and express the differences in gender, economic, social, educational, and political spheres that exist among them. In the following section the emphasis is on gender hierarchy as represented in men–men, men–women, and women–women relationships.

Masculinity and male–male relationships are central and powerful forces that dominate the public sphere of the community. Men gather together in the public domains of the village such as the mosque, the guest house of a kin group (*mandarah*), or the coffee shop. They are seen walking together, sometimes hand-in-hand, discussing some private, personal, or collective problem. Nevertheless, kinship relationships form the basic grounds for *ʿaṣabīyyah*, a patrilineally founded principle that unites males of a kin group in one cohesive collectivity. Masculinity is viewed as an inherited characteristic. A great man is expected to have strong sons. In terms of bodily symbolism, men are associated with the back in which the semen is thought to be located, while women are associated with the stomach or womb. Both men and women describe a brave man as a man begotten from his father's back, *rājil min ḍahr rājil*. A strong, wealthy, and socially prestigious man is *ibn ʿizz*, son of prosperity, as well as *ṭakhīn* and *samīn*, fat and stout from eating good food, especially meat. The image of the fat and stout person is associated with masculinity, strength, self sufficiency, sexual potency, and bigness. Men attempt to dominate other men as well as women for achieving not only specific objectives but also for bolstering their strong character and affirming their masculinity. Through ongoing hospitality in which food and entertainment are offered, notables assert and maintain their hierarchical relationship with kin, friends, or neighbors, who in most cases cannot reciprocate (Mauss 1990; Godelier 1999, 30).

In the community's public zone, friendship between adult males and females, except for relatives and those who work together in a specific place such as a field, school, or otherwise, is not acceptable. A young girl or woman who is frequently and publicly seen accompanying men is colloquially described as *bitāʿit ar-rijjālah*, the friend (follower) of men, meaning that she is lewd and unchaste. By the same token, a man who likes to be around women (outside legitimate relationships) is called *bitāʿ an-niswān*, meaning that he chases after women or is immodest. In public activities, men and women maintain a considerable distance from each other. What is private or inside the house is incompatible with what is public or outside. A man and his wife, who might have a very intimate relationship inside the house, keep distance between themselves in the street or public domain. Although it is common to see men walking hand-in-hand in the village, it is uncommon to see husbands and wives or brothers and sisters walking together in that fashion.

The distinction between male and female worlds is maintained in the early phases of childhood within the family's private zone. Although there is an intimate relationship between parents and children, sons are expected to be connected to their fathers, and daughters to their mothers. Gifts are effective factors in socialization and gender division (Strathern 1988; el-Aswad 1993). Through the symbolic exchange of gifts, gender hierarchy is generated and images of masculinity and femininity are developed. Gender hierarchy here is displayed in two ways: the shape and quality of gifts on the one hand, and the distinctive feature of males as giving agents on the other. It is women who receive gifts from men, mainly fathers, brothers, spouses, prospectus husbands, sons, or fathers-in-law, on different social and religious occasions. It is common to observe that during the Prophet's birthday celebration, for example, various kinds of gifts, made of the same sweet substance, are given to both male and female children. The substance, the homologous component, symbolizes unity. Yet there is great variety in the forms and shapes of the gifts, accentuating the differences between males and females. Gifts given to boys are shaped into horses, lions, camels, knights, officers, soldiers, *fallāḥīn*, cars, ships, airplanes, and the like. On the other hand, gifts given to girls take the shape of a bride, *ʿarūsah*. Evidently, boys have a wider selection and choice of gifts than do girls.

In this context, gifts underpin the cultural universal of female subordination (Ortner 1978) and assert the notion of hierarchy in which males are ascribed a dominant position in public activities. The different shapes of boys' gifts confirm the open world of men associated with different occupations as well as the masculine values of power, leadership, virility, honor, courage, and adventure. The gifts given to girls emphasize the private domain and the image of female identity as that of good wife and mother. The same practice of gift-giving grows as children mature. Again, on the Prophet's birthday celebration a prospective bride receives from her prospective groom a large and well-decorated bride-doll (*ʿarūsah*) embellished with a splendid wedding dress. In everyday activities, a good wife is described as *hadīyah*—a gift, meaning that the husband and his family are blessed with having a virtuous woman. In contrast, a troublesome wife is negatively described as being *razīyah*—a disaster or misfortune.

Villagers widely use a verse from the *Qur'an* (4:24) to emphasize the notion of hierarchical ranking (*al-qawāmah*), according to which, as understood by peasants, men are superior to and have authority over women because Allah has made the one to dominate the other. Men spend their property to support women and are viewed as being necessary for family security. Within female circles, women use the folk saying "*fī al-lail ghafīr wa fī an-nahār ajīr*" (A husband serves his wife as a guard at nighttime and as a laborer during the day). Husbands and wives, though hierarchically differentiated, are seen to play complementary roles in their daily life. Where men are responsible for securing economic resources, women manage the budget of the household. Hierarchical distinction, expressed in bodily symbolism and metaphors,[7] emphasizes that husbands encompass wives. For example, men view themselves as sinew (*ʿaṣab*) or muscles (*ʿaḍal*), while women are looked upon as flesh (*laḥm*). Men are described in terms of power and toughness as represented in the strength of the back and the sharpness of the sword, while women are described in terms of gentleness and vulnerability as represented in the softness of flesh, which is likened to butter (*zibdah*) or dough (*ʿajīn*). Females think that men like women to be as soft, fleshy, and plump as fermented dough, *ʿajīn khamrān*, a term used by women when they compliment and admire their own bodies. Some wedding songs refer to the beautiful body of the female as if it were fermented dough. Although this phrase is used to describe the whole female body, the stomach, in particular, is referred to as *ʿajīn khamrān*. Making bread inside the house is a sign of femininity and nourishment. For instance, women mix flour with water and yeast and knead it to make dough. Three hours after kneading, the female head of the household checks the dough, saying "Oh, ferment, ferment, ferment, your owners have not had their breakfast yet" (*fūr, fūr, fūr ṣiḥābak min ghair fuṭūr*). In play scenarios and to amuse her child, the mother refers to pieces of the dough as the little children of the big dough. She may also make a small doll of dough to give to her child to play with.

There is a sexual connotation implicit in the notion of fermented dough. If dough is associated with women, yeast (*khamīrah*) is associated with men. Villagers make an analogy between yeast and men's semen. Without yeast the dough would not ferment, and without men women would never get pregnant. Yeast is the *baraka* that renders flour into bread (*ʿaish*), which also means "life." Metaphorically, when children are wanted to inhabit the house, *yʿammar al-bait*, husbands provide their wives with seeds or *khamīrah*, yeast (semen). The *khamīrah* causes the dough to rise, as men's semen causes women's stomachs to rise. As dough is baked in the oven, the female body, particularly the womb, is depicted as an oven (furn).[8] I have been told that the pregnant wife tells her husband that she carries his yeast in her stomach. Every household has, or should have, its own yeast (*khamīrah*), exactly as it should have its own man. Both men and women quote the simile, "Without yeast the house would be a wasteland" (*bidūn khamāir al-bait bāir*). Both man and yeast are called "*ʿaṣab ad-dār*," or the sinew of the household. Interestingly, *khamīrah* is also used to refer to monetary savings. A rich man is literally depicted as having *khamīrah kabīrah*, a big yeast or savings. In this context, money saved (*khamīrah*) is used to secure people in times of financial crisis or help them in executing their plans.

Food and food preparation reflect significant aspects of the private relationships between men and women inside the family. Food is cooked and prepared exclusively by women. Cooking is inextricably associated with female identity in the village. A good woman is a good cook who takes care of her husband and family. It is an insult for a woman to be described as a bad cook. The generosity of the man cannot be enacted without the woman's cooperation. The ideal wife is one who honors her husband not only by behaving according to the village's values of chastity and modesty, but also by being always ready to cook and serve food for her husband's guests. Such a woman is called *ṣāḥibat wājib*, the lady who knows her duty. A good wife is called *mā'ūn ṭayyib*, or good food container that should be covered by her husband, *satr wa ghaṭā*, or protector and coverer. It is shameful for a man to cook while his wife, daughter, sister, or mother are living with him in one house. The man who cooks and gossips is described as being womanly (*minaswin*), or the son of (his) mother (*ibn ummuh*). It is also shameful for the woman to let her husband or the male members of her house cook. For women, cooking, associated with nourishment (to feed and to be fed), is not only a duty but also a right that must be maintained and protected. Men are responsible for providing their wives or households with money and other materials necessary for living. This sentiment is widely repeated in the saying *yā gārīya iṭbukhy yā sīdī kallif*, meaning that "for a lady to cook, a man [master] should pay the cost." Women cook and give birth. A productive *fallāḥah* (female rural Egyptian) is described as being as fertile and reproductive as a she-rabbit, *arnabah*. A bachelor is advised by his relatives and friends to marry a woman to cook for him as well as to give him children to inhabit the house, *ti'ammar ad-dār*. Children are a main source of pride and happiness for villagers. A lucky man is the one who is married to a reproductive wife.

The *fallāḥīn* are fond of using certain food items and plants as metaphors to connote certain concepts and values. The metaphorical usage of watermelon (*biṭṭīkh*), which is produced abundantly in the village, is based on the analogy of a closed or sealed body or object that must be opened to know what is inside it. Allegorically, watermelon is used to connote the hidden or invisible aspect of a person, object, or event. A virgin, for instance, is described as being sealed by God, *bikhatm rabbihā*. According to the *fallāḥīn*'s perspective, a woman is like a watermelon. In choosing a wife or in dealing with events and projects with unpredictable results, a common saying is, "Like watermelon, it is either red and delicious or white and tasteless. It is your luck." In some specific contexts, life as a whole is likened to women and luck. Like the heart of a watermelon, luck (*bakht*) or *ḥaẓẓ* (woman or life) is unknown until it is experienced or, as the villagers say, you have to "test your luck" (*jarrab ḥaẓẓak*). Good watermelon is also known by the ripeness of its seeds, *bidhr*. Children are referred to as *bidhr* or *bidhūr*. Bad watermelon is called *mibadhdhara*, meaning that it has numerous bad or unripened kernels. The same adjective, *mibadhdhara*, is used in describing a disliked woman whose children are undisciplined or troublesome.

Women of the same neighborhood maintain good relationships with one another. They exchange services and cooperate in collaborative activities such as baking bread, cooking a big meal, or making the necessary preparations for a wedding. Food is the most common item used as a medium of symbolic exchange among women. When a woman prepares a good meal for her family, she offers a dish to her neighbor, who thanks her by saying, "May this good habit last forever" (*ʿādah mā tingaṭaʿ*).

Tension or conflict, however, frequently occurs among women striving to keep out of the public sphere. The negative scenario among women reaches its climax in the prototypical hierarchical relationship between mother-in-law (*ḥama*) and daughter-in-law (*marat al-ibn*), especially within the extended family.[9] Negative words and accusations of hidden hostility and envy are freely exchanged. There is competition for the love and loyalty of the man who is son of the one and spouse of the other. However, because the son is expected to show love and respect to his mother, his wife in turn must show her the same affection. The mother-in-law, thinking that her daughter-in-law threatens her authority within her own house, assigns her a heavy workload. The daughter-in-law is expected to obey all of her mother-in-law's orders without complaint. Whether or not the daughter-in-law resents her mother-in-law, she represents a potential or actual resentment. Even if she shows none, she is viewed as a swindler, hiding her hatred and anger. This attitude is symbolically expressed by the daughter-in-law who states that her mother-in-law says, "Oh my son's wife, eat and get full, but neither break an unbroken loaf of bread nor eat from a broken loaf of bread" (*yā murāt ibnī, kulī wa ishbaʿī, lakin salīm mā tiksarī wa mikassar mā taklī*). From the point of view of the daughter-in-law, the mother-in-law is envious of her marital relationship with her husband. When the mother-in-law tries to show affection toward her daughter-in-law, the latter considers it false affection, as verbally expressed: "Like geese making noise but having no breast to feed or nothing to give" (*zayy al-wezz ḥinīyya min ghair bezz*).

The relationship between half-siblings and their stepmother is similar to that between mother-in-law and daughter-in-law. Half-siblings and stepmother compete with each other for the love and protection of the man who is the father of one and the husband of the other. It is culturally expected that the stepmother will favor her own children over those of another woman. This hostile relationship is thought to be a cause of envious feelings.

Invisible Forces: *Baraka*, *Ḥasad*, and Folk Healing

Invisible forces are parts of a wider imperceptible world that comprises two domains, one benevolent and superior, the other malevolent and inferior. Anthropological studies have concentrated more on concepts of mystical causes of misfortune such as witchcraft[10] than on notions of mystical causes that result in good fortune. The concealed mysterious forces *quwā ghair manẓūrah*, which represent beneficent and maleficent spheres of influence, respectively, are *baraka* (blessing) and *ḥasad* (envy).[11] *Baraka*[12] and *ḥasad* reflect people's views concerning the cosmos or universe, their psyches or selves, and their social relationships with one another. Eventually, these two beliefs represent two theories of mystical causality, *al-ʿillah al-ghaibīyah*, that mirror significant aspects of people's thought and regulate their interactions with one another. The concept of *ḥasad* represented in the evil power of the envious eye (*ʿain al-ḥasūd*) can best be understood by contrasting it with the opposite but encompassing concept of *baraka*, which represents a cosmic benevolent force. By operating within this simple structure of the invisible cosmos, villagers are able to interpret both the unfortunate and fortunate events that occur to them within the visible world.

As mentioned previously, cosmic capital constitutes a core orientation in peasants' lives. A *fallāḥ* whose crop is abundant believes this to be due either to his observance of religious instruction, to his utterance of divine phrases while cultivating the plant, to his performing a good deed for the poor or needy, or to the birth of a child for whose sake God blessed the crop. On having a child, people say "*Rabbunā lammā ykhlaq al-famm* [or *aṭ-ṭifl*] *ydabbar lahu rizqahu*" (When the Lord creates a mouth [child] He provides its sustenance). If the crop yields less than the normal production, the *fallāḥ* thinks that this failure is a sign of *qillat al-baraka*, the reduction of God's grace caused by either his negligence to his religious obligations or by his misdeeds. But if the crop fails to meet even the minimum expectation, the *fallāḥ* then believes that he and his crop were victims of the envious eye.[13] Here, the negative cosmic-psychic force embodied in the eye is held to be responsible. For instance, when a *fallāḥ* loses his cotton crop to rain, he strongly believes that his crop has been envied. He is unable to offer other explanations as to why the rain came in the summer that year, and why, in particular, it rained extensively on his field, causing such damage to his crop.

There are manifestations of *baraka* and *ḥasad*, represented, respectively, in good and bad events. A hospitable person is called the one who has a generous or open hand (*yad maftūḥa*), while a greedy man is described as a person who has a narrow eye (*ʿain ḍaiyaqah*). *Baraka* is associated with the right hand or *yamīn*, which implies the meaning of *yumn*—good fortune and prosperity. The words *yumn* and *baraka* are virtually synonymous with reference to God's blessing. If the right hand symbolizes *baraka*, the blinded left eye, *a'awar shamal*, is conceived of as *shu'm*, or that which is evil or bad.

People's beliefs concerning *baraka* and *ḥasad* are associated with concepts of the invisible spheres in both the universe and the person. The fundamental theme here is expressed in the popular saying that "*al-khair* [or *al-baraka*] *min rabbunā wa ash-sharr min 'andinā* [or *min anfusinā*]" (Whatever is good is from our Lord, and whatever is evil is from us). *Baraka* belongs to the secret world of heaven or what is sacred, whereas envy originates in the negative or destructive domain of the cosmos and the mundane and inferior aspects of people's selves. Although the ambiguous or ill-defined relationship among members of the community might result in accusations of the envious eye, villagers attribute *ḥasad* to people's negative cosmic-psychic power.[14]

This does not mean that villagers interpret all good fortunes and misfortunes as being caused by the mysterious forces of *baraka* and *ḥasad*. They most certainly know the natural factors or causes of such events. For example, they know that the selection of good seeds, the observing of the suitable time for planting and watering, and the careful and industrious work of weeding result in a good crop yield. This constitutes a mode of thought based on experience or empirical knowledge. But if the yield exceeds or fails villagers' expectations, they immediately think more in terms of *baraka* or the evil eye, the mystical mode of thought, than in terms of luck[15] (*haẓẓ*), good or bad. It is the envious or evil eye by which the occurrences of unexpected or sudden misfortunes are explained.

There are three elements that must work together if the envied person is to be cured. These include the utterance of the appropriate incantation, the use of incense, and the performer, who might be either an ordinary person or a *shaikh* known for his *baraka* or blessed hand, *yad mubārakah*. Of these elements, however, the performer, especially the *shaikh*, is the most important, because he is thought to be the master of hidden knowledge, with cognizance of efficacious methods for restoring health to envied people. For example, a *shaikh* who possesses *baraka* may write some words on a piece of bread and feed it to the sick person to eat. Family members are also integrally involved in the healing process. For example, a picture or image of the afflicted person may be made of paper and poked with holes by the family matriarch while uttering the appropriate *ruqyah*, or incantation. In most cases, parents perform the *ruqyah*; but if the sick person does not show progress, a *shaikh* known for his blessed hand, *yad mubārakah*, is asked to intervene. Villagers believe that ordinary people cannot do successfully what professionals, *shaikhs*, or people of *baraka* can do.[16] It is believed that when the performer passes his hand over the envied person while uttering a suitable formulaic chant and using incense, the negative influence of the *nafs* or psyche vanishes and the sick person's health is restored. What is significant here is that by the touch of the blessed hand, the effect of the envious eye can be expelled from the body.

There are two kinds of touch. First, there is the healing touch made by those who possess *baraka*. The person who possesses *baraka* passes his hand over the sick or envied person in order to cure him. Second, there is a touch made by the receivers[17] of *baraka*. Here, people pass their hand over what is believed to have *baraka*. For example, villagers pay visits to the shrines or tombs of saints to obtain *baraka* so as to have children, to recover from a sickness, to overcome an enemy or the evil eye, or to gain wealth or any number of other desirable things. Using either their right or both hands, but never the left hand alone, people touch the cloth that covers the shrine as well as the pillars and walls inside the shrine, meanwhile saying "*madad yā ahl al-baraka*" (Help and support us O people of *baraka*) or "*yā barakat sayyidnā ash-shaikh*" (O *baraka* of our master, holy man).

The Social Significance of Invisible Cosmological Forces

As invisible cosmological forces, both *baraka* and *ḥasad* are associated, respectively, with the cohesion and weakness of people's social relationships. The word *baraka* and its derivatives such as *mubārak* and *mabrūk* have significant social implications as commonly used in social and public discourse. It is common to hear a host welcoming his guest by saying "*ḥaṣalit lanā al-baraka*," meaning that he (the host) is blessed by the guest. The guest in turn answers, "May Allah bless you" (*Allah ybārik fīk*). Various words used for expressing greetings and congratulations on both private and social occasions are derived from the word *baraka*. Through verbal and public exchanges of blessing, people seek to establish an intimate social relationship with one another. Likewise, the kindly words a husband says to his wife, "*kalimah ṭayyibah*," are considered *baraka* that maintain their matrimonial ties. A good husband or father is metaphorically called *baraka*, meaning that he perpetuates material and immaterial prosperity within the house.

Cooperation, love, and collective actions both privately and publicly or inside and outside the house are believed to generate *baraka* or inspire God to bestow His blessing on people's work and social life. When working together, villagers say "The blessing exists in the gathering" (*al-baraka fī al-*

lammah) or "The blessing is in the hands" (*al-baraka fī al-ayādī*). On the other hand, competition and individualistic attitudes result in *ḥiqd*, hatred, grudge, hostility, and envy that threaten the social order of the community and the family. In addition, the evil eye is associated with what villagers call *an-naq*, which literally means "frogs' croak," but metaphorically indicates people's gossip or negative talk about other people.

The social, cosmological, and religious aspects of villagers' everyday activities are inextricably interconnected. *Baraka* exists when people pray, work, eat together, and love one another. It is believed that uttering the name of Allah and praising the Prophet Muhammad bring about *baraka* and ward off *al-ḥasad*. In the early morning, people greet the day by saying, "May Allah bless this day" (*Allahuma yajʿalahu yaum* [*nahār*] *mubārak* [*mubrūk*]). Before entering a house, a person must praise the Prophet or utter the name of Allah to bring *baraka* and avoid the accusation of *ḥasad*. Likewise, before having a meal, individuals utter *bismillah* or the phrase, "In the name of Allah, the Compassionate, the Merciful." At the end of the meal, they say "*al-ḥamdu lil-lah*" (Praise be to Allah). These and similar utterances are expected to bestow *baraka* on food and make it sufficient for people who are eating.[18] Without such utterances the house would be devoid of *baraka*.

The intimate relationship between parents and children, emphasized by social and religious values, is believed to be both a source and effect of *baraka*. What is significant in this relationship is the attitude of children, especially adult children, toward their parents' invocation. For children, the parents' invocation itself can bring about *baraka* for them. A successful person, for example, interprets his success as a result not only of working hard and good luck or *ḥaẓẓ*, but also of his parents' invocation that, as the villagers say, causes the *baraka* in his health, property, work, and offspring.[19]

Although anybody, kin or nonkin, rich or poor, can be accused of the evil eye, the nature of the social relationship among people determines who might be more frequently accused than others. Privately or within the confines of the family, members of the same family do not usually accuse one another. In specific contexts they do, however. A family member will suspect one of his kin who isolates himself, particularly when there is no justifiable reason for doing so. This person is thought of as having negative attitudes toward the rest of the family and is therefore a potential source of danger. Ambiguous and ill-defined relationships among members of a family are expressed in accusations of the evil eye, such as in the relationship between mother-in-law and daughter-in-law, between half-siblings and stepmother, and between co-wives.

A person who manipulates the envious or evil eye is neither sociable nor religious, but is regarded with suspicion. He does not overtly or publicly praise God and the Prophet when he admires a certain quality or property of someone else. When an unexpected misfortune happens, villagers think of the last person who cast a look at them without praising God or the Prophet. This logic explains people's almost obsessive praising and repetition of the name of Allah and His Prophet. These utterances convey two messages. First, they declare the good intention of the person who admires another person. And second, the person who utters or praises God and the Prophet openly declares that he is not responsible for and should not be accused of any misfortune that might occur to the one whom he admires.

The belief in the eye in particular social contexts, however, results in positive consequences. For example, it is common to observe friends or members of a family who find themselves unexpectedly fighting for insignificant reasons to stop their dispute immediately when one of them says that they (or their good relationships) have been envied by other people—without even defining who those other people might be. Explaining social and economic problems in terms of the evil eye of people outside the family or community reduces the risk of destroying the social relationships among members of that community.

Women are believed to be more preoccupied with the eye than men. Consequently, gossip and mutual accusations of the envious or evil eye are more common among women. Women interact more with one another than with men. The social dilemma here is that as far as the envious eye is concerned, women fear one another more than they fear men. However, because they are not allowed to interact, at least publicly, with men, women have to maintain an ambiguous relationship with other females. Women, using contradictory folk sayings and proverbs, express this problem when saying "If my neighbor were not with me, my gallbladder would burst" (*laulā jārtī lanfaqaʿit marāti*), meaning that a woman would be sick or impatient if she did not have a neighbor to talk to. On the other hand, we hear them say "My neighbor envied me for the length of my gallbladder"[20] (*ḥasaditnī jārtī ʿalā ṭūl marārtī*), indicating, ironically, that because the woman had suffered by enduring a hardship, her neighbor envied her for being patient. This ambiguous and uncertain relationship among women creates the attitude of accusing one another of the envious eye, and in turn they try to protect themselves and their families from the anticipated danger of the eye. In conclusion, both men and women are concerned with minimizing the negative effects of the eye as well as with maximizing their acquisition of *baraka*.

The *Zikr* and the *Zār*: The Enactment of Gendered Cosmology

Fundamental aspects of Egyptian folk cosmology are enacted and experienced, though differently, through two rituals, the *zikr* and the *zār*.[21] These indicate ongoing symbolic exchange and communicative scenarios between human and nonhuman beings. These two rituals deal not merely with the community's moral domains, but also with the unseen beings, spirits and forces that play a significant role in people's daily actions. This world is "based on the twin belief that there exist invisible beings and powers which govern the universe and that humans can sway them by prayer and sacrifices, and by adopting a behavior in accordance with what they imagine to be their desires, their will, or their law" (Godelier 1999, 27).

The *zār* ceremony, locally called *dagat zār*, was introduced into Egypt during the second half of the nineteenth century, yet the social structure and cosmological belief system of Egyptian society facilitated its penetration and spread throughout the country.[22] Although the *zār* is not as widely performed as it was during the past primarily because of the strong waves of Islamic movements that began in the 1970s, it is still secretly performed among women who believe in its efficacy in relieving the possessed person. Although the *zār* ceremony is about such serious concerns as altered states of mind and exorcising spirits, it, like other rituals and ceremonies, encompasses other components related to festivity and the arts of aesthetics, entertainment, joking, and play.[23]

The themes of the superior—benevolent—and inferior—malevolent—aspects of the invisible world are reiterated in different patterns or forms and in different social contexts. The *zikr* is a religious ritual conducted exclusively by men for the purpose of the remembrance of Allah, while the *zār* is a magical ritual[24] performed exclusively by women (except for the involvement of male musicians) as a therapeutic device for dealing with the problem of spirit possession.[25] Spirit possession itself is a private and personal or psychological state, while the *zār* exorcism is a public act, though it seeks to maintain privacy and secrecy. The *zār* cult can be viewed, applying Taussig's terms (1999, 2 [emphasis in original]), as a sort of public secrecy or "*knowing what not to know*." Yet, possession affliction provides an opportunity for public scenarios that go beyond the immediate context of the *zār* cult to trigger broader discourses concerning the hidden and conflicting dimensions of the cosmos, society, and person. The *zār* cult, however, is dealt with here not as a phenomenon confined to possessed women and female participants, but as a cultural medium reflecting multiple differing views of various people, including men and nonparticipants, regarding the cause, function, and significance of spirit possession. In focusing on the attitudes of men and women toward the phenomenon of spirit possession as well as toward one another,[26] the *zikr* and the *zār* can be viewed as opposite axes, signifying two different scenarios in the worlds of religion and magic.

The unseen beings and spirits addressed in both the *zikr* and the *zār* are counter though integrated constituents of the overall cosmological belief system of the community. Except for God, invisible beings and spirits are never adored or worshipped by the villagers. According to the community's overarching cosmology, all invisible creatures and spirits are of two major categories—that is, they are either Muslim or non-Muslim. This broad classification solves the problem of the ambiguity, diversity, and ethnic polarity of unseen beings and spirits involved in the *zār* exorcism. However, invisible beings, Muslim and non-Muslim, causing possession are further classified into *spirits* and *jinn*. *Spirits* are those of the deceased, mainly saints. *Jinn* belong to invisible creatures and related ghosts, demons, or devils who are created of fire, yet behave like humans; they eat, marry, procreate, and live in groups. Locally, all possessing spirits and *jinn* are grouped into one common category and addressed in a masculine and plural form of *asyād* (sing. *sayyid*), the masters, denoting a dominant patriarchical orientation. Invisible beings are not evaluated equally within the social hierarchy. Some are superior, dominant, and beneficent, while others are inferior, subterranean, submissive, and malicious. Within this wider context of Egyptian folk cosmology, both men and women assert the existence of *jinn*, *ʿafārīt*, and spirits[27] who are more powerful than human beings and who can impersonate, transform themselves into, or possess different entities and beings, including humans.[28] However, the *supra*-ability of spirits and *jinn* to transform and possess others is constrained. Practitioners have inherited and developed certain devices and practices to control these forces.

Spirit possession (*istiḥwāz*) is believed to be a result of either a satanic attack (*mass shaiṭānī*) or the earthly (underworld) touch of *jinn* or spirits (*lamsah arḍīyah*). A possessed woman is depicted as *ʿalīyhā asyād*, meaning that spirits or *jinn* are riding her. She is also called *malbūsah*, enclothed by a spirit or *jinn* who penetrates her body and covers it like a garment. Most of the literature on spirit possession suggests that victims of spirit affliction are either spinsters, childless wives "mainly with fertility problems" (Boddy 1988; 1989; 1994, 417), or those who have experienced an emotional disturbance such as deep sorrow or grief.

The cosmological scheme, influenced by Muslim culture, determines the appropriate time and place in which people conduct certain practices and rituals. For example, both men and women share the common belief that all *jinn*, *ʿafārīt*, and evil spirits are shackled during the holy month of Ramadan.

During this month no spirit possession of any sort takes place, nor are any *zār* cults performed. *Zikr* rituals, however, are performed extensively.

During ordinary days, the time in which *jinn*, *ʿafārīt*, and other spirits are believed to be active are carefully noted. People are advised to reduce their activities and movement at night as well as at noon because of the potential danger of invisible beings specifically at those times. Those who must move during these periods of time should utter words seeking God's refuge and protection against malicious invisible creatures. The social significance of these informal instructions is that these are periods of time when people are at rest and should not be disturbed.

People should either avoid places where evil *jinn* and spirits reside or approach them only when guarded by the prescribed behavior and the appropriate protective utterances. For example, it is widely believed that filthy places such as lavatories and animal pens are places where creatures such as *jinn* abide. To approach these places, the *fallāḥīn* utter words that seek God's protection against harmful and invisible beings. Motivated by respect and fear, people use the second- or third-person pronoun rather than the name of Allah when entering unclean places. Furthermore, villagers observe specific ritual movements when approaching certain places. For instance, the person should enter the lavatory with his left leg and leave it with his right leg, which is opposite to his action when entering and leaving a sacred place such as the mosque. From the males' point of view, men are more careful than women in observing these rules. The truly faithful and pious, as villagers maintain, are never victims of spirit possession. This statement implies two messages. First, a person should know the right way to behave not only with people, but also with the environment in which visible and invisible beings exist. And second, invisible creatures are somehow not responsible for their aggressive attitudes toward those who do not observe the customary rules.

In the community there is debate concerning the appropriate way to deal with public and private zones as equated, respectively, with visible and invisible spheres. Men think that possession might affect those who do not observe the customary rules of discursive and nondiscursive actions in their relationship with both social and invisible domains. Socially speaking, disobedient and morally astray females, from men's point of view, are the most vulnerable to spirit possession. In their daily life men seek the protection of God, while women, though they seek Allah's protection, also seek, in certain circumstances or contexts, the pardon of invisible creatures. For example, when a woman discards dirty or hot water into the courtyard at night she utters, "Pardon, O inhabitants of the place" (*dastūr yā sukkān al-makān*), as if she were addressing people. Women also use this phrase when they use the oven for baking bread or when they enter the animal stable. Women think that if they do not observe this usage, they might be harmed or possessed by the offended *jinn*.

There is another important aspect related to the concept of the person in its association with both the macrocosm (universe) and society. Spirit possession is believed to occur not merely by the aggression of the invisible agents, but also as a consequence of the weakness of both the person and social milieu. A woman who has a strong invisible iconic double (*qarīnah*) that mirrors her character is thought to be able to resist the penetration of alien spirits into her body. As was aforementioned, the double of an exceptional person or charismatic saint can exist in two or more places simultaneously. *Zār* practitioners are very concerned to delineate the nature of the possessed person's double in order to be able to locate and disclose the possessing spirit or *jinn*. The same thing is applicable to the unseen brother (*akh*) and sister (*ukht*) that metaphorically reflect social and kinship ties. In brief, it is not only the possessed person that is depicted as being weak and vulnerable, but also her concealed double, brother, and sister. It is interesting to note that in addition to the word *asyād*, the phrase "*yākhūyā*" (O brother) is frequently uttered by possessed women in the midst of their trance, referring to their need of protective siblings. In the *zār*, the cosmological, psychological, and social implications are intricately fused and intermingled.

In addition to social, personal, and emotional troubles, women have to cope with the image of the profane nature of their bodies as well as with the environment within which they interact. Menstruation is considered an impure period of time that renders women vulnerable to spirit affliction.[29] Also, inside the household, women deal more with impure places, such as the courtyard, the lavatory, and the stable, than do men. The narrow, dark alleys surrounding the houses are believed to be inhabited by *jinn* and spirits that can harm or possess women who interact there at night. Spirit possession can also occur near deserted places such as cemeteries, ruins, or the desert, particularly at noon or at night.

Muslim scholars and most male and some female villagers object to *zār* ceremonies, but not to the phenomenon of spirit possession. However, under certain circumstances where modern medicine and other means of traditional healing have failed in treating a possessed woman, the possible alternative is to conduct a *zār* cult. It takes time and effort for women to gain permission from their spouses or close male relatives to perform such a cult. Men believe in spirit possession, yet they refrain from conducting the *zār* cult. They prefer to perform or participate in *lailat zikr*, the night of the *zikr*. In the *zikr*, men follow an established form of the ritual related to a specific *Sūfī* order. Whether or not it is associated with a *Sūfī* order, the *zikr* is a ritual in which men glorify the omnipotence of God by mentioning and repeating His name while swaying their bodies in rhythmical patterns. Although the *zikr* is not fundamentally connected with any device for exorcising spirits, it is used in particular cases for that purpose. Members of certain *Sūfī* orders such as *Aḥmadīyah* and *Rifāʿīyah*, for example, are invited to perform the *zikr* on behalf of a sick person or as a fulfillment of a vow or pledge made by the host. In the *zikr*, men glorify the ultimate creative power and the transcendental oneness of Allah and honor many different famous saints referred to as "people of God" (*ahl Allah*). In the *zār*, on the other hand, women believe that they are under the control of many different and contradictory powers.[30]

The *zikr*, from the point of view of those who perform it, is good for all people, because it brings about *baraka*, attracts angels, and protects people from various kinds of devils. Within this context, the *zikr* might be recommended but not prescribed for attaining spiritual balance and generating positive and desirable outcomes for afflicted or troubled persons. Once during the evening prayer in the village mosque, a man, breaking the solemn silence that followed the prayer leader's (*imām*) recitation of the *fātiḥah*, suddenly made a high shriek that sounded like a dog barking. The *imām* immediately recited a verse of the *Qur'an* stating that *jinn* are created of fire by Allah and must submit to Him. The man immediately stopped screaming. There were no comments from the prayers, who were seemingly aware of the man's case. The only comment I heard from the *imām* was that the man was possessed (or earthly touched) and that the possessing evil spirit was irritated by being in a sacred place. The remedy of such a case, the *imām* asserted, could be achieved through reading or listening to the *Qur'an*, observing daily prayers, participating in the *zikr*, and consulting those who are knowledgeable in applying divine healing.[31]

The *zār* exorcism and not spirit possession as such represents a challenge to the cosmic and social hierarchies through the creation of new scenarios with cosmological forces and beings other than those of Allah and His messengers, and through establishing new interpersonal and social networking other than what is customary.[32] In the *zār*, the spirits or *jinn* that possess women are transformed into powerful forces with social codes seeking to alter the negative female enclosure.

Fundamentally, the relationship between the *zikr* and the *zār* might be understood in terms of oppositions between the sacred and the profane, the abstract and the concrete, order and chaos, unity and disunity, homogeneity and heterogeneity, and creative power and destructive power. These often coincide with oppositions between public and private, men and women, outside and inside, open and closed (secret), manifest and hidden, the attracted and the possessed, compassion and oppression, happiness and misery, heaven and hell, legitimate and illegitimate, profitable and nonprofitable, and good and evil.

In the village, these oppositions work to define certain social and cosmological domains within which people interact with and differentiate themselves from one another. Men are discouraged from participating in the *zār* cult. The leading practitioner is usually a woman assisted by male musicians.[33] The group itself consists of women, and men are not allowed to perform the *zār* with them. Likewise, women are not allowed to participate in the *zikr*. In the *zār*, women, especially the ones afflicted, drink, stain their clothes, or stain their body with blood and perform other actions that are forbidden by religion, while in the *zikr*, men avoid what is forbidden. From the point of view of men, women who violate the religious (Islamic) rules and prohibitions by practicing in the *zār* cult are expected to be punished in the afterlife, while people who follow Islamic rules and perform the *zikr* are expected to be rewarded with paradise.

The *zikr* is performed in a public place such as a mosque or a clean area in the street in front of a *shaikh*'s or host's house, whereas the *zār* is performed inside houses where the women and their behaviors are covered or hidden from men's eyes. For women, the *zār* represents the tension between the private and the public. It displays female public zones akin to those of wedding and *subūʿ* ceremonies in which women find an opportunity to represent themselves in public scenarios. After performing the *zār* ceremony, female participants, coming from different locations or houses, go back and gossip or tell their families and friends stories about the possessed women, about the practitioners, or about the entire *zār* activity. In the *zār*, women, through possessing spirits, negotiate their social position, attempt to achieve personal objectives, and unleash their hidden sentiments. Also, they redefine their identities and establish new relationships with both participant women and spirits. Spirit possession is a unique case in which cultural contradictions and opposing dimensions of the person exist simultaneously. Laughter and tears, happiness and sadness, trilling cries of joy (*zahgāīr*) and shrieks of anger, songs and lamentations, and epilepsy and muteness are all demonstrated by possessed women. Through mimetic behavior[34] women represent the other or alien personalities characterizing possessing spirits. Women's bodies are the mediums through which spirits make themselves visible.[35] In the *zār*, the invisible becomes visible whereby possessed women represent the tangible features of the spirits (*asyād*) through imitating the voices and movements of the possessing *asyād* or spirits, while in the *zikr* men are performing as if they were in the presence of Allah.

Although both rituals imply symbolic exchange, the *zikr* is a nonprofitable ritual performed for the sake of Allah, while the *zār* is a profitable ceremony

TABLE 5.1

DIFFERENCES BETWEEN THE ZIKR AND THE ZĀR AND BETWEEN ASSOCIATED BELIEFS ACCORDING TO MEN'S AND NONPARTICIPANTS' VIEWS

Zikr	*Common features (different in detail)*	*Zār*
men	music, songs,	women
male public domain	swaying and food	female public domain
open		secret, closed
outside		inside
free		captive
sacred domain		secular domain
religion, faith		magic, heretical
God worship		spirit worship
monotheism		polytheism
order		diversity
health		illness
unity		disunity
abstract		concrete
homogeneous		heterogeneous
nonprofitable		profitable
benevolent		malevolent
constructive, creative		destructive
mercy, compassion		anger, hatred
superior		inferior

in which sick women or their families pay money to the practitioner and offer gifts to the possessing spirits. Bargaining between the *zār* practitioner and possessing spirits goes on until satisfactory terms are reached. In the *zār*, women are compelled to perform certain actions, often a dance that turns into hysterical swaying, and respond to the orders of the different spirits possessing them. The most dominant spirits are depicted as males with overwhelmingly masculine features. Through the specific gestures made by the possessed female, the *zār* practitioner announces when the spirits are satisfied with their participation in the dance and gift exchange. Despite their differences, the *zikr* and the *zār* show some common features. In both, music and songs are performed, food is served, and saints are honored (see table 5.1).

Although saints are honored in both the *zār* and *zikr*, there is a significant difference between men's and women's attitudes toward them. Men point out that they honor the saints because they represent the ideal models of and for the true Muslim. In other words, though men believe in the holiness and *baraka* of saints, they, because of their access to literate Islamic tradition through direct connections with the *ʿulamāʾ* (men of learning) and *shaikhs*, do not elevate them to a position close to that of the Prophet Muhammad or God. Conversely, women who practice the *zār* have strong attitudes toward saints within the community. Women address them as powerful and dominant beings for whom they dance and chant their names. On the other hand, from women's point of view, saints possess those who violate or do not fulfill their vow. The strong association between women and saints is illustrated not only in the vows made to them or the visitations paid to their shrines, but also in their daily activities. When involved in heavy household work such as grinding seeds or kneading dough, women attempt to enhance their strength by invoking the names and power of the saints, specifically of Sīdī al-Badawi.[36]

In both the *zikr* and *zār*, the performers go into a trance. However, the trance of the *zikr* differs from that of the *zār* in that it is not caused by spirit possession, but rather by divine sublimity. A man who enters into a trance during the performance of the *zikr* is called *majzūb* (*majdhūb*), meaning "attracted." When a woman becomes entranced in the *zār*, participants say "*illī ʿalīhā ẓahar*" (The one who possesses her appears [or makes himself visible]). In the *zikr*, it is a great honor for a man to go into a trance where he, as *majzūb*, is taken or attracted to Allah, and leaves, though temporarily, this inferior or visible world and enters the sacred domain of the invisible one. Through his trembling body and the white froth at his mouth, while uttering repeatedly and rapidly the name of Allah, the *majzūb* reveals that he is in a distinct state superior to daily experience. He is taken there by *al-jalālah* or Allah's sublime glory. In other words, he is in the state of "being moved," as opposed to the state of "being possessed." The state of being moved denotes, according to Ernst Benz (quoted in Kramer 1993, 60), "an encounter with the divine in its beautific, healing, regenerative form," while the state of "being possessed [means] being overwhelmed . . . by a demonic, infernal or devil spirit which makes itself evident in a person's personality in a harmful and destructive way."

Outside the religious context of the *zikr*, there are men known as *majāzīb* whose minds and behavior appear anomalous. *Majzūb* is a local type of personhood that combines features of abnormality and religiosity. He is believed to have something that connects him directly with Allah. Strange words uttered by the *majzūb* are interpreted by both men and women as revealing or disclosing the secrets of the unseen world. If people do not understand these words, they expect that certain events will occur in the future to clarify his incomprehensible utterances. The *majzūb* is metaphorically depicted as the person for whom the veil that hides or covers the unseen world is disclosed, *makshūf ʿanhu al-ḥijāb*. For him, the cosmos is an open book.

Women's trances in the *zār* are, by contrast, an embodiment of the spirits possessing them. The possessed woman is not attracted to the *jinn*. On the contrary, the *jinn* is attracted to her and symbolically declares his identity through her ecstatic dance. The opposite occurs in the *zikr*, where it is the men who are attracted to the deity. In the spirit possession, then, a transition from the private invisibility of the female into her social visibility is brought into being. In this transformation the secret is exposed "*so as to lead from invisibility into explosive force*" (Taussig 1999, 57 [emphasis in original]). Small children in their play, while imitating women's styles of performing the *zār*, ironically sing: "O present *shaikh*, O present *shaikh*, may the *ʿifrīt* who possesses someone present himself" (*shaikh maḥaḍar yā shaikh maḥḍar wa illī ʿalaih ʿifrīt yaḥḍar*).

Interestingly, women, especially practitioners of the *zār* cult, claim that they are properly observing religious performances, beliefs, and values while conducting the *zār*. For example, a female practitioner claimed that she starts the rituals by reciting the *Fātiḥa*, the opening chapter of the *Qurʾan*, and mentioning the names of God, the prophets, and famous saints. However, this claim is refuted not only by men of religious learning, but also by ordinary Muslims, including women, who assert that the secrecy of the *zār* cult is proof of its heresy.

If we focus on the *zār* ritual as viewed by the women who perform it, we find revealed the following sets of patterned oppositions: the sacred and the profane, good and bad, love and hatred, happiness and unhappiness, unity and diversity, the abstract and the concrete, men and women, health and sickness, freedom and captivity, and so forth. The sacred is expressed by the practitioner's recitation of the *Fātiḥa*, while the profane is expressed in the magical incantations that follow the recitation of the *Fātiḥa*. The holy or sacred is symbolized by uttering the names of Allah, the Prophet, and Muslim saints, while the profane is expressed by uttering the names of great *jinn*. At the beginning of the *zār* the possessive spirits are malevolent, but by the end they become benevolent. Women express their happiness when they recognize that they are possessed by famous, harmless, or good saints, but become frightened when they discover that they are possessed by demons, devils, or the Red Satan. The woman who is possessed is not one person but multiple fragmented identities (or at least two), yet, after coming out of the trance and after the disappearance of the possessing spirits, the woman regains her own personality (or unity). Women who are possessed are slaves of the possessing *asyād*; they become free when the *asyād* depart from their bodies (see table 5.2).

TABLE 5.2

CULTURAL OPPOSITIONS EXPRESSED IN THE ZĀR AS VIEWED BY WOMEN

Religious implication	*Magical implication*
the *Fātiḥa* of the *Qur'an*	magical formula
Allah and His Prophet	*asyād* and *jinn*
saints as religious symbols	satan, demons, spirits
love	hatred
purity—washing before the cult	impurity—staining with blood
sacred	profane

The *Shaikh* and the *Saḥir*: The Enigma of Hidden Knowledge

Among villagers there is a dominant belief, supported by the *Qur'an* and Islamic tradition, that nobody, visible or invisible, alive or dead, can know the future or what is unseen except for Allah. Nevertheless, in their everyday lives people show great curiosity about the unknown (*al-majhūl*) and the future (*al-mustaqbal*), particularly in times of crises. Generally speaking, what is unknown, invisible, or hidden is either feared, revered, or both. This awesome and distressing preoccupation with secret, mysterious, or concealed matters is represented in one of the most widely used sayings, "*rabunā yakfīnā sharr al-mikhabbī idhā* [*izā*] *ẓahar wa bān*," meaning, "We seek our Lord's protection against the concealed when it appears or reveals itself."

For the *fallāḥīn*, as stated earlier, this visible world is surrounded and penetrated by invisible forces and beings that constitute the hidden world. If the structure of the entire universe consists of fourteen layers—seven heavens and seven layers of the earth—only two are visible. Likewise, out of the nine components of the person, only one—the body—is visible. The invisible worlds are conceived of as comprising the sacred, holy, divine, pure, powerful, benevolent, and superior on the one hand, and the profane, impure, defiled, malevolent, and inferior on the other. In dealing with the unseen world, the society requires qualified practitioners who are able to communicate with it. Although people pray and observe religious rituals and magical practices, they believe that direct or immediate communication with unseen forces and beings would be more efficient if it were made on their behalf by specific agents or highly qualified or exceptionally gifted persons. These practitioners are implicitly classified into two major categories: the *shaikh*, a man of *baraka* and/or religious learning; and the *saḥir*, a sorcerer or magician.

It is difficult to distinguish between the *shaikh* and *saḥir* in the village without assistance from the villagers themselves. This is because the *saḥir* in some respects is referred to as *shaikh*. Moreover, some of his actions or practices overlap those of the *shaikh*. It is true that a "person can use the power of the *Qur'an* to heal or to harm, and in this sense its power is prior to judgment about the ethics of its use" (Bowen 1993, 166). But the ethical issue still forms an important standard against which people differentiate the *shaikh* from the *saḥir*. Based on long experience and daily interaction, villagers are able to differentiate between them.

A *shaikh* is a person known for his religious knowledge, whether it is acquired through formal religious education, specifically of the Azhar school, or through self-education that is locally guided by people of learning who live in the village. A *shaikh* plays an important role in people's religious life by leading prayers and teaching the principles of Islam. In addition to its religious significance, the title *shaikh* implies social and moral values. An elderly and highly respected man is called *shaikh*. The *shaikh* represents the social and public zones of the village. For villagers, a *shaikh* is the model "good person" who maintains and perpetuates healthy and balanced relationships with people and who demonstrates social skills in resolving disputes among members of the community. *Shaikhs* are hierarchically demarcated based on their powers of blessing. Only a few are known for their *baraka* or extraordinary ability to manipulate sacred knowledge for the welfare of the community.

The *saḥir* or sorcerer, on the other hand, deals with private domains and abuses sacred knowledge or secretly violates the moral principles of the community by serving some people at the expense of others. For the villagers, the *saḥir* is an enigma who possesses remarkable religious knowledge, which he abuses. Although sorcery, Kapferer maintains, is "the power that human beings exercise," it is inadequate to claim that it is "neither moral nor immoral . . . creative or destructive" (1997, 253).[37] Like the *shaikh*, the sorcerer memorizes the *Qur'an* or at least a great part of it, but, unlike the *shaikh*, he alters the order and meaning of the sacred texts for his own purposes. Neither the magician nor the *shaikh* is isolated from the community. Like the *shaikh*, the *saḥir* interacts with people and is involved in community life but deals with people's affairs privately rather than publicly.[38]

Both the *shaikh* and *saḥir* manipulate, though with different strategies and for different purposes, hidden knowledge and unseen forces and beings. The *shaikh* deals with the sacred, while the *saḥir* deals with the profane. Both the *shaikh* and *saḥir* are symbols of the opposite needs, wishes, emotions, attitudes, thoughts, and worldviews of the people themselves. If the *shaikh* and *saḥir* fail to prove their capacities for fulfilling these needs, they would not exist in the community. The language and practices of both the *shaikh* and *saḥir* tend to nullify each other, though those of the *shaikh* are believed by villagers to be superior to those of the *saḥir*, because the former's power is not his but Allah's. Let us emphasize here that one of the essential features differentiating the *shaikh* from the *saḥir* is that the former refrains from doing whatever might harm people. A benevolent *shaikh* does not accept cases that involve harming people, though he is willing to perform counter-sorcery. Metaphorically, if the *saḥir* ties (*yarbuṭ*) or makes a magical formula (sorcery), the *shaikh* unties (*yaḥill*) or counteracts.

The quintessential attribute of a *super-shaikh* is his *baraka*, which he is believed to have inherited from his pious ancestors whom Allah has blessed. Sīdī Ghānim, a saint whose shrine is located in the village, is ancestor to another famous *shaikh*, ʿĪsā, whose *baraka* is thought to be particularly effective. His reputation attracts a large number of villagers who seek or ask for his holy services. The *saḥir* on the other hand represents an ambiguous phenomenon, and his anomalous attributes are credited by villagers to his self, *nafs*. For the *fallāḥīn*, the *saḥir* has remarkable psychic power and exceptional skills in manipulating destructive or evil invisible forces that cause misfortune to other people. Locally, the characters of both the *saḥir* and *shaikh* are implicitly recognized by villagers, even when they call the *saḥir*, "*shaikh*." In other words, although the *sahir* might be called "*shaikh*," he is, explicitly or implicitly, identified as dealing with underground magic, *as-siḥr as-suflī*.[39]

People seek the *shaikh*'s help in solving problems related to health, barrenness, impotence, envy, marital disputes, lost or stolen property, and protection from evil spirits or magic made by the sorcerer. The *shaikh* works as a medicine man, using his saliva and hands along with some verses of the *Qur'an* in writing charms, *aḥjibah* (sing. *ḥijāb*), among other things to protect and cure people and animals. It is worth noting that the word *ḥijāb* is derived from the root *hajāb*, which means to hide, cover, and protect. However, these charms are intended not only to protect people from evil powers but also to make all activities and enterprises of those who bear them successful. The *baraka* of the *shaikh* and the sacred verses are believed to work together. In addition to charms, the *shaikh* writes verses of the *Qur'an* on a piece of paper or bread, and asks the patient to eat it. The *shaikh* also uses what is known as *al-ḥarf*, or a letter, in his prescriptions whereby he writes certain Arabic letters believed to be efficacious in curing a specific ailment. Ordinary persons who imitate the *shaikh* by writing or reciting verses of the *Qur'an* or letters for preventive or curative purposes are not as successful as the *shaikh*. In this context, people say "*al-baraka fī al-kaff mush fī al-ḥarf*," meaning that the *baraka* exists in the hand, not in the letter. Unlike the *saḥir*, the *shaikh* does not charge people for his service, although he does not reject gifts.

The most common problems the *saḥir* or magician deals with are those that are related to enmity between rivals, accusations of unexpected barrenness, severe illness, or death. For example, if two men compete with each other to marry a woman and one of them succeeds, the other might ask the magician to make a *rabṭ*, or magical tying, to render the winner impotent. The same kind of magic is also requested by divorced women against their ex-husbands. The magical tying is believed to be effective until it is uncovered or its magical formula untied or destroyed by either another magician or a *shaikh*. Unlike the *shaikh*, the *saḥir* is feared by people who are not certain of his motives and intentions. A famous *saḥir* confided that he can cause the sterility of the adult men of the village by putting his magical formula under the thresholds of all mosques of the village during Friday (collective) prayer in which most if not all males participate.

Magical thought and action are viewed as either an affiliation with devils and evil forces or an abuse of hidden knowledge and sacred power. Any magical practice a sorcerer makes, whether it is a knot (*ʿuqdah*) or tying (*rabṭ*) is called *ʿamal*, which is believed to be supported by evil *jinn* or *ʿafārīt* called *khuddām* (servants of the magician). Note here that while *jinn* are considered to be masters (*asyād*) in their relations with the possessed women, they are servants or slaves of the magician to whose command they submit and obey. This sort of magic is known as *siḥr suflī*—lower (underground) magic, suggesting its immoral or contemptible goals as well as its atheistic and inferior invisible assistants who are believed to live underground. Also, in this kind of magic the sorcerer causes disorder both in nature or the cosmos and in people's lives by the intentional violation of sacred books and objects. For example, it is believed that the sorcerer reads the sacred books in the lavatory and washes his feet and genitalia with milk.

Unlike the *shaikh*, who deals publicly with clean, pure objects, the *saḥir* deals secretly with impure and unclean objects such as the bones of dead people and animals, women's menstrual blood (*dam ḥaiḍ*), "hot blood" collected immediately after birth, and so forth. Unlike the *saḥir* who uses the *suflī* method, which seeks the help of devils and spirits of the underworld, the *shaikh*, villagers maintain, applies the spiritual method (*rūḥānī*, also called *ʿulwī* or higher) because it deals with heavenly higher power.

Conclusion

This chapter has concentrated on the public and private zones through discussing the significance of reciprocity and symbolic exchange in people's daily actions. As a cultural medium, symbolic exchange encompasses cosmological, psychological or personal, and social aspects and goes beyond the immediate exchange of gifts to include continuous reciprocity of material and immaterial symbols between people and invisible entities.

The hidden dimensions of the cosmos, society, and person have been demonstrated to be displayed not in abstract concepts, but rather in outward manifestations, in public scenarios, in tangible objects, and in bodily symbols. Whether these symbols are presented as bodily parts such as the hands and eyes, or as bodily behaviors such as gift exchange, or as bodily rituals such as the *zikr* and *zār*, or as identities such as the *shaikh*, *saḥir*, or the *zār* practitioner, they are capable of converting what is invisible, hidden, or private to be visible, social, or public.

The chapter discusses folk healing as related to people's bodily manipulation of invisible cosmological spheres. Also, special attention has been given to gender hierarchy as represented in men–men, men–women, and women–women relationships and enacted in specific practices and rituals such as the *zikr* and the *zār*, among other religious and mundane ceremonies. Cosmic and psychic unseen forces such as *baraka* or blessing and *ḥasad* or envious eye as well as invisible and visible beings such as *jinn*, *ʿafārīt*, angels, *shaikhs*, and magicians are understood by people who believe in them in terms of the hierarchical relationship existent among them. By demonstrating the hierarchical relationship between oppositions of *baraka/ḥasad*, *zikr/zār*, and *shaikh/saḥir*, some significant aspects of social or public and private scenarios have been brought out. The focus has been on the subordination of *ḥasad* (envy), the eye, the *zār*, and the *saḥir* (magician, or the *zār* practitioner) to the *baraka* (blessing), the hand, the *zikr*, and the *shaikh*, respectively.

Although the Egyptian *fallāḥīn* work hard and calculate for their needs, they think and behave as if there were other invisible forces and beings, good or bad, that interfere in the outcome of their plans or actions. Thus symbolic exchange with both people and unseen beings constitutes core ground for the rural Egyptians' cosmological and social orientations in both the public and private domains.

Notes

1. The simplest form of symbolic exchange indicating the unexploitative social relationship is expressed in what villagers call *ʿaish wa malḥ* (bread and salt), which people share or eat together.

2. See chapter 3, which discusses the morning as a cosmic phenomenon.

3. It is difficult to accept the general statement that there is nothing symbolic or that nothing stands for something else in the traditional societies of the Middle East.

The Arabic word *ramz* (symbol) is frequently used by rural Egyptians in various social contexts, especially in those related to gift exchange. Also, the phrase "*shay' ramzī*" (Something symbolic) is used intentionally in contexts whereby the gift is not to be taken literally, but symbolically as something that stands for love, affection, caring, and sincerity.

4. The same gender division is observed in an urban environment in Egypt (El Guindi 1999, 62).

5. Although such phrases, indicating gender division, are also used in the *subū'* ceremony in urban Egyptian communities, they have not been addressed in El Guindi's (1999) rich analysis of that ceremony. In her study of the *subū'* (or El-Sebou') ceremony, El Guindi addresses gender relationships through focusing on the shapes of pots used in that ceremony, yet linguistic or discursive evidence of gender differentiation has not been fully addressed. She points out (1999, 64) that during the ceremony, "the family sing a special El-Sebou' folk song—'Hala'atak Birgalatak' (Earrings and anklets). Its text is gender-neutral language, and the same lyrics are sung by the family during the ceremony for babies of both sexes." However, gender division, as I mentioned, is still reflected in the scenario made by female participants addressing the male baby to listen to his father and the female baby to behave like her mother.

6. Within Islamic tradition *shafā'ah* (mediation) is used in a theological sense, particularly in eschatological descriptions. The intercession of the Prophet Muhammad at the Day of Judgment is frequently mentioned in Muslim tradition. Also, *shafā'ah* is used other than in theological language, such as in laying a petition before a high-ranking official or in interceding for a debtor (Gibb and Kramer n.d., 511–12).

7. Gender differentiation is emphasized through bodily symbolism used by males and females (Bourdieu 1977; Boddy 1988, 1989; Strathern 1996).

8. For a similar concept, consult Boddy's discussion (1988, 1989) of women's blood and men's semen as fluid and substance having complementary roles in the reproductive domain.

9. The same negative relationship is also found between a wife and her sister-in-law. In his analysis of Arab women's patterns of behavior as expressed in their tales, El-Shamy (1999) addresses this problem in detail.

10. See, for example, Kluckhohn (1944), Evans-Pritchard (1966, 1980), Gluckman (1969), Fortune (1959), Douglas (1970), and I. M. Lewis (1970, 1975, 1986).

11. These two concepts have been addressed in chapter 4 with reference to the relationship between the person and the cosmos. The focus here is on the theoretical significance of these concepts as representing two opposite but complementary cosmic outlooks.

12. The concept of *baraka*, in many significant aspects, is synonymous to concepts of *Mana* in Melanesia and Polynesia (Mauss 1990, 108–21; Pitt-Rivers 1974, 2–18; Eliade 1974, 19–23) and *indarra* in Basque (Ott 1981, 87), to mention a few examples, where they are described as being a divine or spiritual (or supernatural) force that causes material and immaterial and negative and positive effects. As regards the importance of the concept of *baraka* in the system of meanings in Egyptian culture, Gilsenan (1973, 33–34) states that *baraka* must be understood "as part of the whole complex of forces, thought in an ultimate sense to constitute as well as to govern the

world. There are maleficent powers to be warded off by the saints, by amulets, talisman, verses of the *Qur'an*, the virtuous life, and trust in God."

13. Ibn Khaldūn (1981, 395–96) argues that the evil eye is a psychic attribute, which is a natural or innate gift of a person causing misfortune to other people. The person who possess an evil eye is not responsible for the negative results of his or her psychic power because he or she does not intend to harm people. The psychic influence is related to the desire of the person who has the envious eye to possess other people's property that seems appealing to him or her.

14. The belief in the cosmic-psychic force is extended to include certain animals such as dogs and cats whose eyes can cause misfortune. For instance, villagers try to avoid dogs' gazing at them at mealtime, thinking that these dogs might envy their food.

15. In her study of the *fellāḥīn* of Upper Egypt, Blackman (1927, 33, 65, 99) broadens the meaning of *baraka* to include blessing, healing virtues, anything that is old or sacred, and good luck. However, the case is different in the village being studied where people do not equate the concept of *ḥaẓẓ* (good luck), which is a secular notion, with that of *baraka*, which is a sacred force.

16. Compare this meaning of *baraka* with the Tunisian (Abu-Zahra, 1978, 5–24) and Moroccan (Westermark 1968, 1:35–261). Westermark defines *baraka*, as used in Morocco, as "a mysterious wonder-working force which is looked upon as a blessing from God" (p. 35).

17. A similar practice of touch was also known to ancient Egyptians, where they "are to be seen in the bas-reliefs transmitting with their hand the vital principle represented by the '*ankh* symbol'" (Hocart 1942, 370 [emphasis in original]). The most significant symbol is that of the Ka, which is represented as two arms or hands extended upwards "as if the palms were raised in adoration" (Clark 1978, 231). Ancient Egyptians recognized and used symbols, such as that of Ka, for "transmission of life power from gods to men" (Hocart 1942, 371). Presently, villagers firmly believe that though prophets, saints, and pious people have *baraka*, the ultimate source of it is Allah.

18. Ammar (1966, 73) says: "To introduce acts of piety or holy symbols into everyday life is the best means of producing 'baraka,' to mention God's name at the beginning of the meal, to thank Him at the end of it, to elicit His help on traveling . . . such religious ritual invokes holiness—'baraka.'" A similar observation is recorded in Lane's study (1966, 148) of Egyptian manners.

19. In order to invoke blessing on their children, villagers name them Baraka, Mabrūk, Mubārak, and Barakāt (for males), and Baraka, Mabrūka, Tabārak, and Ni'ma (for females).

20. Gallbladder (*marārah*) in Egyptian folklore metaphorically means "patience," and the person or woman who is known for his or her patience is described as having a very long gallbladder (el-Aswad 1990a).

21. There are different opinions regarding the origin of the word *zār*. Some writers argue that it is an Arabic word, while others express the opposite opinion. For example, 'Abd al-Raḥmān Ismā'īl (1980) states that the word *zār* might have been derived from where it originated in the town of Zara in northern Iran, or from the village Zar in eastern Yemama, or from the Arabic word *ziyarah*, which means "visita-

tion," referring to the visits of the "masters" or "*al-asyād*" to the possessed person. ʿAbd al-Raḥmān Ismāʿīl and Walker (1934) tend to support the opinion that the *zār* could have been derived from the Arabic word *ziyarah* (Walker 1934, 62). The Arabic origin of the word *zār* is emphasized by Samuel Zwemer, who says that "I have been told that the word is Arabic and denotes 'a (sinister) visitor' (*Zāra Yezuru*) who makes his or her abode and so possesses the victim" (Zwemer 1920, 228). He refutes Snouck Hurgronje's statement that this word (*zār*) is not Arabic and has no plural form. Zwemer (1920, 228) gives an example from Oman in Eastern Arabia, where the plural form, *zeeran*, is used. See also Zwemer (1939). On the other hand, Enrico Cerulli (1934, 1217) states that *zār* is in Arabic "a loan-word from Amharic, as the popular beliefs in the genii Zar were imported from Abyssinia into the Islamic world." This Ethiopian or Abyssinian origin of the *zār* is supported by C. B. Klunzinger (1984, 395–97), Paul Khale, Snouck Hurgronje, N. C. Plowden (Franke 1913, 279–80), D. B. MacDonald (1911), Triminham (1965, 147–76), Messing (1958), and others. However, other scholars maintain that the historical origin of the *zār* is unknown, arguing that "in Ethiopia itself the *zār* spirits are described with great certitude as 'foreign intruders'" (Kramer 1993, 110).

22. Regarding the historical period in which the *zār* was introduced into Egypt, there is a debate among scholars concerning the exact year in which the *zār* spread over Egypt. Some writers, such as Franke (1913, 281) and al-Misrī (1975, 25), depend for their estimation on the negative historical evidence, arguing that some important studies dealing with Egyptian customs and habits such as the French scholars' study *The Description of Egypt* (1820) and E. W. Lane's *The Manners and Customs of the Modern Egyptians* (1966) have not mentioned the *zār*. Ghurbal and al-Misrī argue that before 1820 (in which Egypt conquered and dominated the Sudan), the *zār* exorcisms were not known nor found in Egypt (al-Misrī 1975, 30). Franke (1913, 281), dependent on Kluzinger's study, states that "between 1870–80 the Zar exorcisms spread to such an extent in Upper Egypt that the Government had to put a stop to them."

23. See Boddy (1989), Fakhouri (1968), Kramer (1993), Lambek (1981, 1993), V. Turner (1974, 1980), Turner and Turner (1982), and Rasmussen (1994).

24. A brief description of the *zār* cult might clarify what is meant by its magical characteristics. There are no *zār* practitioners in the village. Those who are possessed either go to a nearby village where they participate in what is called a public *zār*, held every Friday afternoon, or else hold a private *zār* within their houses. The public *zār*, an inexpensive ceremony conducted mostly by male practitioners, attracts those who do not suffer from serious illness, but frequently complain of headache, dizziness, and other symptoms diagnosed as being related to spirit affliction. Women from different rural and urban communities participate in that *zār*. The private *zār*, a costly cult, is held in the village (in the house of the sick woman) where the arrangements with the practitioners, mostly females, are made for that purpose. When a woman manifests the symptoms of being possessed by a spirit or *jinn*, she or her female relatives consult the *zār* practitioner, called a *shaika*, about the problem. The practitioner requires or asks for an *athar*, or something related to the sick woman, such as a scarf or handkerchief. This procedure is common in homeopathic magical acts in the village. The practitioner puts the patient's scarf or handkerchief under her pillow

for two or three nights in order to communicate with the spirit or *jinn* causing the possession. Through her dreams, the practitioner determines the identity of the possessing spirit and informs the patient or her relatives to prepare the necessary offerings and objects, among other things, needed for conducting the ceremony. Then the day of the *zār* ceremony is fixed. The practitioner or the *shaika* accompanied with her assistants (musicians and singers), the patient, and female relatives and friends conduct the ceremony in which the patient as well as other women enter into a trance wherein the *asyād*, or invisible masters, declare themselves through the women's dance. There are two important elements confirming the symbolic exchange without which the *zār* cult cannot be performed. First, the sacrifice of a bird or animal. The important action here is that the practitioner stains the patient's face and clothes with the blood of the scarified animal or bird. Sometimes the patient is asked by the spirit to drink some of that blood. Second, the *kūrsī* literally means the "chair," but here it means the table on which offerings including food items, sweets, candles, and incense among other things are placed. This table symbolizes the altar on which offerings or gifts are offered to gods or spirits.

25. For preventive and therapeutic folk practices in Egypt, see El-Shamy (1972) and Kennedy (1967). The idea that focuses on the spirit inhabitation of the body is discussed in most anthropological literature on spirit possession (Lewis 1966, 1970; Crapanzano and Garrison 1977; Lambek 1981). Raymond Firth (1967, 292), for example, defines spirit possession as "phenomena of abnormal personal behavior which are interpreted by other members of the society as evidence that a spirit is controlling the person's actions and probably inhabiting his body."

26. I. M. Lewis (1966, 1970, 1975) tends to confine the complicated phenomenon of spirit possession to what he calls "sex war," or war between sexes (between men and women). Peter Wilson (1967, 79–93) criticizes Lewis's argument and offers another alternative, which attempts to explain spirit possession as an expression, or result, of the conflict and competition between members of the same sex, not between members of different sexes. To support his argument, Wilson, using examples provided by Lewis, states that "[w]hen a Somali husband takes a new wife, his present wife, we may infer, feels distinctly threatened. But the threat is not her husband, it is the new wife: not a male, but female. The husband is the agent who is instrumental in bringing about the situation of tension, and he remains the focus of the conflict between the two" (1967, 370).

27. Crapanzano (1980) and Crapanzano and Garrison (1977) argue that spirit possession is understood in terms of the existence of spirits as viewed by locals as well as in terms of its total meaning.

28. Spirits and *jinn* cannot impersonate the prophets, especially Muhammad.

29. The relationship between females' impurity and demonic possession has been documented in various studies (Obeyesekere 1981, 1990; Kapferer 1997; el-Aswad 1988).

30. In the *zār* cult, spirits are diagnosed as belonging to different ethnic and cultural backgrounds. There are Muslim, Christian, and Ethiopian spirits, among others.

31. There are certain *shaikhs* known among the villagers for their knowledge and experience in healing possessed persons through applying sacred verses of the

Qur'an; this is to say that "curing is considered to be sanctioned by Islam and to be operating within its norms" (Lambek 1981, 33).

32. A distinction between *spirit possession* and *spirit exorcism* is to be maintained, though it seems that that distinction becomes somehow blurred. Lambek, for example, states that "[s]pirits are challenging the fundamental sociopolitical assumptions and implications of Islamic ideology" (Lambek 1981, 33).

33. The female practitioner of the *zār* shares some basic characteristics of the shaman, especially those of ecstasy and communication with spirits, as defined by Eliade (1964, 4, 5). Eliade, who overlooks the phenomenon of spirit possession, states that shamanism equals the technique of ecstasy.

34. On mimesis and mimetic behavior, see Taussig (1993).

35. On the notion of embodiment—an existential ground of culture—that negates the duality or opposition of mind/body, see Csordas (1990, 1993, 1994).

36. According to Egyptian folk literature, Sīdī Aḥmad al-Badawī, a bachelor and powerful saint, is widely known as "*al-farrāj*," the liberator or the hero who subdued women, as represented in the figure of Fāṭimah bit Barrī, who liberated Muslim captives (*al-asrā*) from Christian captivity. He is considered to be one of the four poles, *aqṭāb* (sing. *quṭb*), governing the universe, which is also known as the gate of the Prophet, *bāb an-nābī*.

37. Kapferer's claim has been refuted and challenged by a recent study (Nabokov 2000) that shows that negative, antisocial, and destructive aspects of sorcery exist in Tamil society.

38. This view does not support the claim of Durkheim (1965) and Mauss (1970) that the sorcerer lives in isolation from the community.

39. It is important to note that when people refer to a "magician," they often use the word *shaikh* followed by his name, then by the adjectival form *saḥir*, such as in "*shaikh Bkkar as-saḥir*."

6

Multiple Worlds

Secularism and Globalization

It has been argued that "modernity," an all-embracing concept that has been associated with secularism, rationality, science, and technology, marks a genuine discontinuity with the traditional world (Giddens 1984, 238–39; 1991). Modernity has become deeply embedded in Western cultural self-understanding in such a way that it provides a broad context within which other analytic descriptions such as "Western modernity," "capitalist modernity," "postmodernity," and "global modernity" are themselves demarcated (Tomlinson 1999, 32).[1]

In a phrase that recalls Weber's distinction between an otherworldly (superstitious) outlook and this worldly (rational) orientation, Shepard (1987, 318) provides a definition of the "traditionalist" within the Muslim context:

> A traditionalist may be defined as one whose allegiance is to what many would consider the particular "mix" of *Shari'a* and *non-Shari'a* elements characterizing his area on the eve of the Western impact, and who has not significantly internalized the Western challenge, that is, who has not felt the attraction as well as the threat of Western ways, and thus has not fully appreciated the depth of the threat. He will probably be more *otherworldly* . . . and certainly more given to traditional *superstitions*. (emphasis added)

The traditionalist is unjustifiably marginalized as not having captured the Western challenge. By the same token, though in a broader tone, Gellner states that the "type of knowledge available to industrial societies is qualitatively so superior to any others that it hardly deserves to be classed under the same name" (1964, 72). From the Western point of view, irrationality or inadequate forms of rationality are the main causes of the "static" nature of traditional societies (Goody 1996, 2–4).

Contemporary global studies in the West confirm that world civilization is a product of many different cultures and not just the triumph of the West or modern Europe (Ahmed and Donnan 1994, 4–5; Mazrui 1997, 91). The preoccupation with Western criteria or "West versus the rest" (Huntington 1993) hinders the objective understanding of traditional and non-Western societies. Jack Goody (1977, lx) points out that "we failed to give full recognition to the achievements of other literate societies because of a preoccupation with the 'uniqueness of the West.'" This kind of thinking is "rooted in a we/they division which is both binary and ethnocentric. . . . We speak in terms of primitive and advanced, almost as if human minds themselves differ in their structure like machines of an earlier and later design" (Goody 1977, 1).

There is no necessary correlation between tradition and irrationality or superstition. Superstitions, based on the belief in the existence of empirically inaccessible or nonexistent entities, are "certainly common among progressivists, secularists, and rationalists but traditionality has been made to bear the obloquy which superstition calls for among progressivists; their own superstitions are spared" (Shils 1981, 5). Tradition cannot be viewed as a residual category attached to premodern societies for the fact that it is historically embedded in different ways in all cultures, modern and premodern alike. As Shils points out, traditions are the "tacit component [of] rational, moral, and cognitive actions, and of affect, too. . . . Tradition enters into the constitution of meaningful conduct by defining its ends and standards and even its means" (1981, 33). Science itself begins by being "traditional" in the sense that any scientific knowledge preserves a "totalitarian" structure that implies cosmogonic, ethical, and existential principles (Marino 1982, 53).

Patterns of thought of rural Egyptians, however, are based not on the evolutionary cosmology but on the cosmology of spirituality and creation that does not dismiss mundane and secular engagement with reality. "The secular bias of modernization theory has had a significant role in deflecting attention from the role of religious practices and values in contemporary societies, particularly in the Muslim majority world" (Eickelman 2000, 119). As being associated with tradition, religious leaders and local Muslim communities have been marginalized by proponents of modernism and secularism as representing an irrational outlook incompatible with those trends. But the fact is that peasants are neither withdrawn from this worldly life nor are they irrationally immersed in the otherworldly life. They do not reject modernization—rather they have developed an indigenous kind of secular modernism. What is rejected, however, is the secularism or secular outlook that negates religious meanings and renders the moral-spiritual human into an ungodly and merciless creature. At the local level, modern technology and development projects have been welcomed and implemented without any objection from people or religious leaders. Modern means of education, communication, and transportation, including schools, telephone networks, electricity, television, paved roads, among others, have been available and accessible to the village. For villagers, who motivate their children to compete for better education, there is no contradiction between modern science or technology and religious faith unrestricted by mundane modes of reason. It is not a matter of refusal to change, viewed by Western secularism as a proof of traditional irrationality, but a matter of appropriateness of the new or modern for the local community. In this context, it becomes clear why villagers reject certain patterns of Western secular behavior, particularly those related to obsession with materialism, inadequate use of freedom, alcohol-abuse, violence, disintegrating social (family) relationships, and unrestricted sexual relationships.

Globalization is a multidimensional phenomenon. To understand it is to grasp the proximity coming from the networking of social relations across large tracts of time-space, causing distant events, powers, and meanings to penetrate people's local experience (Tomlinson 1999, 9). Through migration and mass media, particularly television, villagers become aware of and are exposed to different cultures. Migration provides firsthand experience, the impact of which exceeds the individual to include those who have never gone beyond the borders of their village. However, to understand peasants' modes of thought and actions, we must capture the inside and outside forces affecting them. Political–economic forces, including colonization, Westernization, and globalization, have been playing a decisive role in peasants' lives. For instance, in "the second quarter of the nineteenth century the people of Egypt were made inmates in their own villages" and the village, through a new mode of oppressive authority, was controlled like a military barracks (Mitchell 1988, 34). Only three decades ago—or more specifically, since the advent of the policy of economic liberation in the mid-1970s that coincided with the formation of revolutionary Islamic groups in Egypt—have Egyptian peasants been able to move about locally and globally.

In his discussion of Kabyle traditional society, Bourdieu argues that the *fallāḥ* "refuses to sacrifice a tangible interest in hand . . . to an abstract one which cannot be comprehended by concrete intuition" (1963, 66). He also points out that planning "fails to create incentive, because the plan is based on abstract calculation; it seems as a dream because it belongs in an imaginary realm of possibilities where adherence to actuality must be suspended" (1966, 67). This conclusion, which might be applicable to Kabyle society, cannot be generalized to rural Egypt. It is irrelevant and unconvincing to say that peasants cannot make plans based on abstract calculation or that they cannot conceive the possible consequences of their plans.[2] One argues that what was considered impossible for Egyptian peasants to undertake three decades ago (for political and economic reasons) has become possible today. In fact, the migration of Egyptian peasants to wealthy Arab Gulf countries to work for specified periods of time so as to be able to save the money necessary for planning his life, buying land, and improving his economic resources, renders Bourdieu's argument inadequate. "New possibilities previously hidden are perceived when a tradition enters into a new state" (Shils 1981, 213). The domain of unseen or invisible forces has extended to include not only supernatural, spiritual, and psychological aspects but also material aspects, including advanced technology imbued with invisible power such as credit-card machines and high-tech doors that open automatically. Returning migrants have brought back with them stories of the miracles of modern technology, facilitating a consumerist spirit.

In order to function properly in Muslim societies, the secular or modern should be regulated within the religious outlook. This view is incompatible with the concept of secularism in the West, as represented in the following statement: "We too easily tend to think that people always had our secular understandings of events in homogenous, profane time and then just added some bizarre beliefs about God, eternity, and so on. . . . We don't understand their beliefs, because we no longer grasp the background in which they were held. Eternity, for someone firmly in an understanding of time as exclusively secular, is just the damn thing going on without end" (Taylor 1993, 246).

At both the national and local levels, religious teachings even after the adoption of secular education and modernization in the late nineteenth century have remained essential in school curriculums (Starrett 1998, 56–72). Even when the local discourse was penetrated by the colonial order through its secular education and media, this

> colonising process never fully succeeded, for there always remained regions of resistance and voices of rejection. The schools, universities and the press, moreover, like the military barracks, were always liable to become centers of some kind of revolt, turning the coloniser's methods of instruction and discipline into the means of organized opposition. (Hence the rise after the First World War of disciplinary political movements opposed to European occupation, such as the Muslim Brotherhood in Egypt whose leaders were almost invariably schoolteachers.) (Mitchell 1988, 171)

The divine cosmic power that surpasses any other power is a common theme shared by both Muslim intellectuals and villagers. Although the divine power ensures the preservation of the order of the universe, it is also mandatory (*wājib*) that people, or more specifically, Muslims, strive to prevent the corruption of the cosmos, *fasād al-kaun*, and eliminate whatever causes the cosmos to decay. One of the effective means of doing so is the sermon.

Throughout the cosmic history of Islam, sermons have been explicit and implicit forces in religious identification, social reformation, and political mobilization. Today, in the village, sermons are no longer confined to mosques,[3] but have been disseminated through alternative means of communication such as the mass media (television), audiocassette tapes, and videotapes. These means appeal to a large audience, literate and illiterate. The mass media plays a significant role in unifying people's beliefs in such a way that the distinction between the national and local levels of religious beliefs and practices seems irrelevant. Local Muslim preachers have become interested in faraway countries, peoples, and events, enticed by the proximity provided by advanced means of communication and transportation. They have to cope with the growing expansion of globalization and secularization as well as with the demands of the natives to maintain their Muslim heritage and identity. In their sermons, religious leaders focus on issues related to the overwhelming penetration of Western modes of production and consumption in Muslim societies, especially among the young. They repeatedly warn people of the risk of losing their "religion" and "Muslim identity" through imitating the lifestyles of "unbelievers." They also warn them of the nearness of world collapse and ask them to turn to God in repentance.[4] Issues that range from cosmic–global problems such as cloning and the transplanting of human organs, to local matters such as youngsters' imitation of Western modes of behavior and disobedience of parents' advice, are vigorously addressed by local religious leaders.

The problem of secularism is that it has focused not on life in its totality, but on its fragmentary aspects. It has focused on "this life" without the "other life," on the rational reason without deity, on the body without soul, and on the cosmology without values. In this context, the world as viewed by villagers turns out to be soulless and devoid of meaning and divine grace or blessing (*baraka*), indicating a chronic case of cosmic pathology and near-death. Local as well as global events are interpreted within cosmic, religious, and moral frameworks—that is, when the world moves away from its spiritual and moral realms to confine itself to materialistic objectives, the annihilation of the cosmos will be the inevitable consequence.

Possible Worlds

Among rural Egyptians there is a belief that specific persons such as saints and even magicians are able to communicate with invisible domains through hidden knowledge. While this belief has no foundation in science, it does represent, at least from the natives' point of view, another possibility. Put differently, beyond the scope of the visible and tangible world of experience lies the invisible and imaginary universe from which possible worlds emerge. The concealed or invisible allows for possibility (*mumkin*), rendering the cosmos as a dynamic structure. Although the invisible world is imaginary and imperceptible, it is thought to be real and have its own existence. Possible worlds, within an all-encompassing Egyptian folk cosmology, are themselves systems of meaning that render cosmological, personal, and social experience intelligible. These possible worlds, *ʿawālim mumkihah*, are ordered by a logic different from that used in perceived experience. This logic provides for an open and flexible outlook that provides space for things and events to happen.

Insomuch as possibilities are embedded in the unseen and imaginary world, they can be manifested in everyday practices. If it is possible that a saint can be present simultaneously in two places without any sense of contradiction, and if it is possible for such a saint as the eternal and evergreen man, *al-Khiḍr*, upon whom the divine and Godly knowledge (*ʿilm lādūnny*) is bestowed, to be present, though unseen, whenever people mention his name, it would also be possible for a childless woman, after a long history of barrenness, to conceive and have children. What is thought to be unobtainable in the immediate experience might be achievable in distant and different contexts. In both mundane and transcendental terms, nothing is inaccessible or impossible for God, *mush baʿīd ʿalā l Allah*.

The multiplicity of the cosmos, *taʿaddud al-akwān*, implies that there are possible worlds that are different from one another in ontological, attributional, and relational terms. Ontologically, there are multiple worlds such as the world of spirits (*ʿālam al-arwāḥ*), the world of angels (*ʿālam al-mlāʿka*), the world of *jinn*, and the world of human beings (*ʿālam al-ins*). Attributionally, multiple worlds encompass positive and negative attributes related to specific unseen beings and forces. Positive attributes, for example, are associated with angels, *baraka* (blessing), and *karāmāt*, wonders made by those who are believed to possess hidden, constructive knowledge (religion), while negative attributes are associated with devils (*ḥasad*), envy, and hidden, destructive knowledge (magic). Relationally, the universe or life in its totality is classified into both the mundane world and the otherworld that, in turn, contains the eschatological world, resurrection, and the world of judgment. These worlds, however, are interpenetrating domains and points of reference correlating with cultural constructs that render different levels of experience—real or imaginary—intelligible.

Ontological and attributional aspects of the cosmos have been extensively addressed in previous chapters. In this chapter, however, the focus will be on the relational meaning of multiple worlds, demonstrating how people differentiate the present world from the other that encompasses the world of the tomb (death) and the world to come (resurrection). The main objective here is to examine the extent to which villagers' beliefs about the otherworld influence their worldly life. Through discussing the relationship between these multiple worlds, this study addresses issues related to people's attitudes and reactions toward secularism, modernism, and globalization. The cosmic, religious, and social significance of the world of the tomb is addressed with special emphasis on rural Egyptians' views and concepts concerning the relationship between microcosmic (individual) death and the macrocosmic (collective) end of time.

Triple Worlds

Some domains of experience, imagination, and worldview that seem difficult for people to define are rendered intelligible by applying the analogy of *dār* (house or social unit). For example, the life of this world, *dār ad-dunyā*, which has the connotation of being an inferior abode, is called *dār al-fanā* (The house of evanescence). The otherworld (*al-ākhirah*) is depicted as *dār al-baqā'*, or "the everlasting abode." Between these two worlds exists the world of the tomb, *'ālam al-qabr*, which marks the transition between them.[5] Here reside deceased persons and other creatures, visible or invisible, awaiting the day of resurrection.

Death (*al-maut*) has meanings related to the body (*jasad*, *jism*, or *badan*) and to the soul or spirit (*rūḥ*). The first meaning is related to the condition of the person's body when the breath[6] ceases and the soul departs from it. The body is then described as being motionless or lifeless, *lā ḥayāt* or *lā rūḥ fīh*. The moment at which a person dies is called *ṭulū' ar-rūḥ*, or "the rising of the soul." If the death itself is protracted, it is metaphorically described in terms of the sweetness and dearness of the soul, *ḥalāwat ar-rūḥ*. This phrase also refers to the attachment of the dying person to his or her soul. In the second meaning, death is referred to as a kind of temporal and spatial passage from this world to the otherworld, *kharaj min dār addunyā ilā dār l 'ākhīra*, or, using the *fallāḥīn*'s words, a passage from one *dār* (house) to the other.

This second meaning of death plays a profound part in the villagers' structure of the cosmos or universe. Death is a transition from this visible worldly abode (*dār ad-dunyā*) to the hereafter or otherworldly house (*dār al-ākhirah*), which belongs to *'ālam al-ghaib*, the concealed and unknowable world. In other words, between the present world and the world to come, the world of the tomb (*'ālam al-qabr*) is temporally and spatially located. This world is depicted as a liminal or transitional stage followed by resurrection or the Day of Judgment, *yaum addīn*.

It is interesting to understand how villagers relate the world of death in the tomb to the visible and invisible worlds. Death is related to both the body and soul of a person. After death, the material body is considered impure as it decays and ultimately turns to dust (*turāb*). In funeral scenarios as well as in their daily lives, villagers say, "From dust we are created and to dust we must return." One of the Arabic names for the tomb is *turba*, which stems from the word *turāb*. On the other hand, death is sacred in so far as it is associated with the soul that belongs to *ʿālam al-ghaib* or the invisible and concealed world known only to Allah. The soul (*rūḥ*) is known as a divine secret,[7] *sirr ilāhī*. People understand that the nature of the soul is beyond comprehension, yet they seek understanding through personal experience such as dreams as well as through interpreting the implicit meanings of the divine verses of the *Qur'an*.

The concept of soul, the invisible force, plays a significant role in villagers' cosmological imagery and religious thought. The soul, for instance, exists in corporeal form in this present life, in noncorporeal form in the tomb (*barzakh*), and again in corporeal form, though different from that of this worldly life, in the hereafter.[8] The relationship between soul and body triggers cosmic imagery that is integrated with the image of heaven or macrocosm both in this life and the other life. The soul is the essence (*jawhar*) or inward (*bāṭin*) part of a person, while the body is the outward (*ẓāhir*) appearance. As opposed to the body, which is visible, material, mortal, earthly, dark, and profane, the soul is invisible, immaterial, immortal, heavenly, light, and sacred. (See chapter 4.) These statements imply the following hierarchical oppositions: invisible/visible, soul/body, inward/outward, essence/appearance, immaterial/material, immortal/mortal, heavenly/earthly, light/dark, and sacred/profane. Both the visible and invisible worlds are created by God. So too is death, by which the soul becomes separated from the body. What is implicit here is a set of symbolic hierarchical oppositions between the Creator (Allah) and the created as represented in this visible world and the other invisible world between which death serves as a mediator (see figure 6.1).

Although the fate of dead persons in the tomb, or at the Day of Judgment, is unknown, some specific signs are used to indicate whether or not the dead are at peace in the grave. These signs, associated with certain temporal and spatial qualities, are understood within the spiritual and sacred domains of the cosmos. A person who dies at dawn, *sāʿat al-fajr* (*al-fajrīyah*), is thought to be a good and pious Muslim. Those who die at that time are permitted to be buried on the same day. In contrast to Western culture, where it may take between three and seven days to prepare the deceased for actual burial (considering the process of embalming and viewing the body), it is most honorable for the Muslim to be buried immediately after death, *ikrām al-mayyit dafnahu*. Because of the medical examination and other government proce-

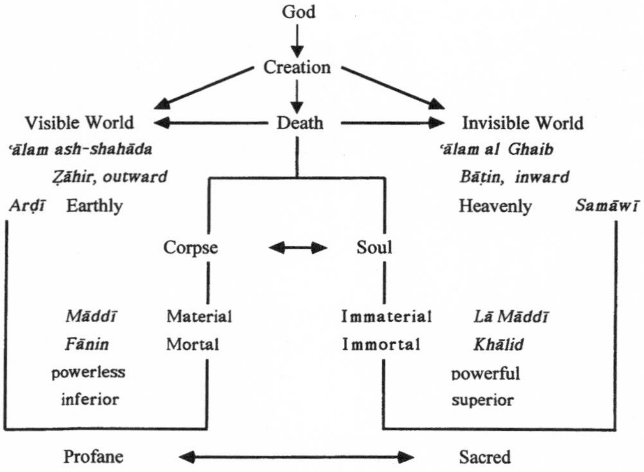

FIGURE 6.1 The relation of death to visible and invisible worlds as conceived by Egyptian villagers.

dures necessary for obtaining a permit of burial, people who die at noon or later in the afternoon cannot be buried on the same day, but are on the next. Villagers resent these complicated and bureaucratic procedures. It happened that an old man died shortly after noontime and his relatives insisted on burying him the same day. They actually hurried to the local medical unit and appealed to the doctor to examine the corpse. The doctor, under pressure, did not hesitate and gave them the permit for burying the corpse immediately after conducting the necessary procedures. It is believed that the soul of the dead resides in the house as long as the corpse remains there. During the first night, known as the "night of loneliness" (*lailat al-wiḥdah*), the dead person's soul seeks temporary reunion with the body in order to be examined by the angels of the tomb. This unity, however, cannot be accomplished until the dead person is buried in the tomb. The night of loneliness signifies the actual separation of the deceased from the social world when he or she alone faces the invisible angels who question his or her faith.

Those who die on the days and months connected with Islamic values are believed to show *karāmah*, grace and honor. For instance, it is a sign of blessing for someone to die on Monday, because the Prophet Muhammad died on that day. Friday, the holy day of Muslims, is also a blessed day from the fact that a significant number within the congregation participate in the burial prayer.

The holy month of Ramadan, especially the last ten days, is the most blessed month of all for the dead. People who show great concern for their afterlife express their wish to die on *lailat al-qadr*, the holy night of the twenty-seventh of Ramadan, on which the *Qur'an* was revealed to the Prophet. It is believed that if a person dies on that night, which is more valuable than a thousand months, he or she will reside in peace both in the grave and in paradise. The quality of being blessed is also attributed to people who die in the month of Rajab, because of the midnight journey of the Prophet Muhammad to the sacred Mosque and to the seventh heaven, *lailat al-isrā' wa al-mi'rāj*. Also, the night of the middle (*an-niṣf*) of *Sha'bān* is highly honored by Muslims. On that night, people's recorded deeds are taken up and shown to Allah, who promises to have mercy on the repentant and pious. It is also socially and religiously meaningful when a person dies in his own house surrounded by his family members, or when he dies during a Muslim holiday or other occasion when a large number of Muslims congregate together. It is believed that the deceased people are blessed on such occasions because of the large number of people who visit and pray for their souls.

Villagers differentiate among four major categories of death: *martyrdom*, *natural death*, *unnatural death*, and *suicide*. These classifications embody certain significant features of the cosmos to which people's souls are ascribed after death. First is *martyrdom*, *al-istishhād*. Following the *Qu'ran* and Islamic tradition, villagers maintain that martyrs are not dead but alive and enjoy the prominent status of being close to Allah. The martyr (*shahīd*) is considered *mujāhid* (related to the concept of *jihād*, holy war), referring to the one who dies defending his religion, country, honor, and property. Moreover, as a mark of blessing, the martyr does not have a ghost (*'ifrīt*) and is freed from the spiritual examination by the angels of the tomb to which all the dead are subject. To be a martyr is considered a sign of eminent standing as well as having God's blessing.

Normal or *ordinary death*, *al-maut aṭ-ṭabī'ī*, results from natural causes such as sickness or aging. When a person dies naturally, peasants say "*māt mautat rabbuh*," which literally means that he died according to his Lord's way. The dead person has a ghost, but the ghost (or *'ifrīt*) is believed to be inactive and harmless. However, not all of those who die naturally have ghosts. Prophets and highly ranked saints who died of natural causes do not have ghosts and their bodies are believed to remain in fine condition after death.

The person who dies by *unnatural* or *violent means*, on the other hand, is believed to have an active and dangerous *'ifrīt* that wanders the earth, causing harm to people. The *'ifrīt* of such a person takes the shape or form of that person exactly as at the moment of death. For example, if a person dies by decapitation, the *'ifrīt* will appear with the head separated from the body. Two demands are made by the soul of such a person: first, it demands to be buried; and second, it seeks vengeance on the killer either through a relative or its

TABLE 6.1

Categories of Death and Beliefs Regarding the Soul, Ghost, and Corpse

Martyrdom	*Natural death*	*Unnatural death*	*Suicide*
no examination in the tomb	examination in the tomb	examination in the tomb	examination in the tomb
no *'ifrīt* (ghost)	nonactive ghost	dangerous ghost	dangerous ghost
the soul enjoys being close to Allah	the soul will be in or out of heaven	the soul will be in or out of heaven	the soul will be out of heaven
alive, the corpse does not decay	the corpse decays	the corpse decays	the corpse decays

ghost. The following is a story from the village. There was a young man who drowned in a canal while he was swimming. A large number of men searched all night for the corpse, shouting loudly, "O, you who wants to be buried turn up" (*yā ṭālib ad-dafnah ḥauuid*) and "If you seek to be buried, appear or manifest yourself" (*idhā kunt ṭālib ad-dafnah iẓhar*). After finding the corpse, the crowd expressed their gratitude to God. Although the bereaved relatives of the dead man were in grief, they showed signs of relief when the corpse was found and buried. When evidence disclosing the mysterious cause of a murdered person is found, it is taken to be a sign of justice from the unseen world. In such cases, people say *'alā rās* (*rā's*) *al-gatīl gandīl*, which metaphorically means that at the dead person's head is a lamp guiding people toward the corpse and toward the cause of death.

Suicide, *al-intiḥār*, as a form of death has never occurred in the village.[9] The person who commits suicide is considered *kāfir*, an atheist or unbeliever, and is described as one who has "lost both this worldly life and the afterlife," *khasar ad-dunyā wa al-ākhirah*. Villagers believe that the one who commits suicide, like a killed person, has an active and dangerous *'ifrīt* that can harm people. Table 6.1 lists the categories and beliefs of death.

The World of the Tomb: A Link between This World and the Otherworld

The world of the tomb is an integral and inseparable part of the villagers' cosmic and religious beliefs as well as of their social life. The location of the cemetery as well as the physical structure of the tomb itself indicates the important place death occupies in villagers' cosmology. The cemetery is located southeast of the village, a location that is associated in part with the *qiblah* (the direction toward which Muslims turn in praying).[10] Houses surround the cemetery on all sides except the north, where there are two schools, a preliminary school and a preparatory school. There is no fence around the cemetery to separate it from the surrounding houses and schools. West of the cemetery there is the shrine of the saint Sidī Ghānim, whose descendants constitute a *DĀR* or kin group in the village. There is a narrow road that runs through the center of the cemetery. It is common to see the *fallāḥīn* take their animals to the fields by using this road. Through their actions, peasants show great respect for the tombs and for the dead who are believed to be conscious within them. When approaching the cemetery, for example, it is not uncommon for a *fallāḥ* to raise his right hand at the level of his head and salute the dead, saying, "Peace on you, O nation of Islam" or "Peace on you, O nation of 'there is no God but Allah'" (*as-salām ʿalaykum yā ummat lā ilāh illā Allah*). People who walk near the cemetery address the dead by saying "*antum as-sābiqūn wa naḥnu al-lāḥiqūn*" (You are the predecessors and we are the followers). They also often recite the *Fātiḥah*, the opening chapter of the *Qur'an*, on behalf of the dead.

The physical structure of the tomb reflects some significant domains of the cosmos, the heaven, the earth, and the underworld. The upper part of the grave takes the shape of a vault or arch, *qabw*. The walls lie on the ground just as the cosmic arch of the heaven, metaphorically speaking, lies down on the earth. The arched or vaulted shape of the sky and the course of the sun (from east to west) are reflected in the structure of tombs as well as in burial rituals. The grave is built on a rectangular spot coinciding with the cardinal points. The length of the grave is about two-and-a-half meters, the width is about one meter, and the height is about two meters, with one of them being dug underground. The length of the tomb runs in an east–west direction; the corpse, as mentioned earlier, is laid in the same direction in the tomb. The entrance of the grave faces east.

The saint's tomb is structured in the same way, with only two differences: The arch or dome of the saint's tomb does not surround the corpse directly as in the case of ordinary tombs. The dome is built upon another building that contains the saint's shrine, which is protected by metal bars. A green sheet of cloth with calligraphy indicating the two Muslim testimonies ("There is no God but Allah and Muhammad is His messenger") covers the shrine. Also, the entrance of the saint's shrine takes the shape of an arch. On the top of the dome there is a pole to which a metal or wooden crescent facing east is attached.[11]

The tomb, sociologically speaking, is a symbol embodying people's concepts of kinship, including those of descent and affinity. It is a sign of blessing and honor as well as a symbol of solidarity that the ancestors of one *DĀR*, descent group (or *Dār*, extended family, or *dār*, nuclear family) are buried together in a tomb. In other words, all members of a *DĀR* (including wives who before marriage belonged to other *DĀR*s and who kept the names of their original *DĀR*s) belong to that *DĀR* not only in this life but also after death. For example, if the dead person is a male, he is buried in the tomb of his family or descent group. If the deceased is an unmarried woman, she is buried in the grave of her father's descent group. But if she is married, she is buried in the tomb that belongs to her husband's *DĀR*. Generally, relatives or members of one family emphasize being buried in one tomb, believing that at resurrection it is easy for them to recognize one another. Married people are more concerned with this point than are other people, because they believe that in the otherworldly *dār* they will continue their marital life.

Family members metaphorically use the phrase the "tomb's bones," *ʿaḍm* (*ʿaẓm*) *at-turbah*, to mean their own ancestors' bones. The tomb's bones are associated with masculinity as well as with a patrilineal principle organizing kinship and social ties. This metaphor is so powerful that when a villager, for instance, tries to settle a fight between members of his family, he asks them to stop fighting for the sake of their tomb's bones. Also, in their daily life, the *fallāḥīn* swear by the "tomb's bones" to attest to the truthfulness of what they say. If the tomb's bones are correlated with masculinity and patriarchy, the tomb itself is associated with femininity and motherhood. It is worth noting that villagers compare the tomb with the womb and the condition of the dead person with that of a newly born child, accentuating the blood relationships associated with both. The Arabic word *raḥim* (womb or uterus, in which life is generated) implies meanings of mercy as well as uterine relationships (el-Aswad 1987, 1988). If people are identified in this world through patrilineal affiliation, they will be identified on the Day of Judgment not through the names of their fathers nor patrilineal ancestors, but through their mothers'.

Also, this Arabic word *raḥim* is related to the word *raḥma*, which means "mercy" as well as to the "offerings" distributed by women in the cemetery on behalf of the deceased's soul. *Ṣilat arraḥim* is a phrase used in contexts where people wish to express their concern for maintaining their kinship relationships. *Ṣilat arraḥim* simply means keeping in touch with relatives through local means of communication, of which visitation or face-to-face bonds are the most significant. A dead person is called *marḥūm* (fem. *marḥūma*), implying the sincere hope that God will bestow His mercy on him or her. Using metaphorical analogies, villagers maintain that as a woman gives birth once each year, so the tomb can be opened only after one year has passed since the last burial. Moreover, both the newly born child and the dead person are naked and wrapped in cloth. For purposes of condolence, the *fallāḥīn* say, "As a person enters this life naked, so he leaves naked." Nakedness here also means having no property. As the newly born child enters this life with no property, so the deceased leaves this world and enters the otherworld. It is worth noting that a poor person who owns nothing is called *ʿuryān*, which means "naked." The intense moment at which a woman delivers a child is analogous to the moments when the corpse is brought from the house to be buried. Distressed female relatives, specifically the mother, sisters, daughters, and wife of the deceased, raise their arms, wail, and smite their cheeks with both hands. They also crouch, dance, and hop, straddling or keeping their legs widely apart with their arms outstretched. Women ease these frantic actions immediately after the corpse has been taken from the house to the grave.

Women's relationships with the cemetery are regulated according to normal and abnormal conditions. One of the abnormal cases within the logic of possibility is related to barrenness. A childless woman (*ʿāqir*), who is socially dead and occupies a marginal role in the household, is threatened by her husband as well as by her mother-in-law (*ḥamah*) of divorce. She cannot participate in the social and sacred process of inhabiting the universe (*tʿamīr al-kaun*) or inhabiting the house (*tʿamīr addār*). A desperate sterile woman is willing to do whatever possible in order to become pregnant. One of the most common folk means for helping a childless woman to conceive is to pay a visit to the cemetery in the full dark of night, with the complete absence of the moon. Superficially, this action implies a belief that the intense and deadly fear of being exposed to the cemetery alone in the dark might result in the possibility of conceiving. By being within the circle of the dead, a physically barren and socially dead woman, who is as fruitless and unproductive as the barren land (*bāirah*), is believed to be able to conceive. While in the graveyard, to lessen her fear and shield herself with the hope of fertility and reproduction, which is not impossible for God, the barren woman repeatedly recites a widely quoted verse of the *Qur'an*, "*yukhriju al ḥayy min al-mayyitt wa yukhriju al-mayyit min al-ḥayy*" (O He [God] brings the living out from the dead and brings the dead out from the living). At a deeper level, however, this action implies a symbolic and analogical relationship between the womb and the grave, denoting the cosmic dynamics of birth and rebirth, or fertility and resurrection within which the possibility of conceiving becomes confirmed. In this context, the symbolic makes the impossible *possible*. Barrenness is akin to death. But death itself is a threshold to resurrection. The idea here is that through the notion of unknowable and mysterious spheres of the cosmos, it is very possible for a thing to be produced, or reproduced by its contrary.

In a normal case, however, the situation is completely different. Taboos and restrictions disassociate women from anything related to the cemetery.

Once a woman delivers a child, she cannot have direct or indirect contact with the dead for at least one month. During the period of thirty days following delivery, a mother is not allowed to see anyone who has just come from the cemetery or who is carrying raw meat. Raw meat symbolizes a lifeless body or corpse. The violation of this taboo threatens the woman with what is locally known as *al-mushāhara*, "being exposed"—meaning the sterility or barrenness that could strike any woman who is exposed to taboos during the first month following delivery.[12] Within this context, the idea is that death opposes life and threatens the new and vulnerable conditions of giving birth.

Death rituals are dealt with here as providing conspicuous clues to villagers' relationships with the dead as well as with one another. Through death rituals, people displace grief and sorrow with the assertion of resurrection and eternal life.[13] Burial rituals, together with prayers, invocations, recitations of the *Qur'an*, and the distribution of food and alms to the poor are considered to be bonds that link the present world with the hereafter. The fate of the dead person in both the tomb and the hereafter is one of the basic concerns of his or her kin. Although the deceased's survivors believe that he or she will be examined according to the deeds of his or her worldly life, they observe and perform such ritual practices as prayers, invocations, recitations of the *Qur'an*, and distribution of food and alms to the poor in order to aid the soul in its endeavor to be accepted by Allah. Villagers show respect for death through the repeatedly discursive uttering of "*al-maut ḥaqq*," which means "Death is true, real, or just." The recitation of the *Qur'an* is expressive of the mourners' piety as well as of their serious concern for the dead person. Villagers consider reciting chapters from the *Qur'an* as spiritual food, *ghadāʿ* (*ghidhāʾ*) *rūḥī*, for the deceased. This spiritual food is a divine means that helps the dead pass the tomb's examination and invokes Allah to have mercy on them.[14]

After burial, the soul is restored to the body for a short time. The deceased is believed to sit up in the grave to be examined by *Nākir* and *Nakīr* (or *Munkar*), the two angels of the tomb.[15] The image of these angels is either kind or dreadful, depending on the deeds and moral or religious qualities of the deceased. They ask about the person's religion, God, prophet, and book. If the deceased passes the religious exam (by responding Islam, Allah, Muhammad, and *Qur'an*, respectively), the angels reassure him or her by saying, "Sleep in peace until the final judgment of Allah." Then the soul departs the body and ascends to heaven where it is received by the good souls of Muslim friends, relatives, and angels. If the deceased fails the examination by saying something that contradicts the principles and teachings of Islam, the two angels threaten him or her with punishment. The soul departs the body, but it is not allowed to ascend. There is a strong conviction among people that ani-

TABLE 6.2

THE REVERSED ROLES OF HOSTS AND GUESTS IN RURAL EGYPTIAN COMMUNITIES

	Hosts	*Guests*
Daily life	Offer food and other services	Receive food and other services
Death rituals	Receive food and other services	Offer food and other services

mals and birds hear the cries of the dead being tormented in the grave. The *fallāḥīn* believe that heavens' gates are closed and armed with powerful angels that keep erring souls away.

Meanwhile, the soul maintains contact with its corpse, as well as with relatives, friends, and enemies by appearing to them in their dreams. It is also believed that the deceased has stronger or extraordinary senses, because now the soul is freed from the prison of the body. The deceased knows who washed his or her body, who prepared and attended burial and funeral rituals, who recited verses or chapters from the *Qur'an* on his or her behalf, and who visited his or her tomb, for example.

Death rituals are an effective means of strengthening social cohesion (Van Gennep 1960, 164). By participating in death rituals, villagers emphasize not only the unity of kinship, but also the unity or *communitas* (Turner 1969) of the village as a whole. A significant example of this unity is manifested in the symbolic reversal roles of hosts (mourners) and guests. Hosts usually offer guests food and other services. And the guests, in turn, show respect and appreciation to hosts for their hospitality. In death rituals, the situation is reversed. Mourners remain in their houses, behaving not as hosts but as guests. They receive food (sometimes money) and other services from their comforters. The food served at the mourning ritual is prepared and cooked by condolers (el-Aswad 1987) (see table 6.2).

At mealtime, for instance, female relatives, friends, and neighbors carry large round trays of food, *ṣawānī* (sing. *ṣaniyya*), to the family of the deceased. The women stand in line in front of the *mandarah*, or guest house, assigned specifically for males, waiting for a signal from one of the oldest guests to enter. Each places the tray on the ground, which has been covered with straw mats, in front of her immediate male relative (father, brother, husband, or son). After almost an hour, the women, without talking, return to take back the empty trays. Food is also served to bereaved women inside their houses. Mourners take notice of who comes and who does not. They also observe the amount of food, money, or services offered by the guests, who are playing the role of hosts. Condolers compete to offer mourners and their visitors trays (*ṣawānī*) full of food. The significance here is that the communication between hosts and guests, which is associated with certain roles, expectations, and meanings and requires specific structural relationships among people within the context of their daily activities, has different meanings and becomes associated with different expectations within the social contexts surrounding death. These two contexts of death and normal life interface and exercise a profound impact on people's thought and action.

There are two important days for observing mourning and memorial rituals: the Little Thursday, *al-khamis aṣ-ṣghir* (the first Thursday following the death), and the Great Thursday, *al-khamis al-kabir* (the second Thursday following the death). On the Little Thursday, bereaved women visit the grave in the very early morning, taking with them bread, rolls (*guraṣ*), and fruits. They distribute food, *raḥmah* (which means "mercy"), to poor people and *fuqahā* (reciters of the *Qur'an*), who gather around the grave waiting for gifts and offerings. Symbolically, women continue practicing their roles of nourishment by offering material food for spiritual purposes. Poor people eat this food, which will be converted to spiritual offerings or merits, *ḥasanāt* (sing. *ḥasanah*), for the dead. On the Great Thursday the same mourning rite is repeated, but on a larger scale.

Signs of the End of the World

In their discourse regarding both this world and the world to come, villagers are concerned with three major events: the end of this world (*nihāyat al-ʿālam*), the period in which the cosmos remains dead or inactive (*al-barzakh*), and the day of resurrection (*yaum al-qiyāmah*). The underlying theme here is that both the individual and the universe partake in the process of transition from one stage to another until they reach the final eternal stage.

Although the *hour*, *sasāʿah*, or end of this world is concealed, there are signs indicating its coming. These signs are believed to belong to the unknowable and invisible world (*ʿālam al-ghaib*) from which visible or concrete messages are sent to people to be interpreted. Peasants' conceptualization and expectation of the signs of macrocosmic death (*ʿalāmāt as-sāʿah*) are consistent with those mentioned in the *Qur'an* and *Ḥadīth* (or Islamic tradition).[16] Underlying villagers' conceptions of the signs of the *hour* are two basic themes: corrupted social cosmology indicating moral, spiritual, and social disintegration, and cosmic reversal. The signs are further classified into those that have already appeared, and those that will occur in the future.

One of the most feared indicators of the corruption of the social cosmology (*fasād al kaun*) is the reversal of men's and women's values and roles. Such indicators are manifested when women wear clothes that uncover their bodies to display attractive physical attributes[17] (*mafātin*) and when they attempt to lead society and compete with men for the domination of outside activities and opportunities. In this context, it is not uncommon to hear a husband, commenting on his wife's argument that questions his leadership, exclaim, "Has the afterlife [resurrection] drawn near?" (*hiya al-ākhirah* [*al-qiyāmah*] *qarrabit?*).

The building of skyscrapers or tall buildings (*tat āwul fī al-bunyān*) by Bedouins (*aʿrāb*) is also viewed as a sign of the nearness of the *hour*. These buildings are associated not with the concept of inhabitation (*ʿamār*), but rather with notions of commodity, consumerism, exploitation, individuality, arrogance, self-interest, and alienation. A further sign are the feelings of bewilderment and alienation experienced by Muslims in Muslim countries. Migrants returning from living in Arab Gulf countries expressed their disappointing experience not of being separated from their families and homes, but of their feelings of inferiority, marginality, and alienation in the hosting countries whose governments and institutions discriminatingly offered Western expatriates more benefits and privileges than those offered Arab Muslims. They also felt stressed and worried that their employment contracts would be terminated and that they would be replaced by cheaper Asian laborers. Moreover, some migrants were victims of false sponsors and organizations that charged them a considerable amount of money for forged labor contracts and black-market visas. Villagers sum up their negative experience with the folk saying, "*man kharag min dāru yanggal migdāru*" (Who goes away from his home will lose his dignity).

Another conflicting and confusing practice that aggravates the feeling of alienation among Muslim migrants in the Arab Gulf countries is the competition between the powerful Western banks and the Islamic banks, which are supposed to be conducting business compatible with Islamic principles. These Islamic banks, in turn, become involved in economic operations and investment outside the Arab Gulf countries. This alienation of Muslims and their wealth is interpreted as a sign of the alienation of Islam (*gharīb fī dārihi*), which in turn is a sign of the nearness of the end of the world. "Those who nowadays hold their religion firmly," a local religious leader affirms, "are like those who hold glowing live coal."[18]

Politically and globally, corruption manifests itself in the dominating forces that seek to replace God through controlling, governing, and manipulating the entire world. Regionally, the same logic of domination and manipulation is reflected in the event that shocked the Muslim world: That a Muslim country invaded and occupied another Muslim country whose liberation, ironically, was essentially secured by Western forces. These events are commented on not merely in political terms, but also in religious terms as being either God's revenge or a sign of the nearness of the annihilation of the world.[19] War, disease, famine, and moral decline are perceived to be consequences of the aggressive global system.

Social disorder, as conceived by villagers, is associated with the West, which is the source of destructive innovations, *al-bida*ʿ. Because of useless or meaningless innovations, material abundance, and vanities of this world (*zakhārif ad-dunyā*), the destructive ignorance of heathens (*jāhliyya*) will spread over the world. This is the era or time of Abu Jahl, a malicious historical figure who antagonized the Prophet Muhammad, used as a metaphor denoting ignorance in which people who possess false knowledge claim that they possess the true one.[20] By ignorance and false knowledge, people mean the use of science and technology for destructive purposes as well as the lack of moral and spiritual values. Moral and religious values and principles are innately or potentially existent and hidden in people. These values and principles are the innate or natural disposition (*fiṭrah*) given to all people by God. When people neglect these values and go astray, Allah will send an animal (*dābbah*) to lead people towards the right way. Not only is the collapse of the social code and moral order associated with the West, but so is the cosmological destruction. One of the cosmic signs of the nearness of the end of the world will be when the sun rises from the west and sets in the east, after which will follow blackness.

After the completion of the signs of the *hour*, Allah will order *Isrāfīl*, the angel of the trumpet, to blow the first blast at which the universe and all its creatures will die except those preserved by God. The microcosmic death of those who die individually and wait in the *micro-barzakh* before the end of the world will be incorporated in the macrocosmic death. *Isrāfīl*, after being resurrected, will blow the second blast and all creatures will rise and gather before God for the Final Judgment. The period between the first and second blasts is considered to be a collective transitional period or *macro-barzakh*. The main point here is that both the individual and the entire universe partake in the same transformation, moving from this present and transitory world to the final and eternal world, passing through the liminal world of the *barzakh*. To put it differently, life, death, and resurrection are stages that both the cosmos and the individual experience (see figure 6.2).

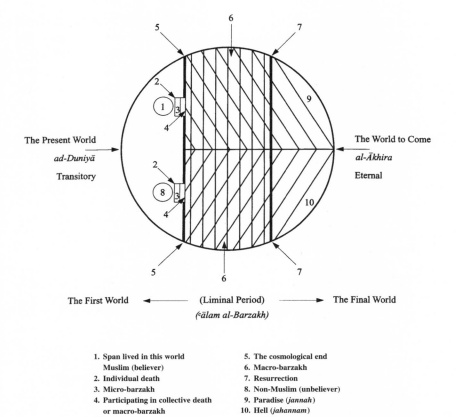

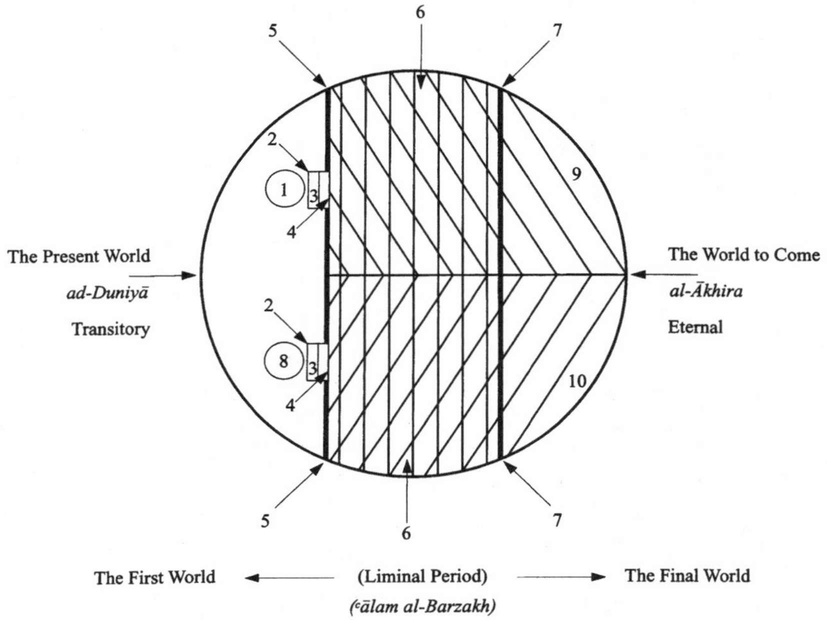

1. **Span lived in this world Muslim (believer)**
2. **Individual death**
3. **Micro-barzakh**
4. **Participating in collective death or macro-barzakh**
5. **The cosmological end**
6. **Macro-barzakh**
7. **Resurrection**
8. **Non-Muslim (unbeliever)**
9. **Paradise (*jannah*)**
10. **Hell (*jahannam*)**

FIGURE **6.2** The connection of the three worlds (the present world, the world of the tomb, and the world to come) as viewed by Egyptian villagers.

The World to Come: Belief and Imagery

In the afterlife, nothing will be hidden, concealed, secret, or invisible. Creatures belonging to different unseen realms in the present world will be visible on the Day of Judgment. On the day of reckoning God will reveal Himself to all creatures. However, believers and unbelievers will see him differently. For believers and pious people God will reveal himself as a merciful and loving light, while for atheists and evildoers He will appear as a blazing light, harming their eyes and bodies. When the imaginary is sanctified through association with an unquestionable and transcendental reality, it becomes not just an idea or ideology, but is as real as a perceptible object. The "imaginary is the birthplace of all beliefs, and at the same time the origin of the distinction between the sacred and the profane" (Godelier 1999, 27).

The vivid and sensory images peasants hold of the things and events that will exist in the afterlife are impossible for an outsider to capture without understanding the power of imagination. To grasp what villagers try to describe, it might be helpful to quote Ibn al-ʿArabi's statement wherein he says that the

> impossible is imagined as a sensory thing and it comes into existence in the hereafter, or wherever God desires, as a sensory thing. That is why this takes place in the "here-after" (*al-ākhira*) not the "here-before" (*al-ūlā*), for imagination stands in a degree posterior to sense perception, since it takes the forms with which it clothes the impossible and other things from sense perception. Hence, whatever it is found, it is only found in the "here-after," or [the] corporeal body exists simultaneously in two places. Just as this is imagined here, so it happens likewise in sense perception in the hereafter. (Chittick 1989, 124)

These images are continuously and repeatedly vivified in both public and private scenarios.

Upon resurrection, people's bodies and souls will be reunited. This reunion is necessary both for the natural conditions of the person and for the final examination or judgment that will include psychological and physical sanctions.[21] The deeds (*aʿmāl*) or actions people do in this worldly life, as well as their bodily organs (*aʿḍāʾ*), will speak or converse in the afterlife. Deeds will be personified in such a way that the good deed (*ʿamal ṣāliḥ*) of a pious or good Muslim will be presented as a kind, shining, and loving person. Conversely, an ugly and terrible image will appear to the evildoer, declaring to be his evil or bad deed, *ʿamal ghair ṣāliḥ*. People' eyes, tongues, hands, and so on will also be witness to their actions in the worldly life. Again, the underlying theme here is that the hidden, covered, and secret actions people perform in the present world will be uncovered and visible in the afterlife.

The afterlife (*dār al-ākhira*) is itself divided into two eternal *dārs*: paradise (*jannah*) and hell (*jahannam*). Villagers, affected by Islamic tradition, have developed unique and significant images of the nature of both paradise and hell. This monumental or grand picture, however, is related to the basic theme of visible/invisible. Paradise and hell are expressed in terms of light (*nūr*) and fire (*nār*), respectively. In the garden one sees what he never saw before and hears what he never heard before, *yajid mā lā ʾayn raʾat wa lāʾ udhunun samaʿat*. In paradise, as opposed to this worldly life, people's thoughts and desires will not be hidden or unknown to other people. Nevertheless, this does not mean that people will read or know one another's thoughts and intentions. Rather, people's thoughts and wishes will be objectified or transformed into perceptible objects. In other words, whatever people in paradise think of, imagine, or want, it will be instantly present in a concrete or tangible form. For example, when a good believer (*mu'min*) desires a specific kind of food, it instantaneously appears in front of him.[22] Another example is that if a Muslim in paradise thinks of a friend or companion, he will find or see him or her instantly or at that moment. Moreover, in the world to come, abstract ideas such as beauty, justice, and goodness are rendered concrete. The theme of the visibility of thoughts and things is profoundly reflected in the description of the *ḥūrī*, black-eyed virgins of paradise. Pious men are promised to be companions to the *ḥūrī* (sing. *ḥūrīyah*), who are created of light. The *ḥūrīyah*'s skin, flesh, and bones are so transparent (*shaffāf*) that a person can see the water running through her throat as she drinks, and also the marrow (*nukhā*ʿ) of her leg.

The visibility of thoughts and desires is applicable to all people in the afterlife. Nevertheless, the unbelievers differ from believers in that when they envision or desire something, they see it but cannot have it. For example, if a *mushrik* (polytheist, unbeliever) desires water while being tortured and thirsty in hell, the water appears in front of him or close to his mouth but he cannot drink it.

Conclusion

This study has examined the cosmology of rural Egypt by showing how ordinary people view their lives in relation to its divine, sacred, profane, and secular spheres. Folk cosmology is profoundly concerned with the multiple or triple universe, which includes the present world, the world of the tomb, and the world to come. Life, death, and afterlife constitute an inseparable totality—it is unconceivable to focus on one world or domain at the exclusion of the others. To concentrate on this world as the sole visible and objective reality toward which rational and secular modes of thought and action are oriented is to rupture the intricate weaving of the multiplicity and sanctity of the cosmos. The study has argued that people's daily practices, death rituals, and beliefs concerning the world to come cannot be clearly comprehended without reference to the relationship between the invisible (divine, spiritual) and the visible (secular, material). Moreover, cosmological concepts and beliefs and death rituals held and performed by peasants are, in many significant aspects, consistent with the tenets of Islam.

The strength of folk cosmology lies not only in its consistency with the tenets of Islam, but also in the profound antithesis of the unseen/seen or invisible/visible through which the divine or the spiritual is protected from being replaced or compromised by the secular. Social and cosmological corruption is viewed as a sign of the end of this world, that will be followed by a purely divine and everlasting world in which righteous people, who suffer in this life, will never suffer again.

The universe and the person contain visible and invisible domains. Of these components or constituents, however, the invisible is the most significant. In so far as the person is concerned, the soul, which is invisible, immaterial, and immortal, is the link between the heaven (above) and the earthly body (below). As far as the universe as a whole is concerned, *al-ghaib*, the invisible or unseen domain, gives meaning to the visible world, *ʿālam ash-shahādah* or *aẓ-ẓāhir*. In this life and through the powerfulness of the concealed and unseen, accentuating ongoing anticipations and expectations, people live in a world of interminable possibilities. In the afterlife, the concealed will cease being unseen. What is invisible, unseen, and imperceptible in this worldly life will be visible and perceptible in the afterlife—nothing will be hidden, invisible, or secret.

Notes

1. Gellner (1987, 14–15) defines modernity as

> a post-traditional order [that refers to] the institutions and modes of behavior established first of all in post-feudal Europe, but which in the twentieth century increasingly have become world-historical in their impact. "Modernity" can be understood as roughly equivalent to "the industrialized world," so long as it be recognized that industrialism is not its only institutional dimension. . . . A second dimension is capitalism, where this term means a system of commodity production involving both competitive product markets and the commodification of labor power.

2. Peasants' rational actions that are based on calculation have been addressed extensively by Popkins (1979).

3. It must be noted that the movements of "re-Islamization" that started in Egypt in the mid-1970s came "mainly 'from below,' from the network of mosques and pietist associations whose tendrils were spreading through civil society" (Kepel 1994, 23).

4. Concerning the issue of repentance, there is a local public debate concerning the phenomenon that has been occurring since the 1980s, indicating a growing trend among some famous female artists and entertainers—including belly dancers—to cover or veil themselves according to Islamic fashion. Although there is no unified agreement among villagers about the motivation behind the adoption of the Islamic dress by famous stars, they were optimistic that these stars might attract unveiled women to follow their example. Abu-Lughod (1998b, 249) points out that like the majority of Egyptian women, these so-called repentant stars have adopted the new modest Islamic dress as part of what they conceive as their religious awakening. However, because "they are such well-known figures, their actions have been publi-

cized and capitalized on by the Islamists to further legitimize the trend toward women's veiling and to support their call for women's return to the home. Secularists and progressives—those opposed to the veiling as a sign of 'backwardness'—suspiciously accuse these actresses of taking fat salaries from the Islamic groups."

5. John MacDonald provides a series of articles (1964a, b, 1965, 1966a, b) about Islamic eschatology. These studies, however, are commentaries on "*Kitāb Ḥaqā'iq wa' l-Daqā'iq,*" whose materials were collected and written by Abū Layth Samarqandī (d. 373/983).

6. Ancient Egyptians reached a similar idea correlating breath with soul and life as created by God, "Lord of Life, he who lets the throat breathe and gives air to every nose" (Morenz 1973, 182). For further information concerning the relationship between breath and the soul or life, see el-Aswad (1987).

7. People frequently refer to one of the verses of the *Qur'an* that states that "the soul is by command of the Lord" (*Qur'an* 17:85).

8. See Jane I. Smith and Yvonne Y. Haddad (1981) for a detailed discussion of what they classify as *traditionalist*, *modernist*, and *spiritualist* writers who deal with problems of the spirit and life after death. However, their study is little concerned with the role of death rituals in clarifying the concept of spirit or soul as viewed within a Muslim context. See A. S. Tritton's study (1938) that, depending on Islamic literature, describes Muslim funeral customs in early Islam.

9. For further information on suicide in Muslim societies, see Franz Rosenthal (1946, 239–59).

10. See chapter 3 for further discussion of this point.

11. In addition to the shrine located in the cemetery, as mentioned earlier, there are two shrines located one mile west of the village. The entrances of the three shrines, however, all face east.

12. Similar notions related to folk means dealing with women's infertility are found in the urban Egyptian environment (Inhorn 1994). For further information on the folk healing and medicine in Egypt, see Kennedy (1967a, b) and Walker (1934).

13. Bereaved men show, or are expected to show, self-control and endurance. Females of the deceased's family are expected to cry loudly, repeating the name (or title) of the dead person.

14. It is believed that the souls of dead relatives, friends, and neighbors, among others, visit people in their dreams and ask them to do some specific deeds and rituals related to prayers, alms, and other good deeds that are believed necessary for the dead to enjoy the mercy of Allah.

15. According to the *ḥadīth*, the Prophet's tradition, the Prophet said that the grave is either a *ḥufrah*, a ditch similar to that in hell, or a garden like those in paradise (al-Ghazālī 1979, 479).

16. Islamic literature on the signs and events preceding *as-sā'ah*, the *hour* or the end of this world, is extensive. The most commonly agreed-upon signs will be: 1) the appearance of *al-masīḥ ad-Dajjāl*, the false messiah or antichrist, who will lead people astray (*ḍalāl*); 2) the descent of *al-masīḥ*, Jesus, to destroy *ad-Dajjāl*; 3) a period of misery and corruption associated with the appearance of *Yā'jūj* and *Mā'jūj*, or the wicked people; 4) the appearance of the *dābbah*, beast, which will guide people toward the right way; and 5) the sun will rise in the west and set in the east (Smith

and Haddad 1981, 128). Ibn Khaldūn (1981, 272–59) states that before the appearance of the antichrist, the *Mahdī*, a male member from the Prophet's family, will appear and lead the people.

17. Within this context, one understands the cosmological meaning of "covering" women's bodies. Hence the significance of the "Islamic veil" as an enclosure and private space within which Muslim women respectably move has been reassured through Muslim public discourse that goes beyond a Muslim locality to reach global spheres. The affair of "the Islamic veil," which erupted in France during the autumn of 1989, showed how far the networks of re-Islamization "from below" had spread in France (Kepel 1994, 37).

18. Carolyn Fluehr-Lobban (1994, 109) observes the same phenomenon in the Arab Peninsula.

19. This point of view was expressed with reference to the Iraqi invasion of Kuwait. From the villagers' point of view, it is the materialistic greed and self-interest that drove a brother to interrogate, invade, and publicly insult his brother.

20. Compare this simple belief with the argument Anderson makes that the "century of Enlightenment, of rational secularism, brought with it its own modern darkness" (Anderson 1983, 19). Another Western intellectual considers modern thought that is "based on the premise that the world is objectively knowable, and that the knowledge so obtained can be reached absolutely generalized, to have reached a 'final' crisis" (Havel, quoted in Eickelman 2000, 121). The way to solve this dilemma is for the intellectual or politician of the future to trust in "soul, individual spirituality [and] in his own subjectivity as his principal link with the subjectivity of the world" (Havel, quoted in Eickelman 2000, 122).

21. Islamic literature dealing with the Day of Judgment is extensive. However, for a comprehensive view, see Sayyid Quṭb's study (1961) of *yaum al-qiyāmah*, the Day of Resurrection, which is based on interpretations of some specific chapters from the *Qur'an*. See also John MacDonald (1966a, b).

22. Ibn Qayyim al-Jawzīyah (1978, 184) mentions one of the Prophet's *ḥadīth* that states that when a believer or Muslim sees a bird and wishes to eat it, the bird instantly falls down roasted between his hands.

7

Conclusion

When tradition is accepted, it is as vivid and as vital to those who accept it as any other part of their action or belief. It is the past in the present but it is as much part of the present as any very recent innovation. (Shils 1981, 13)

"Ordered cosmology" (*kaun munaẓẓam*), a phrase spoken by rural Egyptians in many different contexts, is used with reference to both the macrocosm, *al-kaun al-kabīr* (literally, the grand universe), and the microcosm, *al-kaun aṣ-ṣghīr* (literally, the small universe), or the human being. In this analogical parallel, the inextricable relationship between and the unity of both the universe and individual are embedded.

Both worlds are conceptually divided into the visible or phenomenal and the invisible or supraphenomenal. While the visible represents empirical aspects of life (positivism), the invisible represents cultural or ideological aspects (nonpositivism). The visible, natural, or phenomenal world includes what we would recognize as ecology, environment, climate, and concrete entities (animate and inanimate) that constitute the material conditions of existence. These material conditions are objects of sensory perception. It is this world within which people apply modern, traditional, technical, or secular methods and practices and develop their economic, pragmatic, and materialistic attitudes. This application of modern or traditional technical methods and pragmatic utilization of the world's resources constitute the villagers' secular, mundane, or practical mode of thought. It is also this world in which people make their history and upon which history leaves its marks. Within this framework, in which peasants confirm a sort of secular modernism of their own, it is relevant to assert that this modernity is not to be viewed as being equated with Europe or the culture of positivism, but rather as being "rooted in a dialectic of positivism and non-positivism, a dialectic sustained in different ways by different nation-states" (Gran 1996, 336).

This study highlights the often-neglected potential of folk cosmology for the construction of cultural identity and social memory among rural Egyptians. Cosmic worldviews are not constructed solely by elites or intellectuals, but rather are inherent in the popular imagination and await to be triggered through people's everyday dialectical activities. Folk cosmology is quintessentially a way for people to invest their lives with meaning and the universe in which they live. It is not only with conscious knowledge but also with implicit social and sacred cosmology that this study is concerned. The apparent order of the cosmos can be discerned in terms of the ordering principle or force of the invisible. Beyond the visible world there is a hidden and invisible reality that binds together the multiple apparent and surface entities of the former. This statement explains Egyptian villagers' belief that the known or visible indicates the unknown or invisible. The invisible is reflected in multiple domains of the universe as well as of people's lives. What is visible to the village is explainable in terms of what is invisible but nonetheless present and real. This invisible world refers to what is spiritual, unknowable, imperceptible, and inaccessible in this worldly life. It also refers to the afterlife, including the world of the tomb. The relationship between these two worlds is viewed within three hierarchical levels of encompassment. First, the spiritual domain contrasts with, encompasses, and is superior to the physical or material domain; in other words, what is material, physical, concrete, and perishable is meaningless without that which is immaterial, spiritual, abstract, and eternal.[1] Second, comparing this world with the afterlife, the *fallāḥīn*, influenced by their religious beliefs, consider this worldly life to be inferior to the world to come. The final level of encompassment is that all worlds—visible and invisible, this life and the afterlife—are expressions of the same divine cosmological order in the sense that they are created, dominated, and encompassed by *Allah al-Wāḥid*, the Ultimate One. Egyptian folk cosmology then is a cosmology not of material evolution but of spirituality and divine creation.

The opposition of the visible and the invisible has led us to understand the way people establish links and relationships not only among the person, the society, and the universe, but also between this life and the afterlife, the secular and sacred, the public and private, the outward and inward, and the material and immaterial. In other words, these different and seemingly contradictory domains represented in the oppositions of material/immaterial, body/soul, corporeal/spiritual, mortal/immortal, secular/sacred, and social/private constitute complementary spheres of people's everyday practices. This antithesis between the visible/invisible with other complementary oppositions has shed light on the way villagers conceive and classify the world in which they live.

Although this antithesis has been extensively discussed throughout this study, its multiple and complicated implications can be further rendered. Linguistic evidence shows that the concept of *ghaib*, invisibility or absence, is intrinsically connected with that of *wujūd*, existence. The Arabic word *mawjūd*, a passive form derived from the substantive noun *wujūd*, has two meanings: on the one hand, it means that which is *existent*, *present*, and *in the here and now*. This meaning is used in association with *ʿālam al-ḥawāss*, the world of perception or the senses. The meaning of the phrase, "A person is present [*mawjūd*]" is that he or she is physically in a place at that moment and can be seen, witnessed, or touched. On the other hand, *mawjūd* refers to that which is "existent" but not necessarily present. A person may be existent or alive but not physically present and, therefore, not seen nor witnessed. He is, in other words, *ghāʾib* (*ghāib*), absent. When people talk about a dead person, they say, "*huwa ghāib wa lākin rūḥahu ḥāḍirah*" (He is absent [dead] but his soul or spirit is present).

The word *mawjūd* has further important implications. It refers to those beings, forces, and entities that belong to *ʿālam al-ghaib*, the unseen world, and that are existent and possibly present but not seen or perceptible. In this connection, the word *invisible* (*ghaib*) transcends the common senses (*al-ḥawāss*), and is loaded with cosmological, metaphysical, mystical, and religious meanings. The concept of *ghaib* in this sense is the key theme upon which villagers construct their view of the invisible world. This world transcends the visible realm of the common senses. Angels, souls, and other imperceptible beings and forces are thought of in this sense. Guardian angels are existent and present but not seen nor touched. However, unseen or inaccessible beings and forces can be made accessible through embodiment, spirit-possession, human agents, the hidden knowledge of practitioners, and practices of uttering and writing a certain language, divine or secular. For villagers, the spiritual is inseparable from other domains of life. All in all, *al-ghaib* is defined not only as an eternal or everlasting reality but also as a timeless force that goes beyond the everyday or secular time.

The term *ghaib* is also used in social and interpersonal contexts in connection with other words such as *khafīy* (concealed) or *bāṭin* (inner and private). The word *bāṭin*, "inner," refers to conscience (*ḍamīr*), intention (*niyyah*), and thought (*fikr*) (el-Aswad 1999). In this sense, the theme of invisible and inward (*bāṭin*) and its opposite visible (*ẓāhir*) and outward have important meanings within people's private and public activities. With the exception of God, nobody can presume to ascertain a person's inner states of conscience, thought, or intention, which are surmised by others through discursive actions, deeds, and experiences based on past and present social interactions. The person's behavior is considered *maẓhar* or *ẓāhir*, an apparent and outward or visible side of his or her identity. The *bāṭin* or *makhbar* refers to the intrinsic or essential character of a person. It is the implicit and covert aspects of social knowledge with which people are concerned. What is visible or explicit does not take much time to comprehend compared to what is implicit, hidden, or unseen. Simply put, it is the inward side of people with which villagers are profoundly concerned. It is this deep concern that leads these villagers to develop skeptical attitudes toward strangers, outsiders, or those with whom they are not acquainted.

In both their public and private activities, people do not evaluate another person's inner state solely on the basis of their actions or appearances. They also, and more importantly, rely on their interactions with him or her. Further, people, expressing their doubt as to the accuracy of these actions in revealing an actor's inner or private state, say, "The appearance does not indicate the intrinsic quality [of a person]" (*lā yadul al-maẓhar ʿalā al-makhbar*). When a person's actions create doubt about his or her intention or thought, villagers ironically note, "What is apparent or visible is for us [to know] and what is hidden or concealed is for God" (*aẓ-ẓāhir lanā wa al-khafī ʿalā Allah*). The phrase "false appearances" (*maẓāhir kaddābah*) is commonly used in contexts in which a person pretends that he knows, owns, or does specific things. People who say one thing and do another are suspect. Here, social interaction becomes crucial. It is not enough to hear or see people talking and behaving; it is important to interact with them at greater length. Villagers, in conversation, ask, "Do you know this person?" "Yes." "Have you dealt with him?" "No." "Then, you do not know him." In brief, intention is the most private matter of the individual that can be publicly recognized through his or her interaction with people.

Secrets are private matters that people intend to hide. Those who expose their family's secrets are reprimanded by the widely used folk saying, "*an-nās sirrah fī as-sandūq wa iḥnā sirrinā fī as-suq*" (People's secrets are kept in a box [concealed] and our secret is in the market [revealed]). Also, the inability of an individual to maintain the secrets of friends outside the family is a source of dishonor and mistrust. It is the intricate relationship between what is covered, veiled, or protected (*mastūr*) and what is uncovered or exposed (*mafḍūḥ*) with which villagers, interacting and networking through face-to-face scenarios, are concerned. In this sense, the notion of *satr* (cover or protection) is socially significant. Those who succeed in maximizing their symbolic capital through honorable actions and in minimizing, or hiding, their negative defects are "socially covered."[2] To maintain their social dignity, individuals not only strive to act honorably to demonstrate their positive attributes, but also seek to conceal their moral defects and imperfections. However, in all these circumstances, good intention (*ḥusn an-niyyah*) is important. Allah supports those who consciously recognize their defects, intentionally hide them, and faithfully return to Him in repentance: *illī yasturuh ar-Rabb mā yafḍaḥhūsh al-ʿabd* (The one whom God protects [covers] will never be dishonored [shamefully exposed] by a human being).

Several authors treat such themes related to personhood as mind, self, and body, yet they study them as parts of the person as such—an approach that ties in with the current fashion in anthropology of treating the Islamic Middle East as somehow being individualist. What I am trying to do is to show that in rural Egypt, as in other parts of the world, the individual is part not only of the society but also of the total cosmological system. I have applied this approach in studying various concepts, beliefs, and values in the village. The concept of *as-satr*, or cover, which in most anthropological studies of the Middle East is associated with the virtue or idea of honor, is treated here within the holistic cosmological system of people themselves. The deep concern of rural Egyptians with external and cosmological power extends the concept of the person to be cosmologically significant and articulates the personal or private order as well as the social order with the cosmological order. It is inevitable then, the ethnographic material suggests, to take seriously the triple dimension of the rural Egyptian worldview: person, society, and cosmos. In cosmic, social, and personal or private terms rural Egyptians view their universe as a "shield world," *ʿalam mastūr*. This cosmic worldview, however, is built upon a profound distinction between the invisible, spiritual, subjective, or private and the visible, physical, objective, and public.

Indigenous Paradigm: Religious and Secular Modes of Thought

It is necessary to recognize the role of the folk or peasants in shaping their own worldview as well as in maintaining their cultural identity in a globally dominant and changing world. At the local level, Egyptian villagers are both a worldly and otherworldly minded people. They follow a middle road or way (*ṭarīq wasaṭ*) between spiritualism and secularism—that is, they adopt both secular and religious worldviews and attitudes simultaneously. In this connection, Max Weber's theory of Islam in general is inconsistent with Egyptian Muslim peasants' thought and action. Weber (1964, 182, 202, 203) claims that Islam is not a religion of salvation and is not oriented to this world. He argues that in Islam the belief in predestination results in fatalism and is not rational because it does not eliminate magic from popular religion (1964, 204). Muslims, however, are not as fatalistic as Weber argues. Islam emphasizes full confidence in Allah and requires that Muslims act positively in their everyday lives. One widely used Muslim tradition is to "Act for your worldly life as if you would live forever and act for your afterlife as if you would die tomorrow." Villagers show a deep concern with life in its totality or in its visible, sensory, practical, phenomenal, and transitory as well as invisible, spiritual, and eternal aspects.

Unlike the case in Western society where the sacred cosmos or religion has lost much of its public significance and has increasingly become privatized (Beyer 1994, 70; Luckmann 1967, 103–4), religion in rural Egypt still plays a dominant role in both the public and private spheres. The critical core of the privatization thesis, which is part of the secularization debate in the West, is that "traditional religious forms are no longer definitive for the society as a whole, but can still direct the lives of individuals or subgroups" (Beyer 1994, 70).

In the local context of rural Egypt, religion encapsulates people's social lives. A religious pattern of thought is directed toward and intrinsically concerned with a transcendental and divine reality that is believed to be unquestionably true and that exercises an influence on social and cosmological realities through visible, invisible, external, and internal forces.[3] The relation between religious and nonreligious patterns of thought is simultaneously one of opposition and encompassment. This means that religious thought contradicts nonreligious patterns of thought whether being magical, experimental, or secular, yet it encompasses them as far as they are evaluated by people as being good or bad and relevant or irrelevant in their relations to it. This explains why ethical distinctions are socially and politically powerful.

In their mundane or economic activities, for example, villagers work hard to maximize their material interests and enhance their social positions, yet these activities are validated by the scheme of their religious ideas and values. When a person, for example, succeeds in achieving one of his or her economic goals through legitimate means and hard work, his gain is called *kasb ḥalāl*, a "lawful or legitimate gain." Whatever is religiously and socially acceptable and permissible is called *ḥalāl*, as distinct from what is forbidden and condemned, *ḥarām*. This meaning of *ḥalāl* is so predominant in the everyday life of villagers that they become sensitive toward any illegitimate, unjust, biased, or unfair relationship.[4] In other words, people "come to imagine transcendent cosmic order in terms of the rules that govern their everyday lives and vice versa" (Beyer 1994, 83).

Villagers have a deep sense of their religious and moral beliefs, values, and actions. They are conscious of these beliefs and values to the point that they are cautious of those who violate them. The word "Islam" is explicitly used as a criterion against which people's sayings and actions are evaluated. For instance, it is common to hear a peasant who has not received on time his portion of fertilizers from the agricultural cooperative, or who has witnessed a man mistreating his children or his wife, say "This is not Islam" (*hādhā* [*hādā*] *lais* [*mush*] *Islām*) or "This is forbidden" (*hādhā* [*hādā*] *ḥarām*). These phrases, used in other contexts in which villagers witness a violation of social or moral principles, refer to people's deep understanding and awareness of the fine distinction Islam makes between what is legal or acceptable and what is not. However, let us not forget that the actual decision of what is good and bad is an open argument. What is common is that Islam provides a complete description of the *rights of life*. The language of social judgment is natural and moralizing. But there is no mechanism for producing the definitive collective judgment on practical cases.

As opposed to *religious thought*, which operates within the sacred domain, *magical thought* is viewed by people as either an affiliation with devils and evil forces or a misuse or abuse of the sacred domain. Villagers quote a popular saying, "*khudh min al-Qur'ān mā shi't limā shi't*" (Take from the *Qur'an* what you want for what you want).[5] Although this saying is intended to inspire people to think and act morally, people believe it has an implicit or hidden meaning. In everyday life there are those who use the sacred text and unseen beings and forces for good purposes, and those who use them for evil ones. It is the person's intention, *niyyah*, and his relationship with both people and God, villagers maintain, that determine which way he or she chooses, and it is according to this choice that he or she will be assessed by people in the present world and by God in this life and the afterlife.

The parallel between the universe and the individual is explicitly shown in villagers' beliefs and rituals concerning life, death, and the world to come. Put differently, life, death, and resurrection are stages that both the cosmos and the individual experience. Life moves toward death, and death is the threshold of eternal life. Egyptian peasants consider *al-kaun* (the universe) and *ad-dunyā* (worldly life) as transitory, mortal, inferior, and misleading compared to the world to come, which is *dār al-haqq* (the true world) and *dār al-baqā'* (the eternal abode). As a part of this visible world, society as a whole is also viewed as being imperfect. The limitation of society is manifested in its inability to satisfy its own members' needs. Social and political competitions between units and members of society for dominance of the village's social and economic life are considered manifestations (*maẓāhir*) of the hidden (*bāṭin*) self-interests of these people. However, what makes the present world, in general, and society, in particular, significant is that they are considered by villagers as a place or arena of religious examination or, metaphorically, a field that must be cultivated and its fruits harvested or gained in this life and, likewise, in the afterlife. In a word, the limitation of common-sense experience in this worldly life is overcome by the belief in invisible reality (*al-ghaib*), which is intrinsically a religious concept. The invisible, then, provides for an open and flexible outlook that allows room for things and events to happen.

It is the interconnectedness of the personal, social, and cosmic or divine spheres that explains the deep and emotional engagement of the Egyptian peasant with this world. To save himself and ensure a peaceful life, a person should strengthen his relations not only with people but also with God. For villagers, without God's mercy, which encompasses everything in the universe, *raḥmat Allah wasaʿat kull shaiʾ*, life would be unbearable and meaningless. By relating their mundane social experience to a transcendental and divine reality, people find meaning in what they think, say, and do. In this connection, what is meaningful for people is factual and real whether it is internally conceived and constructed through images and concepts or is externally perceived through concrete symbols. "The propositions, in fact, about the world in which we live," Bateson (1951, 217) says, "are not true or false in a simple objective sense; they are more true if we believe and act upon them, and more false if we disbelieve them. Their validity is a function of our belief."

Scholars who maintain the distinction between literacy or orthodoxy and illiteracy or heterodoxy undermine the significance of the cosmological system in which both literate and illiterate Muslims partake. Unfortunately, anthropological literature on this subject is less than extensive. Cosmic worldviews are not constructed by elite or literate intellectuals; rather they are inherent in the popular imagination and await to be triggered through people's everyday dialectical activities. It is the religious worldview or conceptual system of Muslims that reveals the most common and salient features of their thought and action. This study has concluded that the villagers' main concern is to maintain what is coherent, meaningful, and consistent within the major tenets of Islam.

Egyptian folk cosmology is consistent in many fundamental aspects within the overarching Islamic conceptual system. Local cosmology, religion, the secular, the sacred, the divine, and the profane are interwoven in the everyday actions of rural Egyptians. The entire universe is, through hierarchical relationships, tightly bound together. The universe of rural Egyptians, one concludes by using Dumont's words (1986, 251), "is a universe of faith as against a universe of . . . modern common sense. More precisely, a universe thick with the different dimensions of concrete life, where they have not yet come apart."

This study concludes that the belief in the unknowable and unseen domains of the universe or life is the key to both religion and folk cosmology. In effect, the notion of invisibility and related concepts of spirituality provides the possibility of a more complete cultural and religious experience within a holistic cosmic view. This holistic cosmic view, however, has been maintained by both men of religious learning and common people against the ongoing penetration of secularism and globalization, whose dissenting impacts are depicted as being signs of cosmic corruption leading to the annihilation of this world. The future of the folk cosmology of el-Haddein is not a matter of purely local concern, but is bound up with the future of tradition and religion in Egypt as a whole.

Notes

1. It is interesting to note that a Western intellectual argues that "human rights, human freedoms, and human dignity have their deepest roots outside the perceptible world" (Havel, quoted in Eickelman 2000, 121).

2. See Gilsenan's discussion of the relationship between lying and honor. People's honor, Gilsenan maintains, is threatened by those who make "what should be socially masked and invisible, public and visible" (1976, 201). See also Rappaport's speculation (1979, 223–46; 1999) on sanctity and lies.

3. The unquestionable truthfulness of the divine reality is expressed in, using Rappaport's term (1979, 129, 142), "sacred postulates" such as *lā ilāha illā Allah* as in "There is no God but Allah" and "Muhammad is the messenger of Allah." Ultimate sacred postulates are characterized by their referents usually being nonmaterial (Rappaport 1979, 1999). In Dinka society, for example, "*Wet nhialic*, the 'word' of Divinity, is the truth, or what is really or absolutely is so; and the Dinka think that in certain circumstances men may speak this totally objective 'word,' representing to others the true nature of things, whether of present, or past, or future situations." Also, one of the most common expressions the Dinka use to guarantee and ensure the truth of what they say is "like Divinity" or "as Divinity" (Lienhardt 1976, 47).

4. The meaning of *ḥalāl* is so critical, that when a person kills a domestic animal for consumption, he or she recites the words "*subḥān man ḥallal al-ḥalāl wa ḥarram al-ḥarām*" (Praise the One Who permits that which is legitimate and forbids that which is forbidden or sinful).

5. Ibn Khaldūn (1981, 391–97, 470–82), for example, mentions some practitioners using *ḥurūf* (letters) and verses of the *Qur'an* for good and evil or magical purposes. See also al-Būnī (n.d.), who wrote a book of four volumes showing how people can properly, as he says, use the letters and verses of the *Qur'an* for good purposes.

bibliography

Abou-Zeid, Ahmad M. "Honour and Shame among the Bedouins of Egypt," in *Honour and Shame*, ed. J. G. Peristiany (pp. 243–59). Chicago: University of Chicago Press, 1966.

Abu-Lughod, Lila. *Veiled Sentiments: Honor and Poetry in a Bedouin Society*. Berkeley: University of California Press, 1986.

———. "Islam and the Gendered Discourses of Death." *International Journal of Middle Eastern Studies* 25 (1993): 187–205.

———. "Television and the Virtues of Education: Upper Egyptian Encounters with State Culture," in *Directions of Change in Rural Egypt*, ed. N. Hopkins and K. Westergaard (pp. 147–65). Cairo: American University Cairo Press, 1998a.

———. "The Marriage of Feminism and Islamism in Egypt: Selective Repudiation as a Dynamic of Postcolonial Cultural Politics," in *Remaking Women: Feminism and Modernity in the Middle East*, ed. Lila Abu-Lughod (pp. 243–69). Princeton, NJ: Princeton University Press, 1998b.

Abu-Zahra, Nadia M. "On the Modesty of Women in Arab Villages: A Reply." *American Anthropologist* 72, no. 5 (1970): 1079–88.

———. "Baraka, Material Power, and Women in Tunisia." *Revue d'Histoire Maghrebine* 5, nos. 10–11 (January 1978): 1–24.

———. *Sidi Ameur: A Tunisian Village* (published for the Middle East Center, St. Anthony's College, Oxford). London: Ithaca Press, 1982.

———. *The Pure and the Powerful: Studies in Contemporary Muslim Society*. Reading, Berkshire, UK: Ithaca Press, 1997.

Ahmad, Leila. *Women and Gender in Islam: Historical Roots of a Modern Debate*. New Haven, CT: Yale University Press, 1992.

Ahmed, Akbar S., and Hastings Donnan. *Islam, Globalization and Postmodernity*. London: Routledge, 1994.

al-Bunī, Aḥmad Ibn ʿAlī. *Shams al-Maʿārif al-Kubrā* (4 vols.). Cairo: Muḥammad ʿAlī. Ṣubayḥ wa-Awlādih (n.d).

al-Ghazālī, Abū Ḥāmid. *Iḥyāʾ ʿUlūm ad-Dīn*. Cairo: Dār al-Manār, 1979.

al-Jawzīyah, Ibn Qayyim. *ar-Rūḥ* (The soul). Jiddah: al-Madanī Press, 1984.

al-Maqrīzī, Aḥmad Ibn ʿAlī. *Kitāb al mawāʿiẓ wa al-iʿ tibār fī dhikr al-khiṭaṭ waʾ al-āthār* (1853). Bulāq al-Qāhirah Cairo: Dār al-Tibaʿh al-Miṣriryah, 1970.

al-Miṣrī, Faṭma. *az-Zār*. Cairo: al-Hay'a al-miṣriyah lil-kitāb, 1975.
al-Ms'udi, Abī al-Ḥasan. *Murūj al-dhahab wa-ma'adin al-jawhar*. Bayrut: al-Jāmi'ah al-Lubnāniyah. Qism al-Dirāsāt al-Tārikhiyah. al-Manshurat, 1965.
al-Munūfī, Kamāl. *Al-Fallāḥ al-Miṣrī wa mabdå al-Musāwāh* (The Egyptian peasant and the principle of equality). Cairo: al-Hayå al-Miṣriyya al-'āmma lil-kitāb, 1978.
———. *Ath-thaqāfah as-siyasiyyah lil-fallahin al-Miṣriyyīn* (The political culture of Egyptian peasants). Cairo: Dar Ibn Khaldun, 1980.
al-Sharqāwi, 'Abdel Raḥman. *al-Arḍ* (Egyptian earth), trans. D. Stewart. Reprint, London: Saqi Books, 1990.
al-Tabari, Abi Ja'far Muhammad ibn Jarir. *Tarikh al-Tabari: tarikh al-rusul wa-al-muluk, tahqiq Muhammad Abu al-Fadl Ibrahim*. Cairo: Dār al-Ma'arif, 1960.
Ammar, Hamid. *Growing Up in an Egyptian Village*. London: Routledge/Kegan Paul, 1966.
Anderson, Benedict. *Imagined Communities: Reflections on the Spread of Nationalism*. London: Verso, 1983.
Antoun, Richard. "On the Modesty of Women in Arab Muslim Villages: A Study in the Accommodation of Tradition." *American Anthropologist* 70 (1968): 671–97.
———. *Muslim Preacher in the Modern World: A Jordanian Case Study in Comparative Perspective*. Princeton, NJ: Princeton University Press, 1989.
———. "Themes and Symbols in the Religious Lesson: A Jordanian Case Study." *International Journal of Middle Eastern Studies* 25, no. 4 (1993): 607–24.
Asad, Talal. *The Kababish Arabs: Power, Authority and Consent in a Nomadic Tribe*. New York: Praeger Publishers, 1970.
———. *The Idea of Anthropology of Islam* (Occasional Papers Series). Washington, DC: Center for Contemporary Arab Studies, Georgetown University, 1986.
———. *Genealogies of Religion: Discipline and Reasons of Power in Christianity and Islam*. Baltimore: Johns Hopkins University Press, 1993.
———. "Remarks on the Anthropology of the Body," in *Religion and the Body*, ed. Sarah Coakley (pp. 42–52). Cambridge: Cambridge University Press, 1997.
Ayrout, Henry Habib. *The Egyptian Peasant* (1938). Reprint, Boston: Beacon Press, 1963.
Azdi, Yazid ibn Muhammad. *Tārikh al-Mawṣil*. Cairo: al-Majlis al-A'la lil-Shūn al-Islamiyah. Lajnat Iḥyā' al-Turath al-Islami, 1967.
Baer, Gabriel. *A History of Landownership in Modern Egypt 1800–1950*. London: Oxford University Press, 1962.
———. *Studies in the Social History of Modern Egypt*. Chicago: University of Chicago Press, 1969.
———. *Fellah and Townsman in the Middle East*. London: Frank Cass, 1982.
Bahl, Vinay, and Arif Dirlik. "Introduction" to *History after the Three Worlds*, ed. A. Dirlik, V. Bahl, and P. Gran (pp. 3–23). Lanham, MD: Rowman & Littlefield, 2000.
Barakat, Halim. *The Arab World: Society, Culture, and State*. Berkeley: University of California Press, 1993.
Barnes, R. H. *Kedang: A Study of Collective Thought of an Eastern Indonesian People*. Oxford: Clarendon Press, 1974.
Barth, Fredrik. *Cosmologies in the Making: A Generative Approach to Cultural Variation in Inner New Guinea*. Cambridge: Cambridge University Press, 1987.

Bates, Robert. "People in Villages: Micro-level Studies in Political Economy." *World Politics* 31 (October 1978): 129–48.

Bateson, G. "Conventions of Communication: Where Validity Depends Upon Belief," in *Communication: The Social Matrix of Psychiatry*, ed. Jurgen Ruesch and G. Bateson (pp. 212–27). New York: W. W. Norton, 1951.

———. *Steps to an Ecology of Mind*. New York: Ballantine Books, 1972.

———. *Mind and Nature: A Necessary Unit*. New York: Bantam New Age Books, 1981.

Berger, Morroe. *Islam in Egypt Today: Social and Political Aspects of Popular Religion*. London: Cambridge University Press, 1970.

Berger, Peter L., and Thomas Luckmann. *The Social Construction of Reality*. Garden City, NY: Doubleday, 1966.

Beyer, P. *Religion and Globalization*. London: Sage, 1994.

Binder, Leonard. *In a Moment of Enthusiasm*. Chicago: University of Chicago Press, 1978.

Birks, J. S., et al. "Who Is Migrating Where? An Overview of International Labor Migration in the Arab World," in *Migration, Mechanization and Agricultural Labor Markets in Egypt*, ed. A. Richards and P. L. Martin (pp. 117–34). Cairo: American University in Cairo Press, 1983.

Blackman, Winifred, S. "Some Beliefs among the Egyptian Peasants with Regard to *'afārīt*." *Folklore* 35 (1924): 167–84.

———. *The Fellāhīn of Upper Egypt*. London: Frank Cass, 1927.

Boddy, Janice. "Spirits and Selves in Northern Sudan: The Cultural Therapeutics of Possession and Trance." *American Ethnologist* 15, no. 1 (1988): 4–27.

———. *Wombs and Alien Spirits: Women, Men, and the Zar Cult in Northern Sudan*. Madison: University of Wisconsin Press, 1989.

———. "Spirit Possession Revisited: Beyond Instrumentality." *Annual Review of Anthropology* 23 (1994): 407–34.

Bourdieu, Pierre. "The Sentiment of Honour in Kabyle Society," in *Honour and Shame*, ed. J. G. Peristiany (pp.191–241). Chicago: University of Chicago Press, 1966.

———. *Outline of a Theory of Practice*, trans. Richard Nice. Cambridge: Cambridge University Press, 1977.

Bowen, John R. *Muslims through Discourse: Religion and Ritual in Gayo Society*. Princeton, NJ: Princeton University Press, 1993.

Brown, Nathan. *Peasant Politics in Modern Egypt: The Struggle against the State*. New Haven, CT: Yale University Press, 1990.

———. "The Ignorance and Inscrutability of the Egyptian Peasantry," in *Peasants and Politics in the Modern Middle East*, ed. F. Kazemi and J. Waterbury (pp. 203–21). Miami: Florida International University Press, 1991.

Burke, Edmund. "Changing Patterns of Peasant Protest in the Middle East, 1750–1950," in *Peasants and Politics in the Modern Middle East*, ed. F. Kazemi and J. Waterbury (pp. 24–37). Miami: Florida International University Press, 1991.

Burkhalter, Sheryl L. "Completion in Continuity: Cosmogony and Ethics in Islam," in *Cosmogony and the Ethical Order: New Studies in Comparative Ethics*, ed. R. W. Lovin and F. E. Reynolds (pp. 225–50). Chicago: University of Chicago Press, 1985.

Butler, Alfred J. *The Arab Conquest of Egypt*. Oxford: Clarendon Press, 1978.

Calverley, E. E. "Doctrines of the Soul (*nafs* and *rūḥ*) in Islam." *Moslem World* 33 (1943): 254–64.

———. "Nafs," in *Encyclopedia of Islam*. Leiden, The Netherlands: E. J. Brill, 1960.

The Central Agency for Public Mobilization and Statistics (Egypt), 1976.

———. 1986.

Cerulli, Enrico. "Zar," in *Encyclopedia of Islam*. Leiden, The Netherlands: E. J. Brill, 1960.

Chelhod, J. A. "Contribution to the Problem of the Pre-eminence of the Right, Based upon Arabic Evidence," in *Right and Left: Essays on Dual Symbolic Classification*, ed. Rodney Needham (pp. 239–61). Chicago: University of Chicago Press, 1973.

Chittick, William C. *The Sufi Path of Knowledge: Ibn al-ʿArabi's Metaphysics of Imagination*. Albany: State University of New York Press, 1989.

Clark, R. T. Rundle. *Myth and Symbol in Ancient Egypt* (1959). Reprint, London: Thomas & Hudson, 1978.

Coakley, Sarah. *Religion and the Body*. Cambridge: Cambridge University Press, 1997.

Crapanzano, Vincent, and Vivian Garrison. *Case Studies in Spirit Possession*. New York: Wiley, 1977.

Csordas, Thomas J. "Embodiment as a Paradigm for Anthropology." *Ethos* 18 (1990): 5–47.

———. "Somatic Modes of Attention." *Cultural Anthropology* 8 (1993): 135–56.

———. *Embodiment and Experience: The Existential Ground of Culture and Self*. Cambridge: Cambridge University Press, 1994.

Dalton, George. *Tribal and Peasant Economy*. Austin: University of Texas Press, 1967.

D'Andrade, Roy. "A Folk Model of the Mind," in *Cultural Models in Language and Thought*, ed. D. Holland and N. Quinn (pp. 112–48). Cambridge: Cambridge University Press, 1987.

———. "Culturally Based Reasoning," in *Cognition and Social Worlds*, ed. A. Gellatly, D. Rogers, and J. A. Sloboda (pp. 132–43). Oxford: Clarendon Press, 1989.

Dessouki, Ali E. Hillal. *Islamic Resurgence in the Arab World*. New York: Praeger Publishers, 1982a.

———. "The Politics of Income Distribution in Egypt," in *The Political Economy of Income Distribution in Egypt*, ed. G. Abdel-Khalek and R. Tignor (pp. 55–87). New York: Holmes & Meier, 1982b.

———. "The Shift in Egypt's Migration Policy: 1952–1978." *Middle Eastern Studies* 18, no. 1 (1982c): 53–68.

Douglas, Mary. *Purity and Danger*. London: Routledge/Kegan Paul, 1966.

———. *Natural Symbols*. London: Barrie & Rockliff, 1970.

Dumont, Louis. *Homo Hierarchicus: The Caste System and Its Implications*, rev. English ed. Chicago: University of Chicago Press, 1980.

———. "A Modified View of Our Origin: The Christian Beginning of Modern Individualism," in *The Category of the Person*, ed. M. Carrithers, S. Collins, and S. Lukes (pp. 93–122). Cambridge: Cambridge University Press, 1985.

———. *Essays on Individualism: Modern Ideology in Anthropological Perspective.* Chicago: University of Chicago Press, 1986.

Duncan, D. B. "The Development of the Idea of Spirit in Islam." *Acta Orientalia* 9, no. 4 (1931): 307–51.

Dundes, Alan. "Folk Ideas as Units of Worldview." *Journal of American Folklore* 84 (1971): 93–103.

Durkheim, E. *The Elementary Forms of the Religious Life* (1915). Reprint, New York: Free Press, 1965.

Eickelman, Dale. *Moroccan Islam: Tradition and Society in a Pilgrimage Center.* Austin: University of Texas Press, 1976.

———. "Time in a Complex Society: A Moroccan Example." *Ethnology* 16, no. 1 (1977): 39–55.

———. *The Middle East: An Anthropological Approach.* Englewood Cliffs, NJ: Prentice-Hall, 1981.

———. "The Study of Islam in Local Contexts." *Contributions to Asian Studies* 17 (1984): 1–16.

———. "National Identity and Religious Discourse in Contemporary Oman." *International Journal of Islamic Arabic Studies* 6 (1989): 1–20.

———. "Islam and the Language of Modernity." *Dadelus* 129, no. 1 (2000): 119–35.

Eickelman, Dale, and James Piscatori. *Muslim Politics.* Princeton, NJ: Princeton University Press, 1996.

el-Aswad, el-Sayed. "*at-Turāth ash-Shufāhī wa Dirāsat ash-Shakhṣīy al-Qawmīyah*" (Oral tradition and the study of national character), in *ʿĀlam al-Fikr* 16, no. 1 (1985): 271–94. Kuwait: Kuwait Government Press.

———. "Death Ritual in Rural Egyptian Society: A Symbolic Study." *Urban Anthropology and Studies of Cultural Systems and World Economic Development* 16 (1987): 205–41.

———. "Patterns of Thought: An Anthropological Study of World Views of Rural Egyptian Society." Unpublished Ph.D. dissertation, University of Michigan, Ann Arbor, 1988.

———. *Aṣṣabr fī at-turath ash-shāʿbī al-miṣī dirāsah anthropolojiyyah* (The concept of patience in Egyptian folklore). Alexandria: Munshʾat al-Marʿāf, 1990a.

———. *Ath-thaqāfah wa at-tafkīr rʾūiyah anthropolojiyyah* (Culture and thought: An anthropological view). *National Review of Social Sciences* (Cairo) 27, no. 3 (1990b): 71–114.

———. "The Gift and the Image of the Self and the Other among Rural Egyptians," in *The Gift in Culture*, ed. Rosa Godula (pp. 35–49). Krakow: Prace Etnograficzne, Jagiellonian University Press, 1993.

———. "The Cosmological Belief System of Egyptian Peasants." *Anthropos* 89 (1994): 359–77.

———. *Al-bayt ash-shaʿby, dirsa anthropologiyyah lilʿimāra ash-shʿabiyah wa ath-thaqafa attqlidiya fī mujtma al-Emarat* (The folk house: An anthropological study of folk architecture and traditional culture of the Emirates society. Al Ain: UAE University Press, 1996a.

———. "Ibn Khaldoun's Theory of Civilization and State." *Al-Bahrain Al-Thaqafiyya* 3 (1996b): 150–54.

———. "Archaic Egyptian Cosmology." *Anthropos* 92 (1997): 69–81.

———. "Hierarchy and Symbolic Construction of the Person among Rural Egyptians." *Anthropos* 94 (1999): 431–45.

———. Book review of *Directions of Change in Rural Egypt*, ed. N. Hopkins and K. Westergaard. *Anthropos* 95 (2000a): 600–601.

———. "Muslim Sermons: Public Discourse in Local and Global Scenarios." Paper presented at the 99th Annual Meeting of the AAA (Invited Session: Media-Mediated Islam and the Middle East: Giving the Virtual Reality Check), November 15–19, 2000, Chicago (2000b).

———. "The Ethnography of Invisible Spheres." *AAA Anthropology Newsletter* (Middle East Section) 42, no. 6 (September 2001a): 51.

———. "Invisibility and Possibility: Ethnography of Imaginary Worlds." Invited lecture presented at the American University in Cairo, Department of Sociology, Anthropology, Psychology, and Egyptology, School of Humanities and Social Sciences, November 7, 2001, Cairo (2001b).

———. *Al-anthropolojiya ar-ramziyah: dirāsa naqdiya l-litgāhāt al-mʿuāṣira fī taḥlīl wa ta'wīl aththaqāfa* (Symbolic anthropology: A critical study of the current interpretation of culture). Alexandria: Munshat al-Marʿāf, 2002a.

———. "Sanctified Cosmology: Maintaining Muslim Identity in a Globally Dominant and Changing World." Paper presented at the Society for Anthropology of Religion meeting, April 5–7, 2002, Cleveland (2002b).

———. "Viewing the World through Upper Egyptian Eyes: From Regional Crisis to Global Blessing." Paper presented at the conference on "Social and Cultural Processes in Upper Egypt," October 17–20, 2002, Aswan, Egypt (2002c).

El-Guindi, Fadwa. *Veil: Modesty, Privacy and Resistance*. Oxford: Berg, 1999.

Eliade, Mircea. *Cosmos and History: The Myth of the Eternal Return*. New York: Harper & Row, 1954.

———. *The Sacred and Profane: The Nature of Religion*, trans. W. R. Trask. New York: Harcourt, Brace & World, 1957.

———. *Shamanism: Archaic Techniques of Ecstasy*, trans. W. R. Trask. New York: Bollingen Foundation, 1964.

———. *Patterns in Comparative Religion*. New York: Meridian, 1974.

———. *Symbolism: The Sacred and the Arts*, ed. D. Apostolos-Cappadona. New York: Crossroad, 1985.

el-Messiri, Sawsan. *Ibn Al-Balad: A Concept of Egyptian Identity*. Leiden, The Netherlands: E. J. Brill, 1978.

———. "Tarahil Laborers in Egypt," in *Migration, Mechanization and Agricultural Labor Markets in Egypt*, ed. A. Richards and P. L. Martin (pp. 79–100). Cairo: American University in Cairo Press, 1983.

El-Shamy, H. "Mental Health in Traditional Culture: A Study of Preventive and Therapeutic Folk Practices in Egypt." *Catalyst* 6 (1972): 13–28.

———. *Folktales of Egypt: Collected, Translated, and Edited with Middle Eastern and African Parallels*. Chicago: University of Chicago Press, 1980.

———. *Tales Arab Women Tell and the Behavioral Patterns They Portray*. Bloomington: Indiana University Press, 1999.

el-Zein, Abdul Hamid. "Beyond Ideology and Theology: The Search for the Anthropology of Islam." *Annual Review of Anthropology* 6 (1977): 227–54.

Evans-Pritchard, E. E. "The Intellectualist (English) Interpretation of Magic." *Bulletin of the Faculty of Arts* (Egyptian University, Cairo) 1–2 (1933): 282–311.

———. "Levy-Bruhl's Theory of Primitive Mentality." *Bulletin of the Faculty of Arts* (Egyptian University, Cairo) 2 (1934): 2–36.

———. *Social Anthropology and Other Essays*. New York: Free Press, 1966.

———. *Nuer Religion* (1956). Reprint, Oxford: Clarendon Press, 1974.

———. *Witchcraft, Oracles and Magic among the Azande* (1937). Reprint, London: Clarendon Press, 1980.

Fakhouri, Hani. "The Zar Cult in an Egyptian Village." *Anthropological Quarterly* 41, no. 2 (1968): 49–56.

Fathy, Hassan. *Architecture for the Poor* (1973). Reprint, Cairo: American University in Cairo Press, 1989.

Firth, Raymond. *Tikopia Ritual and Belief*. Boston: Beacon Press, 1967.

Fluehr-Lobban, Carolyn. *Islamic Society in Practice*. Gainesville: University Press of Florida, 1994.

Fortune, R. F. *Sorcerers of Dobu*. New York: E. P. Dutton, 1959.

Foster, George M. "Peasant Society and the Image of Limited Good." *American Anthropologist* 67 (1965): 293–315.

Franke, Elisabeth. "The Zar in Egypt." *Moslem World* 8 (1913): 279–89.

Gaffney, Patrick D. *The Prophet's Pulpit: Islamic Preaching in Contemporary Egypt*. Berkeley: University of California Press, 1994.

Gamst, F. C. *Peasants in Complex Society*. New York: Rinehart & Winston, 1974.

Gardet, L. "Dhikr," in *Encyclopedia of Islam*. Leiden, The Netherlands: E. J. Brill, 1960.

———. "Janna," in *Encyclopedia of Islam*. Leiden, The Netherlands: E. J. Brill, 1960.

Geertz, Clifford. *Islam Observed: Religious Development in Morocco and Indonesia*. Chicago: University of Chicago Press, 1968.

———. *The Interpretation of Cultures*. New York: Basic Books, 1973.

Gellner, Ernest. *Thought and Change*. London: Weidenfeld & Nicolson, 1964.

———. *Saints of Atlas*. Chicago: University of Chicago Press, 1969.

———. *Muslim Society*. Cambridge: Cambridge University Press, 1981.

———. *Culture, Identity, and Politics*. London: Cambridge University Press, 1987.

Gennep, A. Van. *The Rites of Passage* (1911). Reprint, Chicago: Phoenix Books, University of Chicago, 1961.

Georges, Robert A. "Evil Eye," in *Encyclopedia of Folklore and Literature*, ed. M. E. Brown and B. A. Rosenberg (pp. 193–94). Santa Barbara, CA: ABC-CLIO, 1998.

Gerth, H. H., and C. Wright Mills. *From Max Weber: Essays in Sociology*. New York: Oxford University Press, 1980.

Gibb, H. A. R., and J. H. Kramer. *Shorter Encyclopedia of Islam*. Ithaca, NY: Cornell University Press, n.d.

Giddens, Anthony. *The Constitution of Society: Outline of the Theory of Structuration*. Berkeley: University of California Press, 1984.

———. *Modernity and Self-Identity: Self and Society in the Late Age*. Stanford, CA: Stanford University Press, 1991.

Gilmore, David. *Honor and Shame and the Unity of the Mediterranean* (Special Publication of the American Anthropological Association, no. 22). Washington, DC: AAA, 1987.

Gilsenan, M. *Saint and Sufi in Modern Egypt: An Essay in the Sociology of Religion.* Oxford: Oxford University Press, 1973.

———. "Lying, Honor, and Contradiction," in *Transaction and Meaning: Directions in the Anthropology of Exchange and Symbolic Behavior*, ed. B. Kapferer (pp. 191–219). Philadelphia: Institute for the Study of Human Issues, 1976.

———. *Recognizing Islam: Religion and Society in the Modern Arab World.* New York: Pantheon, 1983.

Gluckman, Max. *Custom and Conflict in Africa.* New York: Barnes & Noble, 1969.

Godelier, Maurice. *The Enigma of the Gift*, trans. N. Scott. Chicago: University of Chicago Press, 1999.

Goldberg, Ellis. "Peasants in Revolt—Egypt, 1919." *International Journal of Middle Eastern Studies* 24, no. 2 (1992): 261–80.

Goodenough, W. H. "Sky World and This World: The Place of Kachaw in Micronesian Cosmology." *American Anthropologist* 88, no. 3 (1986): 551–68.

Goody, Jack. *The Domestication of the Savage Mind.* Cambridge: Cambridge University Press, 1977.

———. *The East in the West.* Cambridge: Cambridge University Press, 1996.

Graham, Laura R. *Performing Dreams: Discourses of Immortality among the Xavante of Brazil.* Austin: University of Texas Press, 1995.

Gran, Peter. *Islamic Roots of Capitalism: Egypt, 1760–1840.* Austin: University of Texas Press 1979.

———. *Beyond Eurocentrism: A New View of Modern World History.* Syracuse, NY: Syracuse University Press, 1996.

Granqvist, Hilma. "Marriage Conditions in a Palestinian Village (Part I: Commendations Humanarum Litterarum)." *Helsingfors: Societas Scientiarum Fennica* 3, no. 8 (1931): 1–200.

Haddawy, Husain. *The Arabian Nights* (*alf lailah wa lailah*), trans. Husain Haddawy. New York: Knopf, 1992.

Hall, Edward T. *The Dance of Life: The Other Dimension of Time.* New York: Anchor Books/Doubleday, 1983.

Halperin, Rhoda, and James Dow. *Peasant Livelihood: Studies in Economic Anthropology and Cultural Ecology.* New York: St. Martin's Press, 1977.

Hamdan, Jamal. *Shakhṣīyat Miṣr: Dirāsah Fī ʿAbqīyat al-Makān* (The character of Egypt: A study in the genius of a place), vol. 1. Cairo: ʿĀlam al-Kutub, 1980.

Hanks, W. F. "Exorcism and the Description of Participant Roles," in *Natural Histories of Discourse*, ed. M. Silverstein and G. Urban (pp. 160–200). Chicago: University of Chicago Press, 1996.

Harris, Grage Gredys. "Concepts of Individual, Self, and Person in Description and Analysis." *American Anthropologist* 91 (1989): 599–612.

Harrison, Simon. "Concepts of the Person in Avatip Religious Thought." *Man* 20 (1985): 115–30.

Heinen, Anton M. *Islamic Cosmology: A Study of As-Suyūtîs al-Hay'a as-sanīya fī l-hay'a as-sunnīya.* Beirut: Franz Steiner Verlag, 1982.

Hertz, Robert. The Pre-eminence of the Right Hand: A Study in Religious Polarity," in *Right and Left: Essays on Dual Symbolic Classification*, ed. R. Needham (pp. 3–31). Chicago: University of Chicago Press, 1973.

Hocart, A. M. "The Legacy to Modern Egypt," in *The Legacy of Egypt*, ed. S. R. K. Glanville (pp. 369–93). London: Oxford University Press, 1942.

Hoffman-Ladd, Valerie. "Polemics on the Modesty and Segregation of Women in Contemporary Egypt." *International Journal of Middle Eastern Studies* 19, no. 1 (1987): 23–50.

Hollan, Douglas. "Cross-Cultural Differences in the Self." *Journal of Anthropological Research* 48 (1992): 283–300.

Holland, Dorothy, and Andrew Kipnis. "Metaphor for Embarrassment and Stories of Exposure. The Not-So-Egocentric Self in American Culture." *Ethos* 22 (1994): 316–42.

Hopkins, Nicholas S. "The Social Impact of Mechanization," in *Migration, Mechanization and Agricultural Labor Markets in Egypt*, ed. A. Richards and P. L. Martin. Cairo: American University in Cairo Press, 1983.

———. *Agrarian Transformation in Egypt*. Boulder, CO: Westview Press, 1987.

———. "Anthropology in Egypt." *Anthropology Newsletter* 39 (1998): 50–51.

Hopkins, Nicholas S., and Kirsten Westergaard. *Directions of Change in Rural Egypt*. Cairo: American University in Cairo Press, 1998.

Horton, Robin. "African Traditional Thought and Western Science." *Africa* 37 (1967): I: 50–71; II: 155–87.

Howell, Signe. *Society and Cosmos: Chewong of Peninsular Malaysia*. Chicago: University of Chicago Press, 1989.

Huntington, Samuel. "The Clash of Civilizations?" *Foreign Affairs* 72, no. 3 (1993): 22–49.

Ibn ʿAbd al Ḥakam. *Futūḥ Miṣr wa al-Maghrib* (The conquest of Egypt and Morocco). Cairo: lajnat al-Bayān al ʿArabī, 1961.

Ibn al-ʿArabi, Muḥl ad-Dīn. *al-Futūḥāt al-Makkiyyah* (4 vols.). Cairo: al-Haʾyah al-Miṣriyyah lil-Kitāb, 1972.

Ibn al-Athīr, ʿIzz al-Din. *al-Kamil fi al-tarikh*. al-Qahirah (Cairo): Idarat al-Tibaʿah al-Muniriyah, 1929.

Ibn Hishām. *as-Sīrah an-Nabawiyyah*. Cairo: al-Maktaba at-Tawfīqīyah, 1978.

Ibn Kathīr, Ismāʿīl Ibn ʿUmar. *Tafsīr al-Qurʾān al-ʿAẓīm*. Cairo: Dār Iḥayāʾ al-Kutub al-ʿArabiyyah. 1937.

Ibn Khaldūn. *The Muqaddimah: An Introduction to History*, trans. F. Rosenthal, ed. N. J. Dawood. Princeton, NJ: Princeton University Press, 1981.

Ibn Manẓūr, Muhamad ibn Mukarram. *Lisān al-ʿArab*, 20 vols. Cairo: ad-Dār al-Miṣriyyah lil-Tʾalif wa al-Tarjamah, 1966.

Idris, Yusuf. *al-ḥarām* (The sinners), trans. K. Peterson-Ishaq. Washington, DC: Three Continents Press, 1984.

Inhorn, Marcia Claire. *Quest for Conception: Gender, Infertility, and Egyptian Medical Traditions*. Philadelphia: University of Pennsylvania Press, 1994.

Ions, Veronica. *Egyptian Mythology*. Middlesex, UK: Hamlyn, 1968.

Irvine, Judith T. "The Creation of Identity in Spirit Mediumship and Possession," in *Semantic Anthropology*, ed. D. Parking (pp. 241–60). London: Academic Press, 1982.

Ismāʿīl, ʿAbd al-Raḥmān. *Folk Medicine in Modern Egypt (Tibb al-rikkah)*. New York: AMS Press, 1980.
Isutzu, Toshihiko. *Language and Magic*. Tokyo: Institute of Philosophical Studies, 1956.
———. *God and Man in the Koran: Semantics of the Koranic Weltanschauung*. Tokyo: Keio Institute of Cultural and Linguistic Studies, 1964.
Jackson, Michael. "Introduction: Phenomenology, Radical Empiricism, and Anthropological Critique," in *Things as They Are: New Directions in Phenomenological Anthropology*, ed. M. Jackson (pp. 1–50). Bloomington: Indiana University Press, 1996.
Kapferer, Bruce. *A Celebration of Demons: Exorcism and the Aesthetics of Healing in Sri Lanka*. Bloomington; Indiana University Press, 1983.
———. *The Feast of the Sorcerer: Practices of Consciousness and Power*. Chicago: University of Chicago Press, 1997.
Kazemi, Farhad, and John Waterbury. *Peasants and Politics in the Modern Middle East*. Miami: Florida International University Press, 1991.
Keane, Webb. "Religious Language." *Annual Review of Anthropology* 26 (1997): 47–71.
Kearney, Michael. *World View*. Navato, CA: Chandler Sharp, 1984.
Kennedy, John G. "Nubian Zar Ceremonies as Psychotherapy." *Human Organization* 2, no. 4 (1967a): 185–94.
———. "Mushahara: A Nubian Concept of Supernatural Danger and the Theory of Taboo." *American Anthropologist* 69 (1967b): 685–702.
Kepel, Gilles. *The Revenge of God: The Resurgence of Islam, Christianity and Judaism in the Modern World*. College Park: Pennsylvania State University Press, 1994.
Khafagy, Fatma. "Socio-Economic Impact of Emigration from a Giza Village," in *Migration, Mechanization and Agricultural Labor Markets in Egypt*, ed. A. Richards and P. L. Martin (pp. 135–56). Cairo: American University in Cairo Press, 1983.
———. "Women and Labor Migration: One Village in Egypt." *MERIP Reports* (Middle Eastern Research and Information Project no. 124), 14 (1984): 11–16.
Kiernan, J. "Worldview in Perspective: Toward the Reclamation of Discussed Concept." *African Studies* 40, no. 1 (1981): 3–11.
Kluckhohn, Clyde. *Navaho Witchcraft*. Cambridge, MA: Peabody Museum, 1944.
———. "The Philosophy of the Navaho Indians," in *Ideological Differences and World Order*, ed. F. S. C. Northrop (pp. 356–84). New Haven, CT: Yale University Press, 1949.
———. "Parts and Wholes in Cultural Analysis," in *Parts and Wholes*, ed. D. Learner (pp. 111–33). New York: Free Press of Glencoe, 1963.
Klunzinger, C. B. *Upper Egypt: Its People and its Products* (1878). Reprint, New York: Scribner's, 1984.
Kramer, Fritz W. *The Red Fez: Art and Spirit Possession in Africa*. London: Verso, 1993.
Lambek, Michael. *Human Spirits: A Cultural Account of Trance in Mayotte*. Cambridge: Cambridge University Press, 1981.

———. *Knowledge and Practice in Mayotte: Local Discourse of Islam, Sorcery, and Spirit Possession*. Toronto: University of Toronto Press, 1993.

———. "Body and Mind in Mind, Body and Mind in Body. Some Anthropological Interventions in a Long Conversation," in *Bodies and Persons: Comparative Perspectives from Africa and Melanesia*, ed. M. Lambek and A. Strathern (pp. 103–23). Cambridge: Cambridge University Press, 1998.

Lane, Edward William. *The Manners and Customs of the Modern Egyptians* (1836). Reprint, London: Everyman's Library, 1966.

Lawson, Fred H. "Rural Revolt and Provincial Society in Egypt, 1820–1824." *International Journal of Middle Eastern Studies* 13, no. 2 (1981): 131–53.

Leach, Edmund R. *Humanity and Animality*. London: South Place Ethical Society, 1972.

Lévi-Strauss, Claude. *Structural Anthropology*. New York: Basic Books, 1963.

———. *The Savage Mind*. London: Weidenfield & Nicolson, 1966.

Lewis, Bernard. *The Middle East and the West*. New York: Harper Torch Books, 1966.

Lewis, I. M. "Spirit Possession and Deprivation Cults." *Man* 1, no. 3 (1966): 307–29.

———. "A Structural Approach to Witchcraft and Spirit-Possession," in *Witchcraft, Confessions and Accusations*, ed. M. Douglas (pp. 293–310). London: Tavistock, 1970.

———. *Ecstatic Religion: An Anthropological Study of Spirit Possession and Shamanism*. London: Penguin Books, 1975.

———. *Religion in Context: Cults and Charisma*. Cambridge: Cambridge University Press, 1986.

Lienhardt, Godfrey. "Modes of Thought," in *The Institutions of Primitive Society*, ed. E. E. Evans-Pritchard (pp. 95–107). Chicago: Free Press, 1954.

———. *Divinity and Experience: The Religion of the Dinka*. Oxford: Oxford University Press, 1961.

———. "Self: Public, Private, Some African Representations," in *The Category of the Person: Anthropology, Philosophy and History*, ed. M. Carrithers, S. Collins, and S. Lukes (pp. 141–55). Cambridge: Cambridge University Press, 1985.

Luckmann, Thomas. *The Problem of Religion in Modern Society*. New York: Macmillan, 1967.

Lukes, Steven. "Conclusion," in *The Category of the Person: Anthropology, Philosophy and History*, ed. M. Carrithers, S. Collins, and S. Lukes (pp. 282–301). Cambridge: Cambridge University Press, 1985.

MacDonald, D. B. *Aspects of Islam*. New York: Macmillan, 1911.

———. "The Development of the Idea of Spirit in Islam." *Acta Orientalia* 9 (1931): 307–51.

MacDonald, John. "The Creation of Man and Angels in the Eschatological Literature." *Islamic Studies* 3, no. 3 (1964a): 285–308.

———. "The Angel of Death in Late Islamic Tradition." *Islamic Studies* 3, no. 4 (1964b): 485–519.

———. "The Twilight of the Dead." *Islamic Studies* 4, no. 1 (1965): 55–102.

———. "The Day of Resurrection." *Islamic Studies* 5, no. 2 (1966a): 129–97.

———. "Paradise." *Islamic Studies* 5, no. 4 (1966b): 331–83.

MacLeod, Arlene. *Accommodating Protest: Working Women, the New Veil, and Change in Cairo*. New York: Columbia University Press, 1991.

Marino, Adrian. "Mercia Eliade's Hermeneutics," in *Imagination and Meaning: The Scholarly and Literary Worlds of Mercia Eliade*, ed. N. Girardot and M. L. Ricketts (pp. 19–69). New York: Seabury Press, 1982.

Marsella, Anthony. "Culture, Self, and Mental Disorder," in *Culture and Self: Asian and American Perspectives*, ed. A. Marsella, G. DeVos, and F. Hsu (pp. 281–308). New York: Tavistock, 1985.

Martin, Emily. "Mind–Body Problems." *American Ethnologist* 27, no. 3 (2000): 569–90.

Mauss, Marcel. *A General Theory of Magic*, trans. R. Brain. London: Routledge/Kegan Paul, 1970.

———. "A Category of Human Mind: The Notion of Self," in *The Category of the Person*, ed. M. Carrithers, S. Collins, and S. Lukas (pp. 1–26). Cambridge: Cambridge University Press, 1981.

———. *The Gift: Forms and Functions of Exchange in Archaic Societies*, trans. W. D. Halls. London: Routledge, 1990.

Mayfield, James B. *Rural Politics in Nasser's Egypt: A Quest for Legitimacy*. Austin: University of Texas Press, 1971.

Mazrui, Ali. 1997. "Islam and Islamophobia: Conflicting Images in a Europocentric World," in *Islamic Political Economy in Capitalist-Globalization: An Agenda for Change*, ed. M. A. Choudhury, M. Z. Abdad, and M. S. Salleh (pp. 91–108). Kuala Lampur, Malaysia: Utusan Publications, 1997.

McHugh, Ernest L. "Concepts of the Person among the Gurungs of Nepal." *American Anthropologist* 16 (1989): 75–86.

Meeker, Michael E. "Meaning and Society in the Near East: Examples from the Black Sea Turks and the Levantine Arabs (I)." *International Journal of Middle Eastern Studies* 7, no. 2 (1976a): 243–70.

———. "Meaning and Society in the Near East: Examples from the Black Sea Turks and the Levantine Arabs (II)." *International Journal of Middle Eastern Studies* 7, no. 3 (1976b): 383–422.

———. *Literature and Violence in North Arabia*. Cambridge: Cambridge University Press, 1979.

Meinardus, Otto. *Christian Egypt: Ancient and Modern*. Cairo: French Institute of Oriental Archeology, 1965.

Messing, S. D. "Group Therapy and Social Status in the Zar Cult of Ethiopia." *American Anthropologist* 60 (1958): 1120–26.

Metcalf, Peter. *Where Are You Spirits? Style and Theme in Berawan Prayer*. Washington, DC: Smithsonian Institute Press, 1989.

Mitchell, Timothy. *Colonising Egypt*. Cambridge: Cambridge University Press, 1988.

———. "The Invention and Reinvention of the Egyptian Peasant." *International Journal of Middle Eastern Studies* 22 (1990): 129–50.

———. "The Market's Place," in *Directions of Change in Rural Egypt*, ed. N. S. Hopkins and K. Westergaard (pp. 19–40). Cairo: American University in Cairo Press, 1998.

Mohd, Nor Wan Daud Wan. *The Concept of Knowledge in Islam and Its Implications for Education in a Developing Country*. London: Mansell Publishing, 1989.

Morenz, Siegfried. *Egyptian Religion*, trans. A. E. Keep. London: Methuen, 1973.

Moret, Alexandre. *The Nile and Egyptian Civilization*, trans. M. R. Dobie (1927). Reprint, London: Routledge/Kegan Paul, 1972.

Mortimer, Edward. *Faith and Power: The Politics of Islam*. New York: Random House, 1982.

Nabokov, Isabelle. "Deadly Power: A Funeral to Counter Sorcery in South India." *American Ethnologist* 27, no. 1 (2000): 147–68.

Nash, Manning. *Primitive and Peasant Economic Systems*. San Francisco: Chandler Publishing, 1966.

Nasr, Seyyed Hossein. *An Introduction to Islamic Cosmological Doctrines: Conceptions of Nature and Methods Used for its Study by the Ikhwan al-Safa', al-Biruni, and Ibn Sina*. Cambridge, MA: Belknap Press, 1964.

Needham, Rodney. *Right and Left: Essays on Dual Symbolic Classification*. Chicago: University of Chicago Press, 1973.

Netton, Ian Richard. *Allah Transcendent: Studies in the Structure and Semiotics of Islamic Philosophy, Theology and Cosmology*. London: Routledge, 1989.

Obeyesekere, Gananath. *Medusa's Hair: An Essay on Personal Symbols and Religious Experience*. Chicago: University of Chicago Press, 1981.

———. *The Work of Culture: Symbolic Transformation in Psychoanalysis and Anthropology*. Chicago: University of Chicago Press, 1990.

Ohnuki-Tierney, Emiko. "A Northwest Coast Sakhalin Ainu World View." Ph.D. dissertation, University of Wisconsin, 1968.

———. "Concepts of Time among the Aino of the Northwest Coast Sakhalin." *American Anthropologist* 71 (1969): 488–92.

———. "Spatial Concepts of the Aino of the Northwest Coast of Southern Sakhalin." *American Anthropologist* 74 (1972): 426–57.

Ortner, Sherry B. *Sherpas through Their Rituals*. Cambridge: Cambridge University Press, 1978.

———. "Theory in Anthropology Since the Sixties." *Comparative Studies in Society and History* 26, no. 1 (1984): 126–66.

Ott, Sandra. *The Circle of Mountains: A Basque Shepherding Community*. Oxford: Clarendon Press, 1981.

Owusu, Maxwell. "Ethnography of Africa: The Usefulness of the Useless." *American Anthropologist* 80, no. 2 (1978): 310–34.

Parmentier, Richard J. *Signs in Society: Studies in Semiotic Anthropology*. Bloomington: Indiana University Press, 1994.

Peirce, Charles Sanders. *Collected Papers of Charles Sanders Peirce*, 8 vols., ed. C. Harshorne, P. Weiss, and A. W. Burks. Cambridge, MA: Harvard University Press, 1931–58.

Peristiany, J. G. *Honour and Shame*. Chicago: University of Chicago Press, 1966.

Pitt-Rivers, Julian. *Mana*. Welwyn Garden City, Hertfordshire, UK: Broadwater Press, 1974.

Popkins, S. J. *The Rational Peasant: The Political Economy of Rural Society in Vietnam*. Berkeley: University of California Press, 1979.

Potter, Jack M., May N. Diaz, and George M. Foster. *Peasant Society: A Reader.* Boston: Little, Brown, 1967.
Qāsim, ʿAbd al-Ḥakm. *The Seven Days of Man* (*Ayyā al-Insān al-sabʿah*), trans. J. N. Bell. Evanston, IL: Hydra Books/Northwestern University Press, 1996.
Quinn, Naomi. "The Cultural Basis of Metaphor," in *Beyond Metaphor: The Theory of Tropes in Anthropology*, ed. J. W. Fernandes. Stanford, CA: Stanford University Press, 1991.
Quṭb, Sayyid. *Mashāhid al-Qiyāmah fī al-Qurʾān.* Cairo: Dār al-Maʿārif, 1961.
Rāghib al-Aṣbahānī, Abū al-Qāsim. *al-Mufradāt fī gharīb al-Qurʾān.* Cairo: Maktabat al-Anjlu al-Miṣriyah, 1970.
Rahman, F. "ʿAḳl," in *Encyclopedia of Islam.* Leiden, The Netherlands: E. J. Brill, 1960.
Rapoport, Amos. *House Form and Culture.* Englewood Cliffs, NJ: Prentice-Hall, 1969.
Rappaport, Roy A. *Ecology, Meaning, and Religion.* Richmond, CA: North Atlantic Books, 1979.
———. *Pigs for the Ancestors: Rituals in the Ecology of a New Guinea People* (1968). Reprint, New Haven, CT: Yale University Press, 1984.
———. *Ritual and Religion in the Making of Humanity.* Cambridge: Cambridge University Press, 1999.
Rasmussen, Susan J. *Spirit Possession and Personhood among the Kel Ewey Tuareg.* Cambridge: Cambridge University Press, 1995.
Redfield, Robert. *The Folk Culture of Yucatan.* Chicago: University of Chicago Press, 1941.
———. *The Little Community and Peasant Society and Culture.* Chicago: University of Chicago Press, 1960.
———. *The Primitive World and Its Transformation.* Ithaca, NY: Cornell University Press, 1968.
Reichel-Dolmatoff, Gerardo. *Amazonian Cosmos: The Sexual and Religious Symbolism of the Tukano Indians.* Chicago: University of Chicago Press, 1971.
Richards, Alan. "Egypt's Agriculture in Trouble." *MERIP Report* 84 (January 1980): 3–13.
———. "Ten Years of Infitah: Class, Rent, and Policy Stasis in Egypt." *Journal of Development Studies* 20, no. 4 (1984): 323–38.
Richards, Alan, Philip Martin, and Rifaat Nagaar. "Labor Shortages in Egyptian Agriculture," in *Migration, Mechanization and Agricultural Labor Markets in Egypt*, ed. A. Richards and P. L. Martin (pp. 21–44). Cairo: American University in Cairo Press, 1983.
Rosen, Lawrence. *Bargaining for Reality: The Construction of Social Relations in a Muslim Community.* Chicago: University of Chicago Press, 1984.
Rosenthal, Franz. "On Suicide in Islam." *Journal of the American Oriental Society* 66, no. 3 (1946): 239–59.
Rugh, Andrea B. *Family in Contemporary Egypt.* Syracuse, NY: Syracuse University Press, 1984.
Sahlins, Marshall. *Stone Age Economics.* Chicago: Aldine-Atherton, 1972.
———. *Culture and Practical Reason.* Chicago: University of Chicago Press, 1976.
Said, Edward W. *Orientalism.* New York: Vintage Books, 1979.

———. *Covering Islam*. New York: Pantheon Books, 1981.
———. *The World, the Text and the Critic*. Cambridge, MA: Harvard University Press, 1983.
Ṣāliḥ, Aḥmed Rushdy. *al-Adab ash-Shaʿbī* (Folk literature). Cairo: an-Nahḍah al-Miṣrīyah, 1971.
Saunders, John Joseph. *A History of Medieval Islam*. New York: Barnes & Noble, 1965.
Schulze, Reinhard C. "Colonization and Resistance: The Egyptian Peasant Rebellion, 1919," in *Peasants and Politics in the Modern Middle East*, ed. F. Kazemi and J. Waterbury (pp. 171–202). Miami: Florida International University Press, 1991.
Schwarz, Maureen Trudelle. "Snakes in the Ladies' Room: Navajo Views on Personhood and Effect." *American Ethnologist* 24 (1997): 602–27.
Schwerdtfeger, F. *Traditional Housing in African Cities*. Chichester, NY: Wiley, 1982.
Scott, James C. *The Moral Economy of the Peasant: Rebellion and Subsistence in Southeast Asia*. New Haven, CT: Yale University Press, 1976.
Sharabi, Hisham. *Neopatriarchy*. New York: Oxford University Press, 1988.
Shepard, William E. "Islam and Ideology: Toward a Typology." *International Journal of Middle Eastern Studies* 19, no. 3 (1987): 307–35.
Shils, Edward. *Tradition*. Chicago: University of Chicago Press, 1981.
Short, T. L. "Peirce's Semiotic Theory of the Self." *Semiotica* 91 (1992): 109–31.
Showeder, Richard A., and Edmund J. Bourne. "Does the Concept of the Person vary Cross-Culturally?" in *Culture Theory: Essays on Mind, Self and Emotion*, ed. R. A. Showeder and R. A. LeVine (pp. 158–99). Cambridge: Cambridge University Press, 1984.
Silverstein, Michael, and Greg Urban. *Natural Histories of Discourse*. Chicago. University of Chicago Press, 1996.
Singer, Milton. *Man's Glassy Essence: Explorations in Semiotic Anthropology*. Bloomington: Indiana University Press, 1984.
Skorupski, John. 1976. *Symbol and Theory: A Philosophical Study of Theories of Religion in Social Anthropology*. Cambridge: Cambridge University Press.
Smith, Jane I. "The Understanding of *Nafs* and *Rūḥ* in Contemporary Muslim Considerations of the Nature of Sleep and Death." *Moslem World* 69, no. 3 (1979): 151–62.
Smith, Jane I., and Yvonne Y. Haddad. *The Islamic Understanding of Death and Resurrection*. Albany: State University of New York Press, 1981.
Smith, W. C. *On Understanding Islam*. The Hague, The Netherlands: Mouton Publishers, 1981.
Spiro, Melford E. "Is the Western Conception of the Self 'Peculiar' Within the Context of the World Cultures?" *Ethos* 21 (1992): 107–53.
Spooner, Brian. "The Evil Eye in the Middle East," in *Witchcraft, Confession and Accusations*, ed. M. Douglas (pp. 311–19). London: Tavistock, 1970.
Starrett, Gergory. *Putting Islam to Work: Education, Politics and Religious Transformation in Egypt*. Berkeley: University of California Press, 1998.
Statistical Yearbook (of Egypt). Central Agency for Public Mobilization and Statistics, 1952–1977.
Stewart, Frank H. *Honor*. Chicago: University of Chicago Press, 1994.

Stoddart, William. *Sufism: The Mystical Doctrines and Methods of Islam*. Wellingborough, Northamptonshire, UK: Aquarian Press.

Stoller, Paul. *Fusion of the Worlds: An Ethnography of Possession among the Songhay of Niger*. Chicago: University of Chicago Press, 1989.

Strathern, Andrew. *Body Thoughts*. Ann Arbor: University of Michigan Press, 1996.

Strathern, Andrew, and M. Lambek. "Introduction: Embodying Sociality: Africanst–Melanesianist Comparisons," in *Bodies and Persons: Comparative Perspectives from Africa and Melanesia*, ed. M. Lambek and A. Strathern (pp. 1–25). Cambridge: Cambridge University Press, 1998.

Strathern, Marilyn. *The Gender of the Gift: Problems with Women with Society in Melanesia*. Berkeley: University of California Press, 1988.

———. "Qualified Value: The Perspective of Gift Exchange," in *Barter, Exchange, and Value: An Anthropological Perspective*, ed. C. Humphrey and S. Hugh-Jones (pp. 169–91). Cambridge: Cambridge University Press, 1992.

Tambiah, Stanley J. "Form and Meaning of Magical Acts," in *Modes of Thought*, ed. R. Horton and R. Finnegan (pp. 199–229). London: Faber & Faber, 1973.

———. *Culture, Thought and Social Action: An Anthropological Perspective*. Cambridge, MA: Harvard University Press, 1985.

———. *Magic, Science and Religion and the Scope of Rationality*. Cambridge: Cambridge University Press, 1990.

Tapper, Richard. "Holier than Thou: Islam in Three Tribal Societies," in *Islam in Tribal Societies from the Atlas to the Indus*, ed. A. Akbar and D. M. Hart. London: Routledge/Kegan Paul, 1984.

Taussig, Michael. *The Devil and Commodity Fetishism*. Chapel Hill: University of North Carolina Press, 1980.

———. *Shamanism, Colonialism, and the Wild Man: A Study in Terror and Healing*. Chicago: University of Chicago Press, 1987.

———. *Mimesis and Alterity: A Particular History of the Senses*. New York: Routledge, 1993.

———. *Defacement: Public Secrecy and the Labor of the Negative*. Stanford, CA: Stanford University Press, 1999.

Tax, Sol. "World View and Social Relations in Guatemala." *American Anthropologist* 43 (1941): 27–42.

Taylor, Charles. "Modernity and the Rise of Public Sphere," in *The Tanner Lectures on Human Values*, ed. G. B. Paterson (pp. 205–60). Salt Lake City: University of Utah Press, 1993.

Taylor, Elizabeth, "Egyptian Migration and Peasant Wives." *MERIP Reports* (Middle Eastern Research and Information Project no. 124), 14 (1984): 3–10.

Todorov, Tzvetan. *Symbolism and Interpretation*, trans. C. Potter. Ithaca, NY: Cornell University Press, 1982.

Tomlinson, John. *Globalization and Culture*. Chicago: University of Chicago Press, 1999.

Toth, James. *Rural Labor Movements in Egypt and Their Impact on the State, 1961–1992*. Gainesville: University Press of Florida, 1999.

Traube, Elizabeth G. *Cosmology and Social Life: Ritual Exchange among the Mabai of East Timor*. Chicago: University of Chicago Press, 1986.

Trimingham, J. Spencer. *Islam in the Sudan*. London: Frank Cass, 1965.
———. *The Influence of Islam upon Africa*. New York: Praeger Publishers, 1968.
Tritton, A. S. "Muslim Funeral Customs." *Bulletin of the School of Oriental and African Studies* 9, no. 3 (1938): 653–61.
———. "Man, *nafs*, *ruḥ*, *ʿaql*." *Bulletin of the School of Oriental and African Studies* 34, no. 3 (1971): 491–95.
Turner, Bryan S. *Weber and Islam: A Critical Study*. London: Routledge/Kegan Paul, 1974.
Turner, Terence. "Social Body and Embodied Subject: Bodiliness, Subjectivity, and Sociality among the Kayapo." *Cultural Anthropology* 10, no. 2 (1995): 143–70.
Turner, Victor. *The Ritual Process*. Chicago: Aldine, 1969.
———. *Drama, Fields, and Metaphors: Symbolic Action in Human Society*. Ithaca, NY: Cornell University Press, 1974.
———. *The Forest of Symbols*. Ithaca, NY: Cornell University Press, 1982.
Turner, V., and E. Turner. "Performing Ethnography." *Drama Review* 26 (1982): 33–50.
Tylor, Edward B. *Primitive Culture* (1871). Reprint, New York: Harper Torchbook, 1958.
ʿUways, Sayyid. *Min malāmiḥ al-mujtamaʿ al-Misrī al-Muʿāṣir* (Some features of the Egyptian society). Cairo: Maṭābiʿ ash-Shaʿb, 1965.
———. *al-khulūd fī at-turāth ath-thaqāfi al-Misrī* (The concept of immortality in the Egyptian cultural heritage). Cairo: Dār al-Mʿārif, 1966.
Van Gennep, Arnold. *The Rites of Passage*, trans. M. B. Vizedom and G. L. Caffee (1909). Reprint, Chicago: University of Chicago Press, 1960.
Vatikiotis, P. J. *The History of Egypt*. London: Weidenfeld & Nicolson, 1985.
von Grunebaum, Gustave E. "The Problem: Unity in Diversity," in *Unity and Variety in Muslim Civilization*, ed. G. E. von Grunebaum (pp. 17–37). Chicago: University of Chicago Press, 1955.
Wainwright, William. *Reason and the Heart: A Prolegomenon to a Critique of Passional Mind*. Ithaca, NY: Cornell University Press, 1995.
Walker, J. *Folk Medicine in Modern Egypt*. London: Luzac, 1934.
Waterbury, John. *Hydropolitics of the Nile Valley*. Syracuse, NY: Syracuse University Press, 1979.
———. "Egypt: Islam and Change," in *Change and the Muslim World*, ed. P. H. Stoddard, D. C. Cuthell, and M. W. Sullivan. Syracuse, NY: Syracuse University Press, 1981.
———. "Peasants Defy Categorization (as Well as Landlords and the State)," in *Peasants and Politics in the Modern Middle East*, ed. F. Kazemi and J. Waterbury (pp. 1–23). Miami: Florida International University Press, 1991.
Watt, W. Montgomery. *What Is Islam?* New York: Praeger Publishers, 1968.
Weber, Max. *The Protestant Ethic and the Spirit of Capitalism*, trans. T. Parsons. New York: Scribner's, 1958.
———. *The Sociology of Religion*, trans. E. Fischoff. Boston: Beacon Press, 1964.
Webster, Hutton. *Magic: A Sociological Study*. Stanford, CA: Stanford University Press, 1948.
Wensinck, A. J. *The Muslim Creed: Its Genesis and Historical Development*. London: Cambridge University Press, 1932.

———. "*Al-Khiḍir* (*Al-Khiḍr*)," in *Encyclopedia of Islam*. Leiden, The Netherlands: E. J. Brill, 1960.

Westermark, E. *Rituals and Beliefs in Morocco*, 2 vols. London: Macmillan, 1968.

White, Hayden. *The Content and the Form: Narrative Discourse and Historical Representation*. Baltimore: Johns Hopkins University Press, 1987.

Wiener, Margaret J. *Visible and Invisible Realms: Power, Magic and Colonial Conquest in Bali*. Chicago: University of Chicago Press, 1995.

Wierzbicka, Anna. "Soul and Mind: Linguistic Evidence for Ethnopsychology." *American Anthropologist* 91 (1989): 4–58.

———. *Emotions Across Languages and Cultures: Diversity and Universals*. Cambridge: Cambridge University Press, 1999.

Willcocks, W., and J. Craig. *Egyptian Irrigation*, 2 vols. London: E. & F. N. Spon, 1913.

Williams, John Adam. "A Return to the Veil in Egypt." *Middle East Review* 11, no. 3 (1979): 49–54.

Wilson, John A. "Egypt: The Nature of the Universe," in *The Intellectual Adventure of Ancient Man*, ed. H. Frankfort, H. A. Frankfort, J. Wilson, and T. Jacobsen (pp. 39–70). Chicago: University of Chicago Press, 1946.

Wilson, Peter J. *A Malay Village and Malaysia: Social Values and Rural Development*. New Haven, CT: HRAF Press, 1967.

Wolf, Eric R. *Peasants*. Englewood Cliffs, NJ: Prentice-Hall, 1966.

Younis, M. Abdel Moneim. "The Religious Significance of Miʿraj." *Majallatu'l Azhar* (*Al-Azhar Magazine*) 6 (1967): 5–9.

Zaytun, Muhammad. *Iqlīm al-Buḥayrah* (The Province of Beheira). Cairo: Dār al-Maʿarif, 1962.

Zeghal, Malika. "Religion and Politics in Egypt: The Ulema of al-Azhar, Radical Islam and the State (1952–94)." *International Journal of Middle Eastern Studies* 31, no. 3 (1999): 371–99.

Zuhur, Sherifa. *Revealing Reveiling: Islamist Gender Ideology in Contemporary Egypt* (SUNY Series of Middle Eastern Studies). Albany: State University of New York Press, 1992.

Zwemer, S. M. *The Influence of Animism on Islam*. London: Central Board of Missions and the Society for Promoting Christian Knowledge, 1920.

———. *Studies in Popular Islam: A Collection of Papers Dealing with the Superstitions and Beliefs of the Common People*. London: Sheldon Press, 1939.

index

About the Author

EL-SAYED EL-ASWAD is professor of anthropology and chair of the Department of Sociology, Tanta University (Egypt), and is also adjunct professor at Wayne State University and has taught at Oakland Community College in Michigan. He received his doctorate degree from the University of Michigan, Ann Arbor. Dr. el-Aswad has also taught at the United Arab Emirates University, where he founded and served as head of the Unit of Anthropological and Folkloric Resources. He has been awarded fellowships from various institutes including the Fulbright Program, Ford Foundation, Egyptian government, United Arab Emirates University, and American University in Cairo. He is a member of the American Anthropological Association and the Middle Eastern Studies Association of North America and has published widely in both Arabic and English.